AF705402

The Gender Affirmative Model

Perspectives on Sexual Orientation and Diversity
Maria Lucia Miville, Series Editor

Affirmative Counseling and Psychological Practice With Transgender and Gender Nonconforming Clients
Edited by Anneliese A. Singh and lore m. dickey

The Gender Affirmative Model: An Interdisciplinary Approach to Supporting Transgender and Gender Expansive Children
Edited by Colt Keo-Meier and Diane Ehrensaft

HIV+ Sex: The Psychological and Interpersonal Dynamics of HIV-Seropositive Gay and Bisexual Men's Relationships
Edited by Perry N. Halkitis, Cynthia A. Gómez, and Richard J. Wolitski

Lesbian and Gay Parents and Their Children: Research on the Family Life Cycle
Abbie E. Goldberg

Sexual Orientation and Mental Health: Examining Identity and Development in Lesbian, Gay, and Bisexual People
Edited by Allen M. Omoto and Howard S. Kurtzman

Teaching LGBTQ Psychology: Queering Innovative Pedagogy and Practice
Edited by Theodore R. Burnes and Jeanne L. Stanley

That's So Gay! Microaggressions and the Lesbian, Gay, Bisexual, and Transgender Community
Kevin L. Nadal

The Gender Affirmative Model

An Interdisciplinary Approach to Supporting Transgender and Gender Expansive Children

Edited by
Colt Keo-Meier and Diane Ehrensaft

American Psychological Association
Washington, DC

Copyright © 2018 by the American Psychological Association. All rights reserved. Except as permitted under the United States Copyright Act of 1976, no part of this publication may be reproduced or distributed in any form or by any means, including, but not limited to, the process of scanning and digitization, or stored in a database or retrieval system, without the prior written permission of the publisher.

The opinions and statements published are the responsibility of the authors, and such opinions and statements do not necessarily represent the policies of the American Psychological Association.

Published by
American Psychological Association
750 First Street, NE
Washington, DC 20002
www.apa.org

APA Order Department
P.O. Box 92984
Washington, DC 20090-2984
Phone: (800) 374-2721; Direct: (202) 336-5510
Fax: (202) 336-5502; TDD/TTY: (202) 336-6123
Online: http://www.apa.org/pubs/books
E-mail: order@apa.org

In the U.K., Europe, Africa, and the Middle East, copies may be ordered from
Eurospan Group
c/o Turpin Distribution
Pegasus Drive
Stratton Business Park
Biggleswade Bedfordshire
SG18 8TQ United Kingdom
Phone: +44 (0) 1767 604972
Fax: +44 (0) 1767 601640
Online: https://www.eurospanbookstore.com/apa
E-mail: eurospan@turpin-distribution.com

Typeset in Meridien by Circle Graphics, Inc., Columbia, MD

Printer: Sheridan Books, Chelsea, MI
Cover Designer: Beth Schlenoff Design, Bethesda, MD

Library of Congress Cataloging-in-Publication Data

Names: Keo-Meier, Colt, editor. | Ehrensaft, Diane, editor.
Title: The gender affirmative model : an interdisciplinary approach to supporting transgender and gender expansive children / edited by Colt Keo-Meier, Diane Ehrensaft.
Description: Washington, DC : American Psychological Association, 2018. | Series: Perspectives on sexual orientation and diversity | Includes bibliographical references and index.
Identifiers: LCCN 2018003702 | ISBN 9781433829123 (hardback) | ISBN 1433829126
Subjects: LCSH: Transgender children. | Parents of transgender children. | BISAC: PSYCHOLOGY / Psychotherapy / Child & Adolescent. | SOCIAL SCIENCE / Gender Studies.
Classification: LCC HQ1075 .G3715 2018 | DDC 306.874—dc23 LC record available at https://lccn.loc.gov/2018003702

British Library Cataloguing-in-Publication Data
A CIP record is available from the British Library.

Printed in the United States of America
First Edition

http://dx.doi.org/10.1037/0000095-000

10 9 8 7 6 5 4 3 2 1

To my spouse, who teaches me to think outside of the binaries.
—Colt Keo-Meier

To all my wonderful colleagues in the Child and Adolescent Gender Center and Mind the Gap.
—Diane Ehrensaft

Contents

Contributors

Erica E. Anderson, PhD, is a psychologist in the Child and Adolescent Gender Clinic at the University of California at San Francisco, a professor of clinical psychology at John F. Kennedy University, and is in private practice in Oakland, California.

Demetry Apostle, PhD, is a clinician at inMind, a group practice that provides psychotherapy, assessment, and consultation services. He is an adjunct clinical faculty member at The Wright Institute and is in private practice in San Francisco and Berkeley, where he specializes in working with LGBTQ&Q adults, families, and youth, including sexual and gender nonconforming minorities. His expertise comes from research conducted on the lived experience of homonegativity/homophobia by gay men and the impact on their lives and relationships.

Karisa Barrow, PsyD, is a licensed clinical psychologist who specializes in providing services to gender- and sexually diverse children and their families. She is the founder and clinical director of inMind, a group practice that provides psychotherapy, assessment, and consultation for adults and children. Dr. Barrow is a founding member of the UCSF Child and Adolescent Gender Center and Mind the Gap group, and currently serves as Trustee of the Board for enGender, an organization that supports gender diverse youth and their families through direct services and programming.

Dianne Berg, PhD, is an assistant professor and licensed psychologist at the Program in Human Sexuality at the University of Minnesota. She has been working with gender creative children and transgender adolescents for over 18 years and coordinates the Child/Adolescent Gender Clinical Services program. She is the codirector of the National Center for Gender Spectrum Health and coauthor of the Gender Affirmative Lifespan Approach, the conceptual framework guiding the clinically driven research of the National Center for Gender Spectrum Health. Dr. Berg is also a member of the Child and Adolescent Committee of the World Professional Association for Transgender Health.

Eb. (Ebony) Brown, MSW, is a Black trans-masculine Caribbean interested in supporting transgender, gender nonconfirming, and nonbinary people in addressing internalized oppression, building solidarity, and activating creativity. Eb. has been engaged as researcher, mental health practitioner, and facilitator for the past decade, serving as workshop presenter with various organizations and movements, including Gender Spectrum, Northern California Kaiser Permanente Gender, San Francisco Health Services, Bay Area Black Social Worker Alliance, California Social Work Education Center, LGBTQ Conference at Harvard, and the Move to End Violence. Eb. has worked extensively with Queer and Trans Youth of Color.

Deb Coolhart, PhD, LMFT, is an assistant professor at Syracuse University in Syracuse, New York. Dr. Coolhart's research focuses on trans people and their couple and family relationships, particularly as they relate to adjusting to and supporting trans identities. In her private practice, she has specialized in working with trans people and their families since 1999. She also created and supervises the "Trans Team" at Syracuse University's Couple and Family Therapy Center, providing free therapy services for the community.

Laura Edwards-Leeper, PhD, is an associate professor in the School of Graduate Psychology at Pacific University in Hillsboro, Oregon. She previously worked at Boston Children's Hospital/Harvard Medical School, where she developed an affirmative protocol for assessing readiness in transgender and gender expansive adolescents seeking medical interventions. She served on the American Psychological Association Task Force that wrote the *Guidelines for Psychological Practice With Transgender and Gender Nonconforming People* and served on the panel that assisted the Substance Abuse and Mental Health Services Administration to develop the consensus statement *Ending Conversion Therapy: Supporting and Affirming LGBTQ Youth.* She is currently chair of the World Professional Association for Transgender Health's Child and Adolescent Committee.

Shawn V. Giammattei, PhD, is a clinical psychologist and gender specialist in private practice in San Francisco and Santa Rosa, California, specializing in family therapy with couples, families, and individuals across the lifespan in queer and gender expansive communities. He is an affiliated researcher and past coordinator of training for the Rockway Institute, a national center for LGBT psychology research, education, and public policy, and a professor at the California School of Professional Psychology at Alliant International University, where he teaches graduate courses in LGBT psychology, transgender mental health, distance learning, and family systems.

Elizabeth Glaeser, BS, is a doctoral student at Teachers College, Columbia University, and has worked for the Gender and Family Project at the Ackerman Institute for the Family in New York City since 2012. Her work focuses on multicultural and social justice in mental health specifically with the gender expansive community. Her work has been featured in journals, textbooks on cultural sensitivity, and guides on how to work with transgender individuals.

Randi Kaufman, PsyD, is a clinical psychologist who has been working with gender identity issues since 1998. Currently the team psychologist at the Gender and Family

Project of the Ackerman Institute for the Family in New York City, she worked previously at Boston Children's Hospital/Harvard Medical School, where she provided psychological evaluations to assess readiness for transgender and gender expansive youth seeking medical intervention. Dr. Kaufman founded the Transgender Health Program at Fenway Health in Boston in 2004 to provide mental health and medical care to transgender adults. She has evaluated several inmates in the state of Massachusetts in response to a lack of knowledge and appropriate treatment for incarcerated transgender people, and she was instrumental as an expert witness and a fact witness in helping two inmates win federal lawsuits. Dr. Kaufman is a supervisor for the Institute for Human Identity in NYC, and has a private practice in NYC.

Arlene (Ari) Istar Lev, LCSW-R, CASAC, CST, is a social worker, family therapist, and sex therapist who is the founder and clinical director of Choices Counseling and Consulting (http://www.choicesconsulting.com) and TIGRIS: The Training Institute for Gender, Relationships, Identity, and Sexuality (http://www.tigrisinstitute.com) in Albany, New York. Ms. Lev specializes in issues related to gender and sexuality, including working with LGBTQ couples and families. She is a part-time lecturer at the University at Albany, School of Social Welfare, and is the project director of the Sexual Orientation and Gender Identity Project. Ms. Lev is also the board president for Rainbow Access Initiative, Inc., which provides low-cost therapy to LGBTQ individuals. She also served as a committee member of the World Professional Association for Transgender Health's seventh revision of the Standards of Care.

Jean Malpas, LMHC, LMFT, is the founder and director of the Gender and Family Project of the Ackerman Institute for the Family, director of international training, and a psychotherapist in private practice in New York City. He has presented nationally and internationally on issues of gender, sexuality, addiction, and couple and family therapy. Media appearances include a TEDx Talk, "The Gift of Gender Authenticity," *National Geographic's* "Gender Revolution: A Journey With Katie Couric," and PBS Frontline: "Growing Up Trans."

Kobi Mar, PsyD, is a Chinese American, gender complex, clinical psychologist at Alameda Family Services, in Alameda, California, and a gender therapist in private practice in San Francisco, California. Dr. Mar specializes in working with gender expansive children, their families, and transgender, nonbinary, and gender nonconforming adults. He has served as a workshop facilitator at the Gender Spectrum Conference with a dedicated focus on the intersections of being a transgender person of color. Dr. Mar is also a standing member of the UCSF Child and Adolescent Gender Center, Mind the Gap Group.

Robert J. McLaughlin, PhD, CGP, is dean, School of Allied Health Sciences at Baylor College of Medicine, and an associate professor in allied health and psychiatry and behavioral science. As a clinical psychologist and certified group psychotherapist, he has an extensive history providing service related to LGBTQI experience, including family and individual counseling for children and adolescents, school and organizational consultation, and community education. Dr. McLaughlin is a cofounder of Gender Infinity, Inc., in Houston, Texas, which was formed to empower children, adolescents, and families around diverse gender expressions and identities.

Unique in the Southwestern United States, Gender Infinity has conducted seven annual conferences to cross train professionals in multiple disciplines, and provides affirming spaces for youth and families through empowerment and education and by forging safety networks utilizing a broad range of community resources. Dr. McLaughlin identifies as a White cisgender man.

AndreAs Neumann-Mascis, PhD, is a clinical psychologist who specializes in gender variance, trauma, and physical/psychiatric disabilities. He has worked as a provider, educator, advocate, and activist with complex people in a wide range of settings. Dr. Neumann-Mascis founded and developed The Meeting Point, a collaboration of independent healthcare providers in Jamaica Plain, Massachusetts, which serves the LGBTQ, survivors of trauma, and disability communities.

Robbie N. Sharp, PhD, LSSP, is a clinical assistant professor in allied health and psychiatry and behavioral science. She is experienced in working with those who identify as LGBT in both her clinical practice and as a supervisor and mentor for mental health providers. Dr. Sharp has worked extensively with crisis and trauma victims in Houston area schools and in her clinical practice, many of whom are LGBTQ. She is a cofounder of Gender Infinity, Inc., in Houston, Texas, and continues to work with gender diverse and gender expansive children, youth, and their families through that organization.

Amy Tishelman, PhD, is a clinical psychologist, the director of clinical research, and a senior attending psychologist for the Gender Management Service at Boston Children's Hospital, as well as an assistant professor at Harvard Medical School. She codeveloped the first Boston Children's Hospital clinic for prepubescent youth with gender-related concerns. Dr. Tishelman is an invited member of the Child/Adolescent committee of the World Professional Association of Transgender Health and has been asked by the Board of Directors to serve as the lead for the "Assessment, Support and Therapeutic Approaches of Children" chapter for new transgender health Standards of Care Version 8.

Carolyn Wolf-Gould, MD, has been a family physician in Oneonta, New York, since 1994, and has been practicing transgender medicine as part of general primary care since 2007. She is the founder of The Gender Wellness Center at Susquehanna Family Practice, a multidisciplinary center that has grown rapidly to meet the needs of patients in upstate New York. She and her team of providers are the recipients of a Robert Wood Johnson Foundation Clinical Scholars Grant from 2016 to 2019 to create a rural-based Center of Excellence in Transgender Health for upstate New York.

The Gender Affirmative Model

Colt Keo-Meier and Diane Ehrensaft

Introduction to the Gender Affirmative Model

1

Recently, awareness of prepubertal gender diverse children has increased in the United States among the general population, as well as among psychologists (American Psychological Association [APA], 2014; Ehrensaft, 2011). Major media outlets have likewise increasingly featured transgender children and their families, while hotly debating their treatment needs (Mapes, 2012; Quart, 2008; Speigel, 2008). In the same vein, diverse gender identities, behaviors that diverge from gender stereotypes, and distress at home and school related to these issues are increasingly common presentations in child clinical settings (de Vries & Cohen-Kettenis, 2012; Spack et al., 2012). Thus, the need to prepare psychologists, other mental health professionals and professionals from all disciplines who work with children and families.

Outpatient clinics that specialize in working with transgender and gender expansive (TGE) children have seen a threefold rise in the amount of child referrals they have received over the past 30 years (de Vries & Cohen-Kettenis, 2012; Zucker, Bradley, Owen-Anderson, Kibblewhite, & Cantor, 2008). Recent literature indicates that the vast majority of counseling and education programs fail to prepare practitioners to be competent clinicians to serve the needs of TGE youth (Carroll, 2010; Cole, Denny, Eyler, & Samons, 2000; DePaul, Walsh, & Dam, 2009; Gonzalez & McNulty, 2010; Goodrich & Luke, 2009). Similarly, most public health and medical school training programs fail to

http://dx.doi.org/10.1037/0000095-001
The Gender Affirmative Model: An Interdisciplinary Approach to Supporting Transgender and Gender Expansive Children, C. Keo-Meier and D. Ehrensaft (Editors)
Copyright © 2018 by the American Psychological Association. All rights reserved.

train their students to be gender-sensitive practitioners (Corliss, Shankle, & Moyer, 2007; Obedin-Maliver et al., 2011). Even programs that include lesbian, gay, bisexual, transgender, queer or questioning (LGBTQ) trainings commonly exclude transgender issues or only briefly mention them as an afterthought. The focus is usually on the experiences of adults who transition after puberty, and prepubertal TGE children and adolescents fall off the radar screen completely (Carroll, 2010; Case, Stewart, & Tittsworth, 2009). Because gender identity develops between ages 1.5 and 3 years and sexual orientation develops as early as age 8 (Ehrensaft, 2016), access to information about how to work with TGE children is essential for professionals who work with young children (Gonzalez & McNulty, 2010).

A sea change in gender has been occurring, in such a short time it has hit land and rocked the earth as it has—at home, in communities, in society, and across the globe. In February 2014, Facebook changed its U.S. profile options for gender, extending it from two to 50-plus categories, including transgender, cisgender, agender, gender fluid, intersex, neither, trans female, trans male, trans person, gender variant, gender questioning, bigender, androgynous, pangender, and transsexual. People creating a profile can choose as many categories as they want. In 2012, California passed legislation (Sexual Orientation Change Efforts) prohibiting mental health practitioners from engaging in practices that attempted to change a minor's gendered behaviors. New Jersey soon followed suit, along with the District of Columbia, and as of this writing, 15 other states have similar bills pending. Looking north across the border, Ontario passed a no-reparative-therapy bill in 2015, in the same year that President Obama and the White House issued a statement condemning the practice of reparative therapy. In 2013, California passed another piece of legislation (Pupil Rights: Sex-Segregated School Programs and Activities), ensuring that all students in public schools are allowed to use the facilities and engage in activities associated with their affirmed gender, rather than their natal sex. In 2013, gender identity disorder was removed from the *Diagnostic and Statistical Manual of Mental Disorders* (fifth ed.; *DSM–5*; American Psychiatric Association, 2013), replaced by a more palatable (but still problematic) mental health diagnosis of Gender Dysphoria. In Fall 2011, the World Professional Association of Transgender Health (WPATH) released its new standards of care, which state explicitly that it is unethical and harmful to engage in any form of therapy that attempts to change one's gender. The APA (2015) followed suit and released a large volume of new guidelines for gender affirmative care; however, the majority of the focus of the guidelines and standards are on TGE adults.

New gender clinics have begun to pop up across the United States and beyond to aid children in affirming their authentic gender. The gender affirmative approach has emerged and has become an ascending international model for supporting children's gender health, an effort that we are proud to be a part of. Simultaneously, therapeutic models aimed at altering children's gender to conform to cultural norms or influencing children to accept the gender that matches the sex on their birth certificate have been challenged, declared unethical, and evaluated as harmful to children's well-being. In 2007, Barbara Walters moderated a *20/20* documentary on transgender kids (Goldberg, 2007). It was the first of its kind in TV broadcasts and a transformative turn of events in media history—with transgender children and their families from cities and small towns all over the United States (not just well-known liberal enclaves such as Berkeley, California) portrayed in a positive and empathic light. At the time of this writing (late 2016), it seems that a week does not go by without a new media account of TGE children. The January 2017 National Geographic put out a special issue, "Gender Revolution," that covers the dramatic changes that have occurred in gender identity and expressions. As these changes have rolled out in such a short band of time, we gender specialists, in partnership with the families who are raising the children, can hardly keep up. Every day we learn more and see how much more we have to learn about helping our children discover and fortify their true gender selves.

This book, the first of its kind representing the expertise of a wide number of gender specialists in the field, aims to serve as a substantive guide to inform clinical work with this prepubertal children according to the gender affirmative model (GAM). The authors in this book provide the essential education for psychologists, other mental health providers and professionals from other disciplines to be able to provide culturally competent care to this population of children and their families.

In addition, this book lays the groundwork for further dialogue on and research into developing sound practice for working with TGE children and their families. All chapters examine the issue of TGE children from the perspectives of the individual, the family, and culture. In this volume, national experts review the extant literature on phenomenology, diagnosis, and treatment of children with these presenting concerns; offer case studies from clinical practice; and emphasize the importance of interdisciplinary collaborative practice to address medical, psychosocial, educational, legal, and ethical matters pertaining to their care. One thing is clear: Professionals and families alike need to relearn gender if they are to do no harm to children. This book enables this relearning in the context of clinical guidelines for work with TGE children and their families.

Defining Terms

> Our genders are as unique as we are. No one's definition is the same, and compartmentalizing a person as either a boy or a girl based entirely on the appearance of genitalia at birth undercuts our complex life experiences.
>
> —Janet Mock, *Redefining Realness*

The complexity of gender Mock (2014) referred to, along with the ever changing and not universally agreed upon vernacular of communities and professional associations, especially when referring to children, underscores the daunting task of deciding on the terminology to use throughout this volume. We have created a working language to help the readers conceptualize TGE identities and ways of being. At the same time, we realize other terms—*gender creative, gender nonconforming, gender variant, gender independent*—may be seen throughout academic literature and social media, as well as heard in conversations with and about TGE people, as they describe dynamics and attributes of the children we are talking about. The reader should be prepared for a bit of a language juggling as they read through and gain more experience working with this population, understanding that each of those terms, while nuanced, refers to the same entity. A scan of the professional literature reveals the term *gender nonconforming* to be the most often used. However, similar to the term *gender variant,* many find that *gender nonconforming* has a somewhat negative connotation of "other than normal," not too far off from "deviant," and can serve to reify a normative or "conforming" gender.

No sooner do we think we have all the new terminology about gender clear in our heads than we discover we were all wrong, and that today's words are already passé. With that in mind, we present the map of our current conceptualization of gender terminology. We see *gender diverse* as the umbrella term that refers to this group of children with two subcategories—transgender and gender expansive (TGE).

Gender identity is not visible: It is one's innermost concept of self as boy or girl or both or neither—how individuals perceive and know themselves as well as what they call themselves. It is a biological, psychological, social, and cultural concept. One's *sex* includes several components—chromosomes, relative levels of sex hormones post-puberty, internal genitalia, and external genitalia—the latter used to assign a sex at birth. *Transgender* refers to anyone whose gender identity differs from their sex assigned at birth, that is, everyone else has told you that you are a girl and this is at odds with how you know yourself. A transgender boy was assigned the sex of female at birth and his gender identity is boy. *Cisgender* refers to the majority of the population—individuals whose gender identity aligns with the sex they were assigned at birth, that is, everyone else has told you that you are a boy and that matches how you know yourself. A cisgender boy was assigned the sex of male at birth and his gender identity is boy.

The transgender subcategory includes both binary (either girl or boy) and nonbinary gender identities. Transgender children are those who declare their gender as other than reflected by the sex marker on their birth certificate. They can show up at any age, and as early as the toddler years, as individuals are aware of their gender identity between 18 months and 3 years of age (Golombok & Fivuch, 1994). Transgender children typically consistently, persistently, and insistently express a binary or nonbinary gender and realize that their gender is different from their assigned sex. They may begin talking about their gender as soon as they begin to speak and some may express dissatisfaction with their external genitalia. Transgender children are more likely to experience gender dysphoria (i.e., discomfort related to their bodies not matching their internal sense of gender as well as associated social distress) than other gender diverse children, although some transgender children are comfortable with their bodies. These children may state that they are really the other gender or that someone (e.g., doctor, religious authority) made a mistake in their gender assignment. An important part of affirming these children may include changing relational terms (e.g., *brother* to *sister* or *sibling*), pronouns (e.g., *he* to *she* or *they*), honorifics (e.g., *Mr.* to *Miss* or *Mx.*), and names (*Jerald* to *Jessica* or *Jere*).

The biological basis of gender identity in transgender people has been investigated for decades and found to be more complex than originally anticipated (Erickson-Schroth, 2013; Veale, Clarke, & Lomax, 2010). Although a full discussion of this complexity is beyond the scope of this book, it is important to know that being transgender has no one biological "cause." At the same time, genetic and neuroanatomic influences have been demonstrated. Twin studies of monozygotic and dizygotic twins demonstrate a genetic component where of twin pairs with at least one transgender twin, monozygotic (identical) twins are much more likely to both be transgender than dizygotic twins (Diamond, 2013). Zhou, Hofman, Gooren, and Swaab (1995) focused on a sexually dimorphic region of the brain, the central subdivision of the bed nucleus of the stria terminalis (BTSc), which is about 2 times larger in cisgender men than in cisgender women. They found that the BTSc in transgender women was found to more closely resemble that of cisgender women (gender identity match) than cisgender men (sex match) and proposed this evidence for a neurobiological basis of gender identity. The history of neuroanatomical studies examining brain differences in transgender and cisgender people has been fraught with small sample sizes and the confounding variable of adult exposure to exogenous hormones, as research methods included examining brains of transgender cadavers who had been exposed to exogenous hormones through hormone therapy (Zhou et al., 1995). However, newer neuroanatomical research studies are able to measure living participants using diffusion tensor imaging, which eliminates the confounder of exposure to hormone therapy, as participants are measured before hormone treatment. Rametti and colleagues (Rametti, Carrillo, Gómez-Gil, Junque, Segovia, et al., 2011; Rametti, Carrillo, Gómez-Gil, Junque, Zubiarre-Elorza, et al., 2011) have posited that white matter microstructure pattern may be part of the neuroanatomical basis of gender identity. In their study of transgender men who had not initiated hormone treatment (Rametti, Carrillo, Gómez-Gil, Junque, Segovia, et al., 2011), the white matter microstructure pattern in their brains was closer to that of cisgender men, with whom they share a common gender identity, than that of cisgender women, with whom they share a common assigned sex. It is interesting that their study of transgender women who had not initiated hormone therapy yielded somewhat different results (Rametti, Carrillo, Gómez-Gil, Junque, Zubiarre-Elorza, et al., 2011). The white matter microstructure pattern in the brains of transgender women was in between that of cisgender men and women, a beyond the binary finding. More recent research (Kranz et al., 2014) hypothesizes that white matter microstructure development may be influenced by the hormonal environment in utero during the late stages before birth as well as early during postnatal brain development. Although researchers do not know the exact mechanism or interplay of mechanisms that underlies gender identity development at present, they do know that gender identity has a biological component, supporting the notion that gender identity is not confined to boy or girl only.

Gender expansive refers to anyone whose *gender expression* differs from what is expected, typically based on their gender identity. *Gender expression* refers to readily visible sets of norms, including behaviors, clothing, hairstyle, mannerisms, roles, activities, and so on, that are ascribed to one gender or another—typically referred to as *masculine, feminine,* or *androgynous*. Gender expansive children (also known as *gender creative, gender nonconforming,* or *gender independent*) do not abide by the prescribed gender norms of their culture. Their gender expression is not consistent with socially prescribed gender roles. Their preferences for toys, clothing, sports, activities, playmates, hair length and style, and/or accessories are not expected in the culture based on their sex assigned at birth. Gender expansive children are usually perceived to be "pink boys" and "tomboys."

It is quite possible for an individual to be both transgender in identity and gender diverse in expressions at the same time. For example, a child who was assigned male at birth has a gender identity of girl and expressions consisting of mainly those ascribed as masculine, that is, a tomboy trans girl. Jess is one of those people. Assigned male at birth, Jess, then Jesse, balked at the terrible mistake that had been made, and by age 9 was living in her affirmed gender identity—girl. Yet she never gave up her camouflage pants and short haircut, or the army figures she liked to fight pretend battles with, as she happily lived her life as a girl named Jess.

When we use the *TGE* term in this volume, we refer to all children who challenge and explore gender identity and gender expressions. No matter what language and terminology researchers struggle to develop that will both reflect and be respectful of the multiple ways gender can present itself, children will lead the way in carving out their own self-descriptions, categorizations, and assignations of gender. So, we now build onto preexisting lists (Ehrensaft, 2016) consisting of all the ways we have heard gender described by the children who have come to see us, along with some items borrowed from social media, other people's writing, and word on the street.

- *Gender fluid children.* Children who defy the norms of binary gender and either slide along a gender spectrum or weave their own intricate individual patterns along the gender web. The word *fluid* here refers to the potential for movement through further development of one's understanding of their gender.
- *Gender smoothies.* Gender smoothies are a variation on the theme of gender fluid. As one teenager vividly described it, "You see, you take everything about gender, throw it in the blender, press the button, and you've got me—a gender smoothie."
- *Gender hybrids.* Children who combine or alternate between genders, often in a binary way. Among gender hybrids are the following:
  - *Gender Prius.* Half girl/half boy: This gender label was invented by a school-age child who, from the front, looked like any boy in basketball shorts, tank top, and basketball sneakers, and, from the back, had a long blond braid tied at the end with a bright pink bow: "You see—I'm a Prius, a boy in the front, a girl in the back. A hybrid."
  - *Gender minotaur.* A descriptor for the children who explain that they are one gender on the top and another on the bottom, this usually to account for genitals at odds with the gender they know themselves to be.
  - *Gender-by-season children.* Children who freely express their authentic gender (identity, expressions, or both) during summer and school vacations but never at school, or alternatively use school as the safe place to be their true gender self but keep it under wraps during home-based summers or vacations.
  - *Gender-by-location children.* A close cousin to gender-by-season, a child who knows the locations or is told the locations where free gender expression will be accepted and other locations where it is not, and chooses or is told to keep

their authentic gender muted or under wraps in the unwelcoming locations, such as conservative Aunt Mary's wedding reception.

- *Genderqueer youth.* Not only a category of gender but also a social movement of young people who ask us, "Why do you even bother? We are so beyond gender." They are any and all, never either/or, and they challenge our thinking and carve a new path in which they invite us all to both imagine and embody a world where gender is no longer a defining category. They may also identify with the term *nonbinary*.
- *Protogay children.* Children who start out exploring and pushing the margins of gender on the way to discovering their sexual orientation identity, typically exploring their gender expressions rather than gender identity, though not always.
- *Prototransgender youth.* Children who travel in the exact opposite direction from the protogay children. In the process of exploring their sexual orientation identity, usually in adolescence or young adulthood, they discover, often through their romantic or sexual liaisons, that it is not actually their sexuality but their gender that is in question, and move to understand themselves as transgender.
  - *Gender Tootsie Roll Pops.* Children who exhibit one gender on the outside but experience another gender on the inside. To follow the metaphor, the crunchy outside is often the gender that accommodates to the expectations of the surrounding world, and the soft, gooey inside is the stuff of authenticity and realness. The hard candy is in place to protect or shield the inside chewiness from an unaccepting world or an internalized unaccepting part of one's own self. It should be noted that the gender Tootsie Roll Pops, if not provided with resilience building, are often the most at-risk TGE children.
  - *Gender-ambidextrous children.* Children who use both their girl self and their boy self interchangeably. It may be the child who is a sister to her brother but a male playmate to the boy across the street, or the child who is full-out "femme" one day but totally masculine-style buff the next. If children can use both their left and right hand on par with each other, so too can they use their girl and their boy part of self, not to mention all the parts in between and beyond those two genders; ergo, the gender-ambidextrous child. They may also identify with the term *bigender*.
  - *Gender Teslas.* The gender Tesla is the transgender state some children reach after a stint being a gender hybrid or gender ambidextrous. Some simply go from zero to 60 to get there, meaning from the sex assigned to them at birth to their affirmed gender identity. Some go more slowly. We could say that any child in the transgender category would count as a Tesla, but we are preserving this term for children who are in motion toward an all-one-gender status.
  - *Agender youth.* A close cousin of, if not the same as, genderqueer youth. We can play with the word *agender*, seeing its double entendres—"I'm a gender, but not any particular gender," or "I'm devoid of gender [similar to asexual]," which is the more common referent to the meaning of *agender*. These are youth who, similar to their genderqueer compatriots, are also pushing beyond

> the limits of constricting gender confines to say, "You can't catch me," if it means pinning down a particular gender or any sense of gender at all as being relevant to living a life. Indeed, many agender youth also reference themselves as *genderqueer* or *nonbinary*.

It is important to note that these terms focus on gender, not sexuality. The two are certainly intertwined but are often confused for each other. Not only are the concepts of gender and sexuality intertwined but also ideas about what is normal for one's gender encompass sexuality—cisnormativity, gender conformance, and heteronormativity. For example, when one disentangles what it means to "be a man" (gender identity—man; sex assumed to be male), one realizes that the underlying expectation is that to "be a man," a person should also "act like a man" (gender expression—masculine). This expectation commonly comes along with a concurrent assumption that "acting like a man" also means being sexually attracted to women (sexual orientation identity—heterosexual).

Sexuality and sexual orientation identity (e.g., bisexual, heterosexual) have to do with many things, but at their center is the object of desire—do people desire those who are the same or a different gender as they are, those of any gender, those of fluidly defined gender, those who are transgender, those of no declared gender? Gender identity and expression, on the other hand, have to do with how people incorporate their own culture's definitions about being male or female with their own internal preferences, desires, and recognition of who they are as a boy/man, a girl/woman, a third gender, a fourth gender, and so on. As people reach adulthood, they can think of it this way: Sexual orientation identity has to do with who they get into bed with; gender identity has to do with who they get into bed as. A transgender person can be gay, bisexual, straight, or any other sexual orientation identity—the most common sexual orientation identity of transgender adults is queer, indicating a desire to be understood outside of traditional definitions. A gay person can be cisgender or transgender (gender identity) and gender expansive (e.g., a butch lesbian) or gender conforming (e.g., an effeminate lesbian) in terms of gender expression. And so forth. We hope this differentiation between gender and sexual orientation serves as a helpful compass to hold in hand as this book unfolds and follow the TGE child's journey through the mental health system.

This book focuses on children; because gender identity develops in early childhood and sexual orientation develops closer to puberty, we spend more time discussing gender identity than sexual orientation. Nearly all sexual orientation identities are based on the gender identity of the person and of the people the person is attracted to. For one's sexual orientation to develop, one's gender identity should have already developed. For example, if a person identifies their sexual orientation to be lesbian, then their gender identity is assumed to have already developed as girl/woman. In our work with transgender children, we have begun to see a trend with early and pubertal presentations. The early presenters will typically come in between 4 to 6 years of age with a similar story of always knowing their gender was different than what others were telling them. Their gender identities developed on a similar timeline as those of their cisgender peers. The pubertal presenters will typically come in between 10 to

16 with very confused parents who say my child has never "shown any signs" of being transgender (referring to gender expansiveness). A commonality with the majority of these pubertal presenters is that they come to understand their gender identity was different from their assigned sex as their sexual orientation was developing and as their bodies were changing. The majority of these adolescents identify as both transgender (incongruent gender identity and sex) and not heterosexual (sexual orientation). A mother once called my office in a panic saying, "My 14-year old daughter just told me that she felt that she was a homosexual boy, is that even possible? She has always been so feminine, this just does not make any sense to me." When I met with this teenager, it was clear that he was a gender expansive (i.e., effeminate) gay boy who happened to be transgender. As many pubertal presenters approach the age of burgeoning sexuality and changing bodies that will define their adult sexual selves, they awaken first to the harsh realization that they have been living in a gender that is just plain wrong for them; once realizing that, they can then begin to sort out their sexual orientation and objects of desire after repositioning themselves in their authentic gender selves. It will be important to hold in mind this delicately choreographed developmental footwork as we as mental health professionals see these preadolescents and adolescents in our clinical offices and help their families understand their seemingly sudden turns of gender.

Additional terminology used throughout this volume is listed below.

- *Transphobia/transnegativity.* A range of attitudes, feelings, and behaviors ranging from the idea that being transgender is less optimal than being cisgender to hatred and disgust toward anyone perceived to diverge from gender expectations.
- *Cisnormativity.* The assumption that everyone is cisgender or should be.
- *Heteronormativity.* The assumption that everyone is heterosexual or should be.
- *Passing.* Being perceived by others as the gender one knows oneself to be, regardless of sex assigned at birth. This term has a different meaning in the LGBQ community where passing means being perceived as heterosexual. "Passing" for many today, particularly youth, is a controversial issue, as it is dependent on cis- and heteronormative directives of what counts as a "real" man or woman, directives we are trying to dismantle in a gender affirmative construct of gender in all its imaginative hues and shades.
- *Gender Dysphoria versus gender dysphoria. Gender Dysphoria,* capitalized, is a diagnosis in the *DSM–5,* and *gender dysphoria,* lowercase, is the experience that "something is not right" regarding one's gender. This can include body dysphoria—commonly chest dysphoria and genital dysphoria—as well as distress related to being TGE in a cisgender world.
  - *Clueing in versus coming out. Clueing in* is the experience of coming to an understanding of one's gender and/or sexual orientation as being different than expected (an internal process). *Coming out* is the experience of sharing one's gender and/or sexual orientation with others (an interpersonal process).
  - *Gender transition.* An individual process that may consist of social, legal, medical, and/or surgical changes in gender. A social gender transition can include a new name, pronouns, and honorifics (e.g., *Ms.*) and presenting as one's

true gender self in selected or all environments. Legally, one may get one's new name and/or gender updated on one's identification documents. Medical interventions include puberty-blocking medication and masculinizing and feminizing hormone therapy (see Chapter 12, this volume). More than 10 surgical interventions may be accessed as a part of gender transition—these include facial, chest, and genital surgeries.

- *Binding.* When a person, typically postpubertal and assigned female at birth, attempts to flatten their chest to present the appearance of a masculine chest. Many youth attempt to use ace bandage wrap or duct tape, both of which can cause pain and potential damage to one's health. Several online companies sell chest binders in many different skin tones that are safer for use. *Padding* is the term for adding breast forms to present the appearance of breasts.
- *Tucking.* When a person, typically assigned male at birth, attempts to minimize their genital bulge. Children can be creative, using Band-Aids to tape their penises back. Several online companies sell gaff panties to assist in tucking that are safer for use. *Packing* is the term for adding the appearance of a genital bulge.

Stopping the Harm

> My third-grade teacher called my mother and said, "Ms. Cox, your son is going to end up in New Orleans in a dress if we don't get him into therapy." And, wouldn't you know, just last week I spoke at Tulane University and I wore a LOVELY green and black dress.
>
> —Laverne Cox

Controversy exists as to whether the *DSM–5* Gender Dysphoria diagnosis for children pathologizes normal variations in gender role behaviors and adaptations or represents a psychiatric medical disorder (Lev, 2005; see also Chapter 11, this volume). WPATH and the Endocrine Society have both published guidelines that include treatment of adolescents (Hembree et al., 2009; WPATH, 2011), yet no expert consensus on the treatment of prepubertal children exists. This is a particularly glaring problem because research has indicated that the social support of children in their gender development is directly correlated with mental health outcomes for children. Yet the field of psychology is divided on the form that social support should take and what constitutes "gender health" in children. At the same time, legislative actions have already been taken or are being proposed in three states in the United States (California, New York, New Jersey) that prohibit the use of therapeutic interventions that attempt to change a minor's gender behaviors.

Differing perspectives dictate divergent treatment models for prepubertal and early adolescent children and youth (de Vries & Cohen-Kettenis, 2012; Ehrensaft, 2011; Hidalgo et al., 2013; Hill, Menvielle, Sica, & Johnson, 2010; Spack et al., 2012; Zucker & Cohen-Kettenis, 2008). Prior treatment models have included a "wait and see if these behaviors desist" approach; prohibition of starting adolescents on cross-sex hormones until age 16 (Netherlands model); and attempts to behaviorally modify gender-nonconforming behavior in young children and help them "live in their own skin," that is, the sex assigned to them at birth (the Centre for Addiction and Mental Health model in Toronto; this clinic was recently closed).

In contrast, the GAM, upon which this book is based, is emerging as the treatment of choice of many gender specialists in the United States and in other countries. We posit the GAM to be the best practice for children and adolescents in their gender development. Central to the GAM is the evidence-based idea that attempting to change or contort a person's gender does harm. Instead, the GAM defines *gender health* as follows: the opportunity for a child to live in the gender that feels most real and/or comfortable for the child and the ability for children to express gender without experiencing restriction, criticism, or ostracism. In the model, the role of the mental health professional is a facilitator in helping a child discover and live in their authentic gender with adequate social supports. We as mental health professionals are their translators—striving to understand what they are telling us about their gender in words, actions, feelings, thoughts, and relationships.

Even though transgender people encounter multiple obstacles, including coming out, as well as possibly losing family, friends, partners, and employment opportunities, rates of regret of gender transition in adults are extremely low (0%–2%; Pfäfflin & Junge, 1998), with the majority of transgender adults stating that their only regret is not transitioning earlier. In Beemyn and Rankin's (2011) *The Lives of Transgender People*, a recurring theme was seen across the nearly 3,500 adults they interviewed. The story went something like this:

> If only I had the supports and green light that some of the young children have today, I would have had such a better life. I always knew since I was little that my gender was not what people thought, but there was no place to go with it. So, I had to wait, and wait, with many years of pain and suffering until I could get to the place that was "me."

The GAM is informed by the stories of transgender adults who have been telling us this for years. As more and more providers become proficient in working with TGE children, they won't have to wait near as long to be who they are.

As psychologists and mental health providers, we are bound by the oath that dictates the actions of all medical and mental health professionals: Do No Harm. Yet all around us, physicians, psychiatrists, and child therapists are doing just that—in clinics and private practice consultation rooms where parents are advised to take away their little boys' dolls and pink tights or make their little girls grow out their buzz cuts; mothers and fathers are directed to ignore or punish their children's "inappropriate" gender expressions and pay attention to or reward only the "gender-appropriate" ones; and families are sent home to make sure the TGE children are redirected to same-sex friendships and to their same-sex parent as the main or only parent to identify with. Replacing that viewpoint with the perspective of the GAM provides a new lens through which people can clearly see the vibrant plethora of TGE children. Looking through this lens, one can see children who declare, sometimes at a very early age, that the gender they are is not the one they were assigned at birth.

Ehrensaft (2011, 2016) created the concept of the *gender web* to guide viewing of the children. The gender web is a four-dimensional structure, the three material dimensions being nature, nurture, and culture, and the fourth dimension being time. Imagine a spider web stretched out in a tree to get the visual image, a web that may change its dimensions over time as the spider enhances its home. The gender web is each child's personal creation, spinning together the three major threads of nature, nurture, and culture that interface to allow the child to construct a gender self. Like fingerprints, no two individuals' gender webs will be exactly the same; unlike fingerprints, the gender web is not immutable—it will inevitably change over time. While people are little, to promote individual *gender health*, defined as freedom to explore and live in the gender that feels most authentic, the only person who should be doing that spinning is the child. If parents grab the thread of the web as children are spinning it, and tell them what their gender has to be, rather than listening as children spell out their gender or rather than watching them do their own creative work, the web risks ending up as a tangled knot of threads rather than a beautifully spun web that shimmers and glows. Alternatively, if parents and the surrounding environment facilitate, protect, and respect children's creative spinning, they stand to grow up gender healthy and proud. It is the role of the gender affirmative clinician to assure that the latter occurs.

The Gender Affirmative Model: Theoretical Basis

The major theoretical bases informing the GAM of clinical practice are: (a) no gender identity or expression is pathological; (b) gender presentations are diverse and vary across cultures, requiring our cultural sensitivity; (c) according to current knowledge, gender involves an integration of biology, development and socialization, and culture and context, with all of these bearing on any individual's gender self; (d) gender may be fluid, and is not binary, both at a particular time point and if and when it changes within an individual over time; and (e) any pathology that is present is more often caused by cultural reactions to gender diversity (e.g., transphobia, homophobia, sexism) than by internal psychological disturbances within the child (Hidalgo et al., 2013). Implicit in this model is a focus on resilience, coping, and wellness. The GAM serves to assist in facilitating gender health, not labeling any part of gender as an illness. We do not see gender diversity as an illness, but rather a variation of health. We define *gender health* as a child's opportunity to live in the gender that feels most real or comfortable to that child and to express that gender with freedom from restriction, aspersion, or rejection (Hidalgo et al., 2013). Recent emerging research indicates that those children who are not allowed these freedoms are at later risk for negative psychosocial outcomes (Ryan, Huebner, Diaz, & Sanchez, 2009). The GAM is supported by this research, as it also finds that family acceptance acts as a protective factor against these negative outcomes and that building gender resilience helps a child be confident in a world that may be far from accepting TGE people.

The GAM holds several tenets. Primary to these tenets is that we, as care providers, need to be able to reevaluate our social constructs of gender and sexuality within our cultural context and the positions we impose on children. We see gender identity and expression as a basic human right. GAM practitioners should remain open to fluidity and changes overtime and listen closely to our children's best attempt to explain themselves and respond in affirming way. As there is no way to know with complete certainty what the gender and sexuality of a child will be once they reach adulthood, much of the work of GAM clinicians involves helping parents cope with the "not knowing" and moving forward to deal with what is known. As therapists, we should increase our ability to make use of the countertransference and manage our own biases and minimize the risk in collapsing our clinical judgment. One priority is to tease out what is gender dysphoric stress and something else and treat in a triage and harm reduction fashion, as well as go deep into the psychological and social experiences of the children we treat in the context of the family, community, and culture in which they live. As GAM practitioners, we aim to increase our capacity to not know, be curious, and celebrate human diversity.

Guide to This Volume

To that end, we have organized this volume to guide all of us in accomplishing this goal. We have had the privilege of working with a group of experts from coast to coast in the United States to bring this work together. Some of us are transgender ourselves, some have raised TGE children, some have TGE romantic partners, and all of us have been touched by the lives of TGE people around us. We lecture, train, write, advocate, build a professional community, and conduct research on the lives of these TGE people who have been our greatest teachers.

Each of the following chapters is designed to be its own independent learning module about psychological, social, and community issues as we get in clearer focus the infinite variety and rapidly growing population of TGE children across the globe. Chapters 2 through 6 focus on the individual child in development and psychotherapy. This section brings the reader through developmental theories of gender development, provides tools to sharpen skills at differentiating gender identity and expressions, increase consciousness about issues impacting TGE children of color, considers the accompanying psychological factors that often show up alongside gender creativity, and delves into trauma-informed practice through the GAM lens. Chapter 7 is a comprehensive child and family assessment guide that includes guidance for using both gender-specific and general instruments with TGE children. Chapters 8 through 10 center on family dynamics and family therapy. This section highlights the importance of therapeutic intervention focused on the parents' emotional response to discovering they have a TGE child, building family resilience through using multiple therapeutic modalities, and navigating clinical work with families in conflict. Chapters 11 and 12 cover the interdisciplinary, collaborative, and intersectional nature of GAM providers, as it truly takes a village to create the conditions necessary for gender health. These chapters discuss creating a network of professionals across disciplines, advocating on the front lines for TGE children and their families and best practices for coordinating care with medical providers. Chapter 13, our conclusion, brings up the current limitations of the GAM as well as ideas on where to go from here.

A Final Note Before We Start

A problem facing untrained providers in the mental health community is that more and more TGE children and their families are seeking the services of psychologists and other mental health providers to help gender explorations or conundrums. Although many resources have been developed to address the needs of transgender adults, mental health providers typically have not received adequate training to guide them in supporting and treating the younger cohort of TGE children and their families.

The source of the lack of professional training is multifaceted: (a) graduate mental health and health care education rarely addresses issues pertinent to working with these children and their families; (b) little to no attention to this topic is paid by primary psychological and medical journals; (c) very few educational resources exist on this topic; (d) formal training on this issue is exceedingly rare; and (e) training that does exist is often outmoded, incorrect, and/or endorses practices that are likely to cause harm rather than promote health. Much of the available research has focused on the etiology of being transgender and research on transgender adults. Although affirming practice interventions and protocols for working with transgender adults are widely available, very little guidance exists for therapists who are working with children and families. Consequently, mental health providers increasingly face daunting challenges in the diagnosis and treatment of these children, who are showing up in larger numbers each year (de Vries & Cohen-Kettenis, 2012; Spack et al., 2012; Zucker et al., 2008), and providers are at risk for providing substandard care because of lack of access to proper training.

Recognizing a need for clearer guidance for mental health professionals providing services for children with gender-related concerns, this edited book is a compilation of the work of a mental health and medical group of experts who have experience working with TGE children, with the aim of increasing the clinical and cultural competence of psychologists and allied mental health professionals who will be treating these children.

References

American Psychiatric Association. (2013). *Diagnostic and statistical manual of mental disorders* (5th ed.). Washington, DC: Author.

American Psychological Association. (2014). *Fact sheet: Gender diversity and transgender identity in children.* Washington, DC: Author. Retrieved from http://www.apadivisions.org/division-44/resources/advocacy/transgender-children.pdf

American Psychological Association. (2015). Guidelines for psychological practice with transgender and gender nonconforming people. *American Psychologist, 70,* 832–864. http://dx.doi.org/10.1037/a0039906

Beemyn, G., & Rankin, S. (2011). *The lives of transgender people.* New York, NY: Columbia University Press.

Carroll, L. (2010). *Counseling sexual and gender minorities.* Upper Saddle River, NJ: Pearson.

Case, K. A., Stewart, B., & Tittsworth, J. (2009). Transgender across the curriculum: A psychology for inclusion. *Teaching of Psychology, 36,* 117–121. http://dx.doi.org/10.1080/00986280902739446

Cole, S. S., Denny, D., Eyler, A. E., & Samons, S. L. (2000). Issues of transgender. In L. T. Szuchman & F. Muscarella (Eds.), *Psychological perspectives on human sexuality* (pp. 149–1954). New York, NY: Wiley.

Corliss, H. L., Shankle, M. D., & Moyer, M. B. (2007). Research, curricula, and resources related to lesbian, gay, bisexual, and transgender health in U.S. schools of public health. *American Journal of Public Health, 97,* 1023–1027. http://dx.doi.org/10.2105/AJPH.2006.086157

DePaul, J., Walsh, M. E., & Dam, U. C. (2009). The role of school counselors in addressing sexual orientation in schools. *Professional School Counseling, 12,* 300–308. http://dx.doi.org/10.5330/PSC.n.2010-12.300

de Vries, A. L. C., & Cohen-Kettenis, P. T. (2012). Clinical management of gender dysphoria in children and adolescents: The Dutch approach. *Journal of Homosexuality, 59,* 301–320. http://dx.doi.org/10.1080/00918369.2012.653300

Diamond, M. (2013). Transsexuality among twins: Identity concordance, transition, rearing, and orientation. *International Journal of Transgenderism, 14,* 24–38. http://dx.doi.org/10.1080/15532739.2013.750222

Ehrensaft, D. (2011). *Gender born, gender made: Raising healthy gender-nonconforming children.* New York, NY: The Experiment.

Ehrensaft, D. (2016). *The gender creative child: Pathways for nurturing and supporting children who live outside gender boxes.* New York, NY: The Experiment.

Erickson-Schroth, L. (2013). Update on the biology of transgender identity. *Journal of Gay & Lesbian Mental Health, 17,* 150–174. http://dx.doi.org/10.1080/19359705.2013.753393

Goldberg, A. B. (Producer). (2007, April 27). *My secret self: A story of transgender children* [Television program]. Houston, TX: ABC News.

Golombok, S., & Fivuch, R. (1994). *Gender development.* Cambridge, England: Cambridge University Press.

Gonzalez, M., & McNulty, J. (2010). Achieving competency with transgender youth: School counselors as collaborative advocates. *Journal of LGBT Issues in Counseling, 4,* 176–186. http://dx.doi.org/10.1080/15538605.2010.524841

Goodrich, K. M., & Luke, M. (2009). LGBTQ responsive school counseling. *Journal of LGBT Issues in Counseling, 3,* 113–127. http://dx.doi.org/10.1080/15538600903005284

Hembree, W. C., Cohen-Kettenis, P., Delemarre-van de Waal, H. A., Gooren, L. J., Meyer, W. J., III, Spack, N. P., . . . Montori, V. M. (2009). Endocrine treatment of transsexual persons: An Endocrine Society clinical practice guideline. *The Journal of Clinical Endocrinology and Metabolism, 94,* 3132–3154. http://dx.doi.org/10.1210/jc.2009-0345

Hidalgo, M. A., Ehrensaft, D., Tishelman, A. C., Clark, L. F., Garofalo, R., Rosenthal, S. M., . . . Olson, J. (2013). The gender affirmative model: What we know and what we aim to learn. *Human Development, 56,* 285–290. http://dx.doi.org/10.1159/000355235

Hill, D. B., Menvielle, E., Sica, K. M., & Johnson, A. (2010). An affirmative intervention for families with gender variant children: Parental ratings of child mental health and gender. *Journal of Sex & Marital Therapy, 36,* 6–23. http://dx.doi.org/10.1080/00926230903375560

Kranz, G. S., Hahn, A., Kaufmann, U., Küblböck, M., Hummer, A., Ganger, S., . . . Lanzenberger, R. (2014). White matter microstructure in transsexuals and controls investigated by diffusion tensor imaging. *The Journal of Neuroscience, 34,* 15466–15475. http://dx.doi.org/10.1523/JNEUROSCI.2488-14.2014

Lev, A. I. (2005). Disordering gender identity: Gender identity disorder in the *DSM–IV–TR. Journal of Psychology & Human Sexuality, 17*(3/4), 35–69. http://dx.doi.org/10.1300/J056v17n03_03

Mapes, D. (2012, February). More transgender kids seeking help, getting treatment. *MSNBC.* Retrieved from https://vitals.nbcnews.com/_news/2012/02/20/10450683-more-transgender-kids-seeking-help-getting-treatment?d=1

Mock, J. (2014). *Redefining realness: My path to womanhood, identity, love, and so much more.* New York, NY: Atria.

National Geographic. (2017). *Gender revolution* [Special issue]. Available from https://www.nationalgeographic.com/magazine/2017/01/

Obedin-Maliver, J., Goldsmith, E. S., Stewart, L., White, W., Tran, E., Brenman, S., . . . Lunn, M. R. (2011). Lesbian, gay, bisexual, and transgender-related content in undergraduate medical education. *JAMA, 306,* 971–977. http://dx.doi.org/10.1001/jama.2011.1255

Pfäfflin, F., & Junge, A. (1998). *Sex reassignment: Thirty years of international follow-up studies after SRS: A comprehensive review, 1961–1991.* Düsseldorf, Germany: Symposium Publishing.

Pupil rights: Sex-segregated school programs and activities, S., 1266, § 221.5 (2013).

Quart, A. (2008, March 16). When girls will be boys. *The New York Times.* Retrieved from http://www.nytimes.com/2008/03/16/magazine/16students-t.html

Rametti, G., Carrillo, B., Gómez-Gil, E., Junque, C., Segovia, S., Gomez, Á., & Guillamon, A. (2011). White matter microstructure in female to male transsexuals before cross-sex hormonal treatment: A diffusion tensor imaging study. *Journal of Psychiatric Research, 45,* 199–204. http://dx.doi.org/10.1016/j.jpsychires.2010.05.006

Rametti, G., Carrillo, B., Gómez-Gil, E., Junque, C., Zubiarre-Elorza, L., Segovia, S., . . . Guillamon, A. (2011). The microstructure of white matter in male to female transsexuals before cross-sex hormonal treatment: A DTI study. *Journal of Psychiatric Research, 45,* 949–954. http://dx.doi.org/10.1016/j.jpsychires.2010.11.007

Ryan, C., Huebner, D., Diaz, R. M., & Sanchez, J. (2009). Family rejection as a predictor of negative health outcomes in white and Latino lesbian, gay, and bisexual young adults. *Pediatrics, 123,* 346–352. http://dx.doi.org/10.1542/peds.2007-3524

Sexual orientation change efforts, S., 1172, § 865 (2012).

Spack, N. P., Edwards-Leeper, L., Feldman, H. A., Leibowitz, S., Mandel, F., Diamond, D. A., & Vance, S. R. (2012). Children and adolescents with gender identity disorder referred to a pediatric medical center. *Pediatrics, 129,* 418–425. http://dx.doi.org/10.1542/peds.2011-0907

Speigel, A. (2008, May 7). Two families grapple with sons' gender identity: Psychologists take radically different approaches in therapy. *National Public Radio: All Things Considered.* Retrieved from https://www.npr.org/2008/05/07/90247842/two-families-grapple-with-sons-gender-preferences

Veale, J. F., Clarke, D. E., & Lomax, T. C. (2010). Biological and psychosocial correlates of adult gender-variant identities: A review. *Personality and Individual Differences, 48,* 357–366. http://dx.doi.org/10.1016/j.paid.2009.09.018

World Professional Association for Transgender Health. (2011). *Standards of care for the health of transsexual, transgender, and gender nonconforming people* (7th version). Retrieved from https://www.wpath.org/media/cms/Documents/Web%20Transfer/SOC/Standards%20of%20Care%20V7%20-%202011%20WPATH.pdf

Zhou, J. N., Hofman, M. A., Gooren, L. J., & Swaab, D. F. (1995, November 2). A sex difference in the human brain and its relation to transsexuality. *Nature, 378,* 68–70. http://dx.doi.org/10.1038/378068a0

Zucker, K. J., Bradley, S. J., Owen-Anderson, A., Kibblewhite, S. J., & Cantor, J. M. (2008). Is gender identity disorder in adolescents coming out of the closet? [Letter to the editor]. *Journal of Sex & Marital Therapy, 34,* 287–290. http://dx.doi.org/10.1080/00926230802096192

Zucker, K. J., & Cohen-Kettenis, P. T. (2008). Gender identity disorder in children and adolescents. In D. L. Rowland & L. Incrocci (Eds.), *Handbook of sexual and gender identity disorders* (pp. 376–422). Hoboken, NJ: Wiley. http://dx.doi.org/10.1002/9781118269978.ch13

Erica E. Anderson

The Unfolding and Exploration of Gender From a Gender Affirmative Perspective

2

Few aspects of human development have undergone such radical scrutiny and exploration in the early 21st century as gender. One of the factors that may have previously restrained more open inquiry is that the dominant gender schema ("biology is destiny") "ideologically links sex to both gender and to sexuality through a purportedly biologically controlled connection" (Devor, 1994). This model of gender development, prevalent until the recent past, asserts that "biological facts" (sex assigned at birth) automatically determine the gender that a person will be. Such determination occurs as early as a detection at birth (assigned sex) or in developed countries in utero, assuming it matches observation of external genitals at birth. One's assigned sex has been presumed by the dominant gender schema to explain the development of gender, with variations in the connection between sex and gender typically regarded as not normal.

The dominant gender schema has come under attack from a variety of perspectives. Feminist scholars have questioned the dominant gender schema as being male centric and inadequate to account for female gender and sexual development, let alone development in those now known as transgender or genderqueer. Similar scholarship in the study of lesbian, gay, bisexual, or queer (LGBQ) cisgender people has pointed out that the dominant gender schema

http://dx.doi.org/10.1037/0000095-002
The Gender Affirmative Model: An Interdisciplinary Approach to Supporting Transgender and Gender Expansive Children, C. Keo-Meier and D. Ehrensaft (Editors)
Copyright © 2018 by the American Psychological Association. All rights reserved.

cannot account for the development of same-gender attractions and consolidation in one's gender identity.

More recently, scholars working with transgender and gender expansive (TGE) children have observed early disclosure of a transgender identity on the part of many such children, even in the absence of factors that previously were used to account for such variation (e.g., in the case of transgender girls, father absence). To more fully understand TGE children, scholars have proposed an alternative gender affirmative model (GAM) of development to the dominant gender schema. On the one hand, with the dominant gender schema and biology-is-destiny view, children explore gender by expressing themselves in society having been assigned and told by many in their lives that they are male or female. As such communication and social experience occur, each child is affirmed in one or the other sex assignment. Such confirmation occurs from a very early age and is continuous and unremitting. For the vast majority of children, such experience reinforces their own gender identity and growing self-concept as either a boy or a girl, based on their sex assignment at birth.

However, those engaged in clinical work with TGE children report that some children resist the efforts of others to teach and reinforce expectations of masculine or feminine behavior in society. In some cases, the gender identity of a child can motivate them to resist accepting a gender identity consistent with sex assigned at birth, as the latter is at odds with who they know themselves to be. In such cases, the development of a transgender identity can occur across childhood and can exhibit not only resistance to conventions but also persistence in such transgression. In other cases, the expansive gender expression of a child motivates their resistance to adopting expected masculine or feminine behaviors (Butler, 1990). For example, a child whose gender identity of boy is aligned with the male sex he was assigned at birth may refuse to play with trucks, insist on playing female roles in play, communicate that he loves playing with Barbies, and want to grow his hair long "like mommy." Virtually every child is gendered within familial and social relationships, as well as in their exposure to and interactions with others in the larger social environment (Bronfenbrenner, 1986). TGE children can be expected to likely confront the expectations of other children, who in most cases have fully adopted the dominant gender schema for themselves and presume that all other children do so as well.

As TGE children experience more of their social life outside of the family, their individual gender expression and exploration as well as its variation from the dominant gender schema become more and more apparent to others. The gender exploration conducted by any individual child will eventually be highly interactive with others inside and outside the child's family. As each child's cognitive, social, and psychological development progress, the interaction between a child's capability and feedback from society will mold, shape/reshape, and in many cases, challenge the child's gender identity. The willingness of any individual child to explore expansive gender expression will be a by-product of many factors, including, at a minimum, the child's level of assertiveness, confidence, flexibility, and openness to do so openly in full view of others. At the same time, the social ecology in which children might find themselves is itself shifting as society exhibits more or less tolerance for those whose gender exploration diverges from the expected exploration of traditional binary gender identities and expressions.

It is unfortunate that few longitudinal studies exist to guide researchers in tracking the developmental pathways of TGE children. Efforts to monitor and document the life course of TGE individuals (e.g., The Shine Study, being conducted through the San Francisco Department of Public Health) are just beginning. Revised theories of gender development are needed to inform those studies. To that end, I turn to a discussion of existent theories of gender development.

Theories of Gender Identity Formation/ Stages of Development

At least three clear perspectives or theories exist that address how and, to some extent, why gender develops.

BIOLOGICAL

This approach to gender development concerns itself with a number of factors related to biology. These include an evolutionary perspective, a genetic perspective, a hormonal perspective, and a neuroscience perspective. In the biological view of gender development, genes (chromosomes), sex hormones, and brain development collaborate in their impact on sex differences in physical function and behavior (Hoyenga & Hoyenga, 1993; Piaget, 1964). Differences in the hypothalamus of cisgender male and females result from differences in exposure to androgens (e.g., dihydrotestosterone) in utero, which is also responsible for differentiation of internal and external genitalia. Some research exists that describes effects of exposure to atypical levels of prenatal hormones for one's sex. For example, girls with congenital adrenal hyperplasia and exposure to androgens exhibit expressions known to be more common among boys. These include interest in "boy" toys, higher activity levels, greater physical aggressiveness, and less interest in internally focused activities than is typically expected of girls (Berenbaum, 1999; Berenbaum & Hines, 1992; Berenbaum & Resnick, 1997; Berenbaum & Snyder, 1995; Leveroni & Berenbaum, 1998).

Within the biological perspective is evolutionary theory (Buss & Kenrick, 1998; Kenrick & Luce, 2000), which posits that differences between the two genders have existed for millennia and serve the evolutionary purpose of survival and propagation of the species. Modern sex differences, when they exist, are thus said to descend from such needs for the species to survive. Those who most successfully perform the behaviors necessary for such survival are selected favorably and are hence more likely to pass along their genetic strains.

SOCIAL

The second significant theory of gender development concerns socialization approaches. In this theory, it is presumed that the differential treatment of children by parents, family members, peers, and others in the larger social environment shapes the development of male and female children differently (Fagot, Rodgers, & Leinbach, 2000; Ruble, Martin, & Berenbaum, 2006). Such approaches began significantly with Freud's (1986/1905) biosocial theory, in which he introduced the idea of penis envy as a construct to account for emerging awareness of anatomical differences between boys and girls. In Freud's view, socialization entered with the child's identification with same sex parents that developed as a child came to know genitals. He believed that the knowledge of anatomical differences, the experience of constancy of persons, and identification with the same sex parent coalesced in the acquisition of a child's stable gender identity. Research has now revealed that conscious knowledge of genitals and their significance more typically comes later in development than believed by Freud and after a child's socialization into a particular gender. For example, a child's demonstrated affinity for toys, activities, and playmates typically shows up before a child's self-knowledge of the genitals they have but after they have comprehended that they are being socialized as one gender or the other, that is, "I am girl" or "I am boy," known in the 20th century literature on gender development as "core gender identity" (Bem, 1989; McConaghy, 1979).

Learning theory and reinforcement paradigms, in particular, the work of Bandura (1977), provided a social engineering model of gender. According to this perspective, much behavior, including gender-related behavior, is learned from the social environment. In this paradigm, children pattern their gender behavior after "models," socialization agents who show the children how they are to behave through modeling, teaching, and shaping behaviors through reinforcement strategies. Regarding gender formation, it is assumed that the vast majority of male children observe and imitate older males, and the vast majority of female children observe and imitate older females.

At the same time, significant others directly and indirectly communicate gender expectations to the child through both verbal and nonverbal means. As an example of subjectively based gender expectations, mothers in one study estimated the crawling ability of 11-month-old infants differentially on the basis of the sex of the child: Boys were believed to be capable of crawling faster than girls, although the evidence shows no such difference (Mondschein, Adolph, & Tamis-LeMonda, 2000). So, within the learning theory of gender development, gender-specific expectations by socialization agents in turn affect interactions with the children, with the result of shaping gender behavior in children, whether with or without conscious intent.

COGNITIVE

The third theory concerning gender development is the cognitive theory. In this framework, the knowledge acquired by children about gender, gender stereotypes, and norms influences how children think and then behave. In this view, each child acquires a gender schema, which is modified over time as the child gains more experience and becomes much more sophisticated. Over time, the evolving schema of one's gender organize themselves into a solid and stable gender identity (Kohlberg, 1966).

Binary and Nonbinary Gender Development

The development of gender in the binary has presumed either that biology is destiny or that the combination of nature and nurture (perhaps with a leavening of culture) yields in most cases a predictable and linear course with the healthy outcome of a boy or girl gender identity along with masculine and feminine gender expressions, respectively. Under this framework, the normative result is gender development consistent with sex assigned at birth. Children who vary from this have been perceived as "abnormal" and typically exposed to interventions to get onto or resume the "normal" course of gender development, despite evidence that such efforts to convert or repair gender development to conform to their binary sex assignment and expectations not only do not work but are also harmful (Substance Abuse and Mental Health Services Administration [SAMHSA], 2015).

In contrast, expansive gender development can take many paths and proceed at a highly individual pace. Nonbinary and expansive gender development accommodates a spectrum of gender identities and expressions (Ehrensaft, 2010, 2016; Hidalgo et al., 2013; Simons, Leibowitz, & Hidalgo, 2014). Scholars studying both gender development and same-gender sexual orientation argue that rather than account for variations as deviations, science must recognize the primacy of variations as inherently natural. The original work of Kinsey, Pomeroy, Martin, and Sloan (1948) addressed this; more recently, the SAMHSA (2015) report on conversion therapy, among other sources, asserted the current view that developmental variations in gender identity, gender expression, and sexual orientation (outside of the binary and heteronormative paradigm) are essentially normal, albeit far from the mean.

In the traditional cisnormative binary gender model, children are assigned one of two genders, boy or girl. In nearly every country in the world, formal documentation of live births records a sex, male or female. This results in the schema of a child's "assigned" sex and presumed gender. Hence, each child is said in this model to be either male or female. Those children whose physical appearance at birth (i.e., external genitalia) does not easily yield a conclusion by medical personnel present at the birth of the child as male or female are evaluated further to determine their sex, and historically in Western countries, recommendations have been made to surgically, in infancy, alter the genitals in accordance with one sex or the other, a practice that is presently in disfavor as against the best interests of the child (Rosenthal, 2014).

This binary model also is predicated on the view that the future lived experience of those whose gender and physical presentation does not conform to binary gender norms will most likely result in stigmatization and marginalization (Zucker & Bradley, 1995; Zucker, Wood, Singh, & Bradley, 2012). Experts abiding by this model argue that children can be assisted to align their gender with their assigned sex at birth and that these efforts are likely to result in such children avoiding multiple medical interventions and distress that results when one is TGE. Although some have argued that such interventions are efficacious as well as humane (Zucker, 2008; Zucker et al., 2012), controversy exists about such interventions, with a conclusion that such interventions are harmful to a child's development (Coleman et al., 2012; Ehrensaft,

2011; Hill, Menvielle, Sica, & Johnson, 2010; Pyne, 2014; SAMHSA, 2015; Travers et al., 2012).

I now turn to perception of children and their needs, using a nonbinary construct of gender development. Research indicates that an uncertain percentage of children who demonstrate gender diversity and have received a diagnosis of Gender Dysphoria (or Gender Identity Disorder, in the *Diagnostic and Statistical Manual of Mental Disorders*; fourth ed.; American Psychiatric Association, 1994) persist in a gender identity different from assigned sex at birth. Percentages vary from 12% to 50% in estimating the proportion of such children who persist in gender diversity into adolescence and adulthood (Drummond, Bradley, Peterson-Badali, & Zucker, 2008; Steensma, McGuire, Kreukels, Beekman, & Cohen-Kettenis, 2013; Wallien & Cohen-Kettenis, 2008). A fault in this research is that nonpersistence includes those who are lost to follow-up in research studies or do not for whatever reason return to the clinics conducting patient follow-ups. The inherent assumption that most such children who drop out of gender services no longer identify with a gender different from that assigned at birth, a questionable assumption at best and certainly unacceptable in terms of research data accountability (Steensma, McGuire, Kreukels, Beekman, & Cohen-Kettenis, 2013; Wallien & Cohen-Kettenis, 2008; Zucker, 2008). See Chapter 3, this volume, for further discussion of persistence/desistence.

Additional issues arise in the case of the evaluation of adolescent gender development. Some adolescents will have exhibited gender dysphoria or gender expansiveness since early childhood. Sometimes dysphoria or expansiveness only surfaces with the onset of puberty. Emerging gender dysphoria or expansiveness may first become apparent in the co-occurrence with psychological problems (see Chapter 5, this volume), such as suicidal ideation and self-injurious behaviors (Liu & Mustanski, 2012; Mustanski, Garofalo, & Emerson, 2010), drug and alcohol abuse (Garofalo, Deleon, Osmer, Doll, & Harper, 2006), and/or autism spectrum disorder (de Vries, Noens, Cohen-Kettenis, van Berckelaer-Onnes, & Doreleijers, 2010; Jones et al., 2012). Although new complications confront medical personnel and families with adolescents, more expert consensus is emerging concerning adolescent gender development and accompanying clinical practice (Coleman et al., 2012; Vance, Ehrensaft, & Rosenthal, 2014). In this view, more seem willing to accept the TGE adolescent's gender identity as developmentally sound; hence, less controversy exists about making available some of the medical intervention options for TGE persons in this age group. Regardless of where along the ages and stages of development scholars and practitioners acknowledge the child's ability to self-determine their authentic gender, those operating within or influenced by the GAM are being guided by the more recent developmental paradigm in which sex assignment does not dictate authentic gender identity and in which the binary male/female is not set in stone.

Case Study

CJ was a 13-year-old teenager, assigned female at birth, who had come out as gay to their parents 1 year before going to a gender specialist for therapy. Their parents had struggled with the issues associated with this revelation, because this heterosexual couple was active in a very conservative religious tradition and faith community. Many months after the family had come to accept their daughter/sister as a gay female, CJ began to experiment with gender presentation and announced a desire to be referred to as *he/him/his*. At that point, a referral was sought to a psychologist who was a gender specialist.

In the course of the evaluation and monitoring of the client, CJ expressed a desire to move away from a binary (masculine) gendered presentation and began to assert a nonbinary gender identity. In turn CJ requested the use of *they* and *them* pronouns in reference to themselves. All parties were prepared to accommodate CJ's wishes about this, including CJ's parents, having worked through the conflicts between this acceptance and the beliefs of their religious community.

Nevertheless, at this point a consultation with the parents was arranged during which the psychologist facilitated the discussion of this recently asserted identity, pronoun use, and corresponding appeals that family, friends, and school personnel accept this version of CJ's gender identity. In the intervening months, CJ had been active in their school's gay/straight alliance, found support for their fluidity and choices, and made such declarations and choices having considered alternatives. By the psychologist's determination, CJ exhibited no obvious distress or dysphoria. They would continue to explore gender identity. The psychologist's evaluation was informed by the nonbinary model of gender development, in which variations and "living in the middle" are embraced as healthy ways of being in child development.

Evidence of Nonbinary Development Among Children

Recently, clinicians have observed TGE children adopting inventive terms to explain their differences from binary gender constructions, such as "I'm a princess with a penis" and "I'm a boy in the front and a girl in the back, kind of a Prius-hybrid" (Ehrensaft, 2012). Ehrensaft (2012) called such children "gender creative." H. Schreier (personal communication, November 2013) reported that these children, having had to negotiate the social milieu of gender conformity, exhibit intelligence, especially social and emotional intelligence, beyond any reasonable standard for their ages. An interesting trend is also appearing among older adolescents and young adults who not only reject the binary construction of gender identity and expression but also refuse the linguistic parallel to binary construction in the use of pronouns, physical appearance, and clothing, asking, among other things, to be called *they/them* rather than *he/him* or *she/her*. Practitioners such as Ehrensaft and her colleagues have been writing that a spectrum or a web of gender identities exists that cannot be accounted for on the basis of binary gender norms and construction. Perceived expansiveness in not only gender expression but also gender identity calls into question previous developmental theories regarding the permanence and certainty of gender identity. In its stead, the GAM of multiple gender pathways now presents challenges of identifying the differing pathways a child may be on—transgender, gender fluid, protogay, and so forth.

In sum, professionals working in the GAM have proposed a developmental model of gender in which a spectrum exists. Such a spectrum can accommodate a range of gender expressions, permit an uncoupling of gender expression from gender identity, and accommodate for changes in both over time. The nonbinary model integrates aspects of development related to gender in such a way as to accentuate the individual nature of gender and create the flexibility to fully embrace individual developmental pathways. Rather than prematurely forcing choices of a binary nature (i.e., girl or boy) to be made with respect to gender identity, masculine or feminine with respect to gender expression, and sexual attractions to the "other gender," those adopting this model argue for a period of extended observation and support for children to explore their gender. At the same time, when it is clear that a child is confidently self-knowledgeable about their true gender self, no attempts are made to hold that child back in the expression of that self. Accepting a spectrum of genders (i.e., a potentially unlimited variety) enables individuals to espouse unique gender identities and expressions, which many believe are already present in the population and which to the knowing eye present themselves in the form of young TGE children every day. Next, I discuss the developmental exploration of gender in the context of the GAM.

Exploration of Gender Expression and Gender Identity

The young child's social world is initially oriented around family, including parental figures and siblings. To the extent that a child expresses themselves at variance from the dominant gender schema, they will typically first do so with family members. Based on the reaction of their family members, such children may feel comfortable with a more elaborated presentation of themselves to the family. Feedback from parents and siblings, whether encouraging and supportive or disapproving and shaming, affects the experience of the child and can cause children to modify or change how they present themselves in the future.

Ambiguous reactions from family that are less clearly positive or negative or that are difficult to decipher for the child can, of course, be even more challenging. This can be especially true for a child who does not model themselves after anyone else in their immediate life experience and may not have language for their thoughts, feelings, or intentions. For a child whose parents accept the child's choices in play, toys, clothing, and activities different from those in conformance to the dominant gender schema, such interests may continue, increase, and become more varied and nuanced. Efforts to suppress expansive gender expressions on the part of parents may result in a variety of reactions by such children. Some children, fearing disapproval of parents, may refrain from expressing alternative choices in the future and may begin to internalize shame. Healthy gender development necessitates opportunities to "try on" gender expressions and potentially new names and pronouns for a child to determine if these feel right for them. Some of these children who sense that their environment is not supportive may then adopt a pattern of secret interest in such gender expressions and then activate that interest only when out of the view of parents, siblings, or others who the child expects to disapprove. In a few cases, such children become more insistent or even combative with those who oppose them or may develop any one of a variety of psychologically damaging reactions, including depression, anxiety with panic, or extreme behavioral problems, both at home and in other environments (e.g., school). Many will develop a secret place in which they can express themselves authentically, creating a shield against feared rejection or disapproval but not relinquishing their inner desires. Although this strategy preserves the core of the child's true gender self, such secrecy may also result in an early and then chronic course of personal conflict over gender identity and public presentation (expression). Such conflict and ongoing difference between gender identity and expression can in fact sow the seeds of shame and trauma in the child's developmental trajectory, with the possible outcome of complex posttraumatic stress disorder, especially in the face of social hostility, prejudice, or marginalization throughout the course of an individual's childhood.

If, by contrast, the response a TGE child receives is more positive, it can permit such a child a more complete and spontaneous exploration of gender identity and expression. As a child expresses interests and impulses, they try out ways to be, for themselves and with others. Interaction with others in the social environment is the means through which the social constructions of gender norms are experienced. However, for TGE children, presenting themselves differently in social interactions in effect facilitates such children's ability to present in ways other than those dictated by the dominant gender schema. The positive response of others can in effect grant children permission to be themselves and to act upon their own predilections, even when such affinities challenge dominant expectations and roles about gender. Developmentally, such permission experienced by the child inclines them less toward satisfying the expectations of others and more toward acting upon their own initiatives. In this way, children can become idiosyncratically creative and more fully themselves. Fantasy play, ideas, verbalizations, dressing, activities and so on provide an outlet for such creativity of the children.

Just as children can be creative in play, so too, can they be creative with gender. Children play and experiment with fantasy, and participate in both solitary activities and interactively with others to act out their fantasies, TGE children can exhibit to themselves and others the gendered possibilities for themselves. They can, in effect, try out in a supportive environment, the identity and more tangibly the gender expression that they wish/aspire to or are curious about.

It should be noted that experts agree that not all exploration of gender, whether in identity or expression, persist and endure past a period of exploration, be it a few hours, days, weeks, or months. Also, it is common for children to have recurrent themes or scenes that they act out over and over or from time to time. Professionals can take note of such themes and derive additional understanding of such children as a result, not unlike the work of child clinicians in play therapy or sand-tray approaches.

The vexing part for parents and professionals is that, developmentally, it is impossible to predict with precision the course of a child's creative gender play or its ultimate outcome. No matter how insistent a child might be at a specific point in time about their identities, and likewise no matter how assertive a child's presentation, developmentally any or all the components of this presentation may be subject to change over time as the child's authentic gender unfolds. On the other hand, a TGE child's explorations are rarely "just a phase"; they may simply be the present stopping point along the developmental gender pathways or they might be quite stable and impermeable.

Over time, parents and professionals will have the opportunity to track the course of a child's authentic gender identity and their more public gender expression. In addition to children whose gender expression may be consistent with their gender identity, some children clearly exhibit gender expressions that do not align with their gender identity. For example, a 9-year-old child who was assigned female at birth, identifies as a girl, prefers boys' clothes, and is pleased when perceived as a boy may never indicate a gender identity other than that of a girl. This child illustrates that many TGE children not only distinguish between gender identity and expression; they make personal choices that are meaningful to them, with thoughtful reasons for making such choices. Further, children's experimenting with gender expression does not necessarily result in such children pairing the culture's normative gender expression, with the gender identity that child knows themselves to be.

Children creatively explore gender expression and even gender identity within an environment they perceive to be safe. In the GAM, parents, siblings, peers, and various adults (e.g., teachers/health professionals) play a vital part in providing support and facilitating exploration and creative expression by a child. Alternatively, developmental outcomes will be skewed or compromised if others in the child's life criticize, challenge, and shame such exploration and creative expression. The underlying premise is that each child deserves the opportunity to be their authentic gender self, with freedom to fully express themselves (assuming personal safety and respect from others) and to ultimately arrive at the best place for themselves insofar as identity is concerned; it is thus important to identify the developmental barriers to such exploration so these barriers can be removed.

Barriers to Healthy Gender Development

Such developmental barriers to healthy gender development are potentially more numerous than any limited list can convey; a few obvious barriers are highlighted here.

FIRST: LACK OF SAFETY

Most children who do not feel safe and loved will react with fear and apprehension. Children who do not feel accepted and cared for in general may likely not reveal weakness to others, which may coalesce around hiding their true gender selves from harm. Basic survival instincts will motivate most children to concentrate on meeting basic needs before exploring the more vulnerable aspects of themselves—in this case, their authentic gender.

SECOND: FAILURE TO IDENTIFY DIFFERENCES IN THREAT/ DANGER BETWEEN PRIVATE AND PUBLIC SPACES

It is imperative that adults recognize differences in threat or danger levels between creativity explored (a) in private among those who know and have established a basis of trust with the child and (b) in more public settings. Within those public settings, others may be known to the child, but the child may not feel safe because they do not have control over the environment and feel uncertain about whether they might be negatively exposed in some ways, including to those who may mistakenly take it upon themselves to enforce the dominant gender schema.

Whether interventions to help a child conform to normative gender expectations are motivated by a sincere desire to provide helpful, even loving, direction to a child or are motivated by transphobia and bigotry, the effects can be very negative. Hence, gender expansiveness at home may naturally be freer than at school or in public places. Just as the risks of disapproval, or worse, exist for the TGE child outside the family, many children may experience less than total acceptance even within their own immediate family, as well as within their extended family. Parents often do not agree upon the level of acceptance for a child in their own immediate family, and extended family may vary in their acceptance levels as well. A sibling can be an ally but sometimes, out of their own anxieties, an adversary in a TGE child's gender explorations. Other dynamics among children and between children and parents can obscure or mask real feelings of shame and disapproval that can affect the gender creative child and, conversely, their siblings as well. Work with TGE children must therefore include work with the entire family to ensure healthy gender development (see Chapters 8, 9, and 10, this volume).

THIRD: LACK OF CONSENSUS AMONG PROFESSIONALS

One of the intentions of the authors in this book is to create consensus among professionals working with TGE children (Edwards-Leeper & Spack, 2012). Many of the issues raised by work with such children have been highly controversial. It is not surprising that professionals in psychology, pediatrics, and education have debated how to respond to such children (American Psychological Association, 2015). Ongoing controversy among the specific professionals involved with an individual child must be addressed and cannot be ignored without risking deleterious effects upon the child. Everyone understands how ongoing fundamental conflict between parents about child rearing practices and values affects a child negatively. A similar dynamic of frustration and disagreement is also detrimental when it is professionals responding to a TGE child. Absent a model (e.g., the GAM, discussed in this volume) and practical guidance supported by all parties, continued controversies can do nothing but harm a TGE child's unfolding development.

FOURTH: DISPARITIES IN THE ACCEPTANCE OF TRANSGENDER AND GENDER EXPANSIVE CHILDREN IN THE LARGER COMMUNITY

When parents of a TGE child begin to support the child's authentic gender presentation in their school, religious organization, and larger community, disparities are revealed in the position of others outside the family. Such differences, unaddressed, can also compromise and derail family plans and interventions. Care must be given to communicate and, at times, negotiate with school officials. Parents must exert a watchful oversight beyond that usually practiced even by the most competent of parents (Angello, 2013). Venturing out into community programs and activities presents new challenges, including the need to communicate and problem solve to support a child's unfolding gender development.

FIFTH: REJECTING THE GENDER AFFIRMATIVE MODEL AS DISRUPTIVE TO SOCIETY

All involved in supporting these children must recognize that, like it or not, we are all involved in disrupting society's tacit and strong devotion to the dominant gender schema. Although we may not have chosen to be social activists, we have become so, by default perhaps. Advocating for what is best for these children, giving permission for them to become their authentic selves, even with the attendant costs, can test the resolve of even the most ardent advocate of individual self-expression. Parents and professionals who come to support the GAM of development for gender creative children must reckon with a society largely resistant to changing the adherence to the dominant gender schema. The authors of this book have borne witness to hundreds of families and their children who have struggled to do the right thing for the children. It is for them that we struggle to open a new path for the development of authentic and healthy gender identity and expression.

References

American Psychiatric Association. (1994). *Diagnostic and statistical manual of mental disorders* (4th ed.). Washington, DC: Author.

American Psychological Association. (2015). Guidelines for psychological practice with transgender and gender nonconforming people. *American Psychologist, 70,* 832–864. http://dx.doi.org/10.1037/a0039906

Angello, M. (2013). *On the couch with Dr. Angello: A guide to raising and supporting transgender youth*. Philadelphia, PA: Author.

Bandura, A. (1977). Self-efficacy: Toward a unifying theory of behavioral change. *Psychological Review, 84,* 191–215. http://dx.doi.org/10.1037/0033-295X.84.2.191

Bem, S. L. (1989). Genital knowledge and gender constancy in preschool children. *Child Development, 60,* 649–662. http://dx.doi.org/10.2307/1130730

Berenbaum, S. A. (1999). Effects of early androgens on sex-typed activities and interests in adolescents with congenital adrenal hyperplasia. *Hormones and Behavior, 35,* 102–110. http://dx.doi.org/10.1006/hbeh.1998.1503

Berenbaum, S. A., & Hines, M. (1992). Early androgens are related to childhood sex-typed toy preferences. *Psychological Science, 3,* 203–206. http://dx.doi.org/10.1111/j.1467-9280.1992.tb00028.x

Berenbaum, S. A., & Resnick, S. M. (1997). Early androgen effects on aggression in children and adults with congenital adrenal hyperplasia. *Psychoneuroendocrinology, 22,* 505–515. http://dx.doi.org/10.1016/S0306-4530(97)00049-8

Berenbaum, S. A., & Snyder, E. (1995). Early hormonal influences on childhood sex-typed activity and playmate preferences: Implications for the development of sexual orientation. *Developmental Psychology, 31,* 31–42. http://dx.doi.org/10.1037/0012-1649.31.1.31

Bronfenbrenner, U. (1986). Ecology of the family as a context for human development: Research perspectives. *Developmental Psychology, 22,* 723–742. http://dx.doi.org/10.1037/0012-1649.22.6.723

Buss, D. M., & Kenrick, D. T. (1998). Evolutionary social psychology. In D. T. Gilbert, S. T. Fiske, & G. Lindzey (Eds.), *Handbook of social psychology* (4th ed., Vol. 2, pp. 982–1026). New York, NY: Oxford.

Butler, J. (1990). *Gender trouble: Feminism and the subversion of identity.* New York, NY: Routledge.

Coleman, E., Bockting, W., Botzer, M., Cohen-Kettenis, P., DeCuypere, G., Feldman, J., . . . Zucker, K. (2012). Standards of care for the health of transsexual, transgender, and gender-nonconforming people: Version 7. *International Journal of Transgenderism, 13,* 165–232. http://dx.doi.org/10.1080/15532739.2011.700873

de Vries, A. L., Noens, I. L., Cohen-Kettenis, P. T., van Berckelaer-Onnes, I. A., & Doreleijers, T. A. (2010). Autism spectrum disorders in gender dysphoric children and adolescents. *Journal of Autism and Developmental Disorders, 40,* 930–936. http://dx.doi.org/10.1007/s10803-010-0935-9

Devor, H. (1994). Toward a taxonomy of gendered sexuality. *Journal of Psychology & Human Sexuality, 6,* 23–56. http://dx.doi.org/10.1300/J056v06n01_03

Drummond, K. D., Bradley, S. J., Peterson-Badali, M., & Zucker, K. J. (2008). A follow-up study of girls with gender identity disorder. *Developmental Psychology, 44,* 34–45. http://dx.doi.org/10.1037/0012-1649.44.1.34

Edwards-Leeper, L., & Spack, N. P. (2012). Psychological evaluation and medical treatment of transgender youth in an interdisciplinary "Gender Management Service" (GeMS) in a major pediatric center. *Journal of Homosexuality, 59,* 321–336. http://dx.doi.org/10.1080/00918369.2012.653302

Ehrensaft, D. (2010). I'm a Prius: A child case of a gender/ethnic hybrid. *Journal of Gay & Lesbian Mental Health, 15,* 46–57. http://dx.doi.org/10.1080/19359705.2011.530571

Ehrensaft, D. (2011). Boys will be girls, girls will be boys: Children affect parents as parents affect children in gender nonconformity. *Psychoanalytic Psychology, 28,* 528–548. http://dx.doi.org/10.1037/a0023828

Ehrensaft, D. (2012). From gender identity disorder to gender identity creativity: True gender self child therapy. *Journal of Homosexuality, 59,* 337–356. http://dx.doi.org/10.1080/00918369.2012.653303

Ehrensaft, D. (2016). *The gender creative child: Pathways for nurturing and supporting children who live outside gender boxes.* New York, NY: The Experiment.

Fagot, B. I., Rodgers, C. S., & Leinbach, M. D. (2000). Theories of gender socialization. In T. Eckes & H. M. Trautner (Eds.), *The developmental social psychology of gender* (pp. 65–89). Hillsdale, NJ: Erlbaum.

Freud, S. (1986). Three essays on the theory of sexuality. In J. Strachey (Ed. & Trans.), *The standard edition of the complete psychological works of Sigmund Freud* (Vol. 7, pp. 7–243). London, England: Hogarth. (Original work published 1905)

Garofalo, R., Deleon, J., Osmer, E., Doll, M., & Harper, G. W. (2006). Overlooked, misunderstood and at-risk: Exploring the lives and HIV risk of ethnic minority male-to-female transgender youth. *Journal of Adolescent Health, 38,* 230–236. http://dx.doi.org/10.1016/j.jadohealth.2005.03.023

Hidalgo, M. A., Ehrensaft, D., Tishelman, A. C., Clark, L. F., Garofalo, R., Rosenthal, S. M., . . . Olson, J. (2013). The gender affirmative model: What we know and what we aim to learn. *Human Development, 56,* 285–290. http://dx.doi.org/10.1159/000355235

Hill, D. B., Menvielle, E., Sica, K. M., & Johnson, A. (2010). An affirmative intervention for families with gender variant children: Parental ratings of child mental health and gender. *Journal of Sex & Marital Therapy, 36,* 6–23. http://dx.doi.org/10.1080/00926230903375560

Hoyenga, K. B., & Hoyenga, K. T. (1993). *Gender-related differences: Origins and outcomes.* Boston, MA: Allyn & Bacon.

Jones, R. M., Wheelwright, S., Farrell, K., Martin, E., Green, R., Di Ceglie, D., & Baron-Cohen, S. (2012). Brief report: Female-to-male transsexual people and autistic traits. *Journal of Autism and Developmental Disorders, 42,* 301–306. http://dx.doi.org/10.1007/s10803-011-1227-8

Kenrick, D. T., & Luce, C. L. (2000). An evolutionary life-history model of gender differences and similarities. In T. Eckes & H. M. Trautner (Eds.), *The developmental social psychology of gender* (pp. 35–64). Hillsdale, NJ: Erlbaum.

Kinsey, A., Pomeroy, W., Martin, C., & Sloan, S. (1948). *Sexual behaviour in the human male.* London, England: W. B. Saunders.

Kohlberg, L. (1966). A cognitive developmental analysis of children's sex-role attitudes. In E. Maccoby (Ed.), *Development of sex differences* (pp. 82–173). Stanford, CA: Stanford University.

Leveroni, C., & Berenbaum, S. A. (1998). Early androgen effects on interest in infants: Evidence from children with congenital adrenal hyperplasia. *Developmental Neuropsychology, 14,* 321–340. http://dx.doi.org/10.1080/87565649809540714

Liu, R. T., & Mustanski, B. (2012). Suicidal ideation and self-harm in lesbian, gay, bisexual, and transgender youth. *American Journal of Preventive Medicine, 42,* 221–228. http://dx.doi.org/10.1016/j.amepre.2011.10.023

McConaghy, M. J. (1979). Gender permanence and the genital basis of gender: Stages in the development of constancy of gender identity. *Child Development, 50,* 1223–1226. http://dx.doi.org/10.2307/1129354

Mondschein, E. R., Adolph, K. E., & Tamis-LeMonda, C. S. (2000). Gender bias in mothers' expectations about infant crawling. *Journal of Experimental Child Psychology, 77,* 304–316. http://dx.doi.org/10.1006/jecp.2000.2597

Mustanski, B. S., Garofalo, R., & Emerson, E. M. (2010). Mental health disorders, psychological distress, and suicidality in a diverse sample of lesbian, gay, bisexual, and transgender youths. *American Journal of Public Health, 100,* 2426–2432. http://dx.doi.org/10.2105/AJPH.2009.178319

Piaget, J. (1964). Part I: Cognitive development in children: Piaget development and learning. *Journal of Research in Science Teaching, 2,* 176–186. http://dx.doi.org/10.1002/tea.3660020306

Pyne, J. (2014). The governance of gender non-conforming children: A dangerous enclosure. *Annual Review of Critical Psychology, 11,* 79–96. Retrieved from https://thediscourseunit.files.wordpress.com/2016/08/5-governance1.pdf

Rosenthal, S. M. (2014). Approach to the patient: Transgender youth: Endocrine considerations. *The Journal of Clinical Endocrinology and Metabolism, 99,* 4379–4389. http://dx.doi.org/10.1210/jc.2014-1919

Ruble, D. N., Martin, C. L., & Berenbaum, S. A. (2006). Gender development. In N. Eisenberg, W. Damon, & R. M. Lerner (Eds.), *Handbook of child psychology: Vol. 3. Social, emotional, and personality development* (6th ed., pp. 858–932). Hoboken, NJ: Wiley.

Simons, L. K., Leibowitz, S. F., & Hidalgo, M. A. (2014). Understanding gender variance in children and adolescents. *Pediatric Annals, 43,* e126–e131. http://dx.doi.org/10.3928/00904481-20140522-07

Steensma, T. D., McGuire, J. K., Kreukels, B. P. C., Beekman, A. J., & Cohen-Kettenis, P. T. (2013). Factors associated with desistence and persistence of childhood gender dysphoria: A quantitative follow-up study. *Journal of the American Academy of Child & Adolescent Psychiatry, 52,* 582–590. http://dx.doi.org/10.1016/j.jaac.2013.03.016

Substance Abuse and Mental Health Services Administration. (2015). *Ending conversion therapy: Supporting and affirming LGBTQ youth* (HHS Publication No. SMA 15-4928). Rockville, MD: Author.

Travers, R., Bauer, G., Pyne, J., Bradley, K., Gale, L., & Papadimitriou, M. (2012, October 2). *Impacts of strong parental support for trans youth: A report prepared for Children's Aid Society of Toronto and Delisle Youth Services.* Retrieved from http://transpulseproject.ca/wp-content/uploads/2012/10/Impacts-ofStrong-Parental-Support-for-Trans-Youth-vFINAL.pdf

Vance, S. R., Jr., Ehrensaft, D., & Rosenthal, S. M. (2014). Psychological and medical care of gender nonconforming youth. *Pediatrics, 134,* 1184–1192. http://dx.doi.org/10.1542/peds.2014-0772

Wallien, M. S., & Cohen-Kettenis, P. T. (2008). Psychosexual outcome of gender-dysphoric children. *Journal of the American Academy of Child & Adolescent Psychiatry, 47,* 1413–1423. http://dx.doi.org/10.1097/CHI.0b013e31818956b9

Zucker, K. J. (2008). Enfants avec troubles de l'identité sexuée: Y-a-t-il une pratique la meilleure? [Children with gender identity disorder: Is there a best practice?]. *Neuropsychiatrie de l'Enfance et de l'Adolescence, 56,* 350–357. http://dx.doi.org/10.1016/j.neurenf.2008.05.010

Zucker, K. J., & Bradley, S. J. (1995). *Gender identity disorder and psychosexual problems in children and adolescents.* New York, NY: Guilford Press.

Zucker, K. J., Wood, H., Singh, D., & Bradley, S. J. (2012). A developmental, biopsychosocial model for the treatment of children with gender identity disorder. *Journal of Homosexuality, 59,* 369–397. http://dx.doi.org/10.1080/00918369.2012.653309

Diane Ehrensaft

3 Exploring Gender Expansive Expressions Versus Asserting a Gender Identity

In the gender affirmative model (GAM), emphasis is put on gender diversity. Beyond two boxes, a child's gender can unfold in an infinite variety of hues and textures. In other writing (Ehrensaft, 2011, 2012, 2016), I have referred metaphorically to each child's evolution of their authentic gender self as a spinning activity: Each child spins their own unique gender web based on three major categories of threads: nature, nurture, and culture. Some children will spin a cisgender web with gender expressions conforming to gender identity and sex assigned to them at birth (e.g., a cisgender girly girl), some a transgender web, also with gender expressions conforming to gender identity but not congruent with the sex assigned to them at birth (e.g., a transgender girly girl), and so forth. This complicated new paradigm that replaces the traditional model of binary gender development based on sex assigned at birth presents some complicated clinical challenges: How do we as clinicians ascertain what a child's authentic or true gender self is? What measures do we take to support it? Subsequent chapters in this volume address assessment protocols for answering these two questions, but for the purpose of this chapter I focus on the conceptual paradigm for creating pathways for differentiating children who are exploring gender expressions (i.e., children who accept the gender associated with the sex assigned to them at birth but do not conform to the social expectations for gender roles and behavior)

http://dx.doi.org/10.1037/0000095-003
The Gender Affirmative Model: An Interdisciplinary Approach to Supporting Transgender and Gender Expansive Children, C. Keo-Meier and D. Ehrensaft (Editors)
Copyright © 2018 by the American Psychological Association. All rights reserved.

from children who are affirming a gender identity that is other than that associated with the sex assigned to them at birth, from yet a third group of children who are interweaving both a transgender gender identity and gender expansive expressions. This conceptualization is not just an intellectual exercise. Significant and sometimes heated controversy has surfaced within the first 2 decades of the 21st century revolving around three questions: (a) Can a young child really know their gender identity? (b) Can we as mental health professionals accurately detect a child's authentic gender identity? and (c) Would it be against a child's best interests to allow a transgender and gender expansive (TGE) young child to socially transition from one gender to another when existing clinical research repeatedly indicates that most children assessed with gender dysphoria early in life do not persist with this dysphoria by the end of their childhoods?

Answers to each of these questions are addressed within the GAM by focusing on the differentiation between the three groups of children: those who question and explore their gender identities (hereinafter, "apples"), those who question and explore their gender expressions (hereinafter, "oranges"), and those who question and explore both (hereinafter, "fruit salads"). Intervention recommendations will be made for each of the three groups of children, depending on where they position themselves across the groups. It should be noted from the outset that these three groupings are not fixed categories, and any child can traverse from one to another over a period of time or stay firmly embedded in one of them. Further, in the spirit of gender infinity, we are continually spotting interstices between and among the apples, oranges, and fruit salads that bring us back to the underlying premise that gender is fluid, full of surprises, with each gender diverse child as their own unique snowflake.

Persisters/Desisters; Apples/Oranges

For many years, researchers at the gender clinic at the Vrije Universiteit University Medical Center in Amsterdam, the Netherlands, under the leadership of Peggy Cohen-Kettenis, have documented the trajectory of children who have come to their program for services. Using measures that assessed whether the child qualified for a diagnosis of Gender Dysphoria (*Diagnostic and Statistical Manual of Mental Disorders*, fifth ed.; American Psychiatric Association, 2013), and before the change in diagnosis, whether they qualified for a diagnosis of Gender Identity Disorder (GID; *Diagnostic and Statistical Manual of Mental Disorders*, fourth ed.; American Psychiatric Association, 1994), their data indicated that the majority of the children coming to their clinic at an early age, somewhere between 70% and 80%, qualified as "desisters," meaning that by adolescence their earlier assessed "gender dysphoria" as defined by meeting criteria for GID would no longer be in evidence (Steensma, Biemond, de Boer, & Cohen-Kettenis, 2011). Only a minority of the children, somewhere between 20% and 30%, would carry that diagnosis with them into adolescence, and those would be the "persisters." The latter group would become good candidates for puberty blockers and then later for hormone therapy, culminating in an affirmed transgender identity.

However, because the clinical researchers in the Netherlands could identify no solid predictive factors that would sort out the desisters from the persisters in early childhood, the conclusion, and subsequent clinical recommendations, were that the most auspicious path was to wait and see, because as Steensma et al. (2011) described,

> Feelings of gender dysphoria persisted into adolescence in only 39 out of 246 of the children (15.8%) who were investigated in a number of prospective follow-up studies. . . . Results unequivocally showed that the gender dysphoria remitted after puberty in the vast majority of children. (p. 500)

The thought process was that if by adolescence the child was persistent in their cross-gender identifications, actions could be taken to help them socially transition and receive medical interventions to better align their bodies with their transgender psyche, but before the onset of adolescence, it would be too early to tell. Because only a small number of gender dysphoric children will continue to be gender dysphoric in adolescence, this is not a reliable predictor of later transgender outcome. Therefore, they reasoned, give children a chance to explore their gender, but do not promote an early and potentially premature or inappropriate gender transition, as most of these children will grow out of their gender dysphoria and will not grow up to be transgender.

The World Professional Association for Transgender Health (WPATH) abided by that cautionary stance when it released the seventh version of the *Standards of Care* (WPATH, 2011):

> Mental health professionals can help families to make decisions regarding the timing and process of any gender role changes [social transitions] for their young children. They should provide information and help parents to weigh the potential benefits and challenges of particular choices. Relevant in this respect are the previously described relatively low persistence rates of childhood gender dysphoria. A change back to the original gender role [assigned sex] can be highly distressing and even result in postponement of this second social transition on the child's part. For reasons such as these, parents may want to present this role change [social transition] as an exploration of living in another gender role, rather than an irreversible situation. Mental health professionals can assist parents in identifying potential in-between solutions or compromises (e.g., only when on vacation). It is also important that parents explicitly let the child know that there is a way back. (p. 17)

The concern was that children given a green light to change their gender early in life may have a hard time turning back; given that most young children do not continue on a path that results in a transgender identity, it would behoove professionals to take a conservative stance, forestalling any social transitions until it is certain that the transgender identity is an authentic one.

As a developmental and clinical psychologist, reviewing these studies left me confused, and to be honest, somewhat miffed. The term "apples and oranges" kept coming to mind; that is, that the children identified as the desisters early in life were always a completely different group from the group identified as persisters, from the get-go, a differentiation that might clearly be demarcated if the proper measuring tools are utilized, and the appropriate clinical/developmental question is asked: What can you tell me and what can I learn about your gender identity and your gender expressions?

Can Young Children Know Their Gender?

Starting with this question may be the most robust way to move on to the task of differentiating children in different gender categories and matching them with the supports and interventions most beneficial to their gender health. Typically, the question "Can a young child really know their gender?" is not in reference to cisgender children but rather to the children who declare at an early age that their gender is neither the one everyone thinks it is nor the gender that matches the sex assigned at birth. Further, this question is typically not posed dispassionately but is often accompanied by a skeptical if not disparaging tone. Regarding the TGE group of children implicitly referenced when the question "Can a young child really know their gender?" is asked, inferences from a macrostudy of 3,474 transgender adults conducted by Beemyn and Rankin (2011) provided a partial answer. In their online survey, 82.6% of the transgender respondents reported that they were aware before age 12 that they felt different. In follow-up interviews with 419 of the sample, 67% of the transgender men and 62% of the transgender women felt that from a young age they were different from the gender matching the sex assigned to them at birth. This finding was corroborated by a more recent World Health Organization field study in which participants ($N = 250$) reported first awareness of their transgender identity at a mean age of 5.6 (Robles et al., 2016). Returning to the Beemyn and Rankin study, most of their respondents expressed that they hid this self-knowledge from those around them, acknowledging their affirmed gender only in hiding. The reported effect was chronic psychological pain and suffering.

It must be acknowledged that these are retrospective data, and people often have the tendency to color their history with the tint of the historical lens from which it is being observed. Yet, collective clinical observations across pediatric gender clinics and programs internationally yield the same information: Parents of TGE children report that their child has been indicating both in word and action from a very early age, as young as toddlerhood, that someone had gotten it wrong and they were not the gender people thought they were. Mirroring the findings from the studies of adults, this declaration was often accompanied by stress, distress, frustration, or anger, particularly if they experienced that no one was listening or taking them seriously. The children themselves will offer the same narrative through their play or with their words (Ehrensaft, 2014; Malpas, 2011). For example, a 6-year-old who had been assigned male at birth but had refused anything "boy" since 2 years old reported that she always knew she was a girl, even when she was still in diapers and when she learned that boys had penises. She just assumed hers would go away as soon as she changed her name from George to Ginny, which occurred at age 5, when she said that her parents "finally stopped being so silly and calling me a boy." The point here is that she knew, and she knew early, with hardly enough years behind her to become a revisionist of history.

Not just transgender research participants who are not minors but who are over the age of majority indicate early knowledge of their transgender identities. Transgender adult patients, bearing witness to the trajectories of the younger cohort of transgender children today, especially those who have socially transitioned at an early age, often express envy and sadness that, because they were born in a different era, they were never afforded the opportunity to expose their transgender self but were instead forced to hide it, sometimes even from themselves. Yet they are quite clear that their transgender identity was there, from an early age. This circles back to the research on persisters and desisters. Would some of these young children be equally clear, at a young age, whether they were going to be a persister or a desister?

In 2013, the Dutch researchers released a publication with a reevaluation of their persister/desister data (Steensma, McGuire, Kreukels, Beekman, & Cohen-Kettenis, 2013). The following findings were reported: (a) the percentage of desisters was adjusted down to 63%; (b) the persisters had a complete childhood diagnosis of GID at higher rates than desisters, showed more gender nonconforming behavior (i.e., gender expansive expressions) and a greater degree of gender dysphoria throughout childhood, indicated that they believed they were the other gender, rather than wanted to be the other gender, and had greater discomfort with their sexed bodies and incongruence between their body and gender identity; and (c) the desisters, in contrast, showed fluidity in their gender expressions and only said they wished they were the other gender, rather than they were the other gender, and later, in adolescence, they were more likely to express attractions to people of the same gender as themselves (Steensma et al., 2013). In other words, the persisters and desisters were already looking different in early childhood, and if they had been looked at through a different lens, it would likely be discovered that they were actually on two different trajectories from early on, the persisters being our youngest cohort of transgender children, the desisters being the children who would qualify as gender expansive in gender expressions but not transgender in gender identity and would most likely, as indeed documented by the outcome data of desisters, grow up to be gay, lesbian, or queer cisgender adults.

These findings of Steensma et al. (2013) were completely coincident with the rapidly accumulating clinical observations among gender affirmative practitioners engaged with prepubertal children. A cluster of behaviors and feelings separated the children who were ripe for a social transition to a different gender identity from the children who were exploring gender expressions, but not their gender identities, which I address shortly in looking at the profiles of the "apples," "oranges," and "fruit salads." Circling back to the studies on persisters and desisters, the fault line in these studies is precisely related to the lens used to look at the child. Put differently, the researchers failed to measure the most salient variables that would enable them to differentiate between the so-called persisters and desisters, not with 100% accuracy, but certainly with robust validity. Rather than taking measures of gender stress and distress, which is essentially what researchers are doing when they assess gender dysphoria, the more salient measures would involve evaluating whether the child is primarily exploring or grappling with gender identity (who I am as boy, girl, or other), with gender expressions (how I want to "do" my gender), or with both. Unlike gender dysphoria (or GID before that), measures of gender identity and gender expressions are neutral categories, rather than assessments of pathology or psychological malfunctioning. The groundbreaking research of Kristina Olson at the University of Washington has done exactly that: taken as an independent measure the child's affirmed gender identity, and as dependent variables, mental health measures of these children in comparison with two control groups (Olson, Durwood, DeMeules, & McLaughlin, 2016; Olson, Key, & Eaton, 2015). This is an issue not only for research but also for clinical practice. If one wants to know a child's gender, find out about how they experience themselves as boy, girl, or other, and find out how they "do" their gender—their modes of dress, play, friendship patterns, activities, and so forth.

In sum, the approach and conclusions emanating from the persister/desister research are not in alignment with the GAM of care, and troubling in their inferences that (a) we as researchers cannot determine a child's authentic gender early on, and (b) even if we could, we might be damaging a child by boxing them into a corner too early if we facilitate social transitions to another gender before puberty. The GAM perspective instead posits that (a) a small number of children emerge early on who are cross-gender or "another gender" in their identifications and transgender in their identities (the so-called persisters); (b) predictive variables do exist to identify these children and differentiate them from the children who are exploring gender expressions but not gender identity; (c) the risks of allowing a child to socially transition at an early age are overblown and are primarily operative only if we do not open an accepting pathway of transition to some other gender identity or authentic gender self later in life if a child so desires; and (d) in comparison, the risks are higher of preventing a child from fully living in their affirmed gender identity, resulting in psychological stress or distress.

Separating Apples, Oranges, and Fruit Salads

Before delineating approaches for separating out the apples and oranges, to replace the more traditional approach of casting children as either persisters or desisters, a necessary footnote to the apples and oranges typography is in order. As time moves forward and the public becomes more aware of gender as a spectrum, a rainbow, or a multiple rather than binary construct, with it has come a whole new genre of youth—nonbinary children and adolescents who live between, among, or beyond the two-gender trope—of boy/girl—in their gender selves. Further, gender expansive binary transgender children (e.g., tomboy transgender girls) have necessitated an asymmetrical re-framing of the persister/desister model—apples are to persisters as oranges are to desisters, but now we must add on fruit salads who neither persist nor desist but creatively assemble a diverse sense of gender, both in identity and expressions.

Let us imagine two parents coming to a therapy office for a first visit. They have a 6-year-old child and they are puzzled about what their child is attempting to tell them about the child's gender. They only want to do the right thing for their child, but they do not know what that is. Assigned female at birth, their child will only wear clothes bought in the boys' section of the local department store, has attempted to urinate standing up in imitation of their older brother, and is distraught because, according to the rules, they will not be allowed to try out for the boys' junior softball team. Rather than immediately assessing for gender dysphoria, consider instead the following questions a clinician might ask the parents about their child.

1. How long has your child been communicating cross-gender identifications or behaviors?
2. Has it been consistent over a period of time?
3. If able to express their sense of their own gender, how does your child articulate it and with what feeling?
4. Does your child say, "I *want to be* a girl [boy] [other]," or do they say, "I *am* a girl [boy] [other]"?
5. How insistent is your child in declarations and demonstrations of gender? How persistent?
6. Does your child show distress or stress about the body they have?
7. Is your child making serious statements rather than playful gestures when gravitating toward the toys/activities/dress codes/and so on typically designated for the "other" gender within your culture?
8. Does your child express distress when someone "misgenders" them?
9. Does your child show delight when someone perceives them as a gender other than the one that matches the sex assigned to them at birth?
10. How do you as parents, and how do other people in your child's life, respond to your child's gender messages?

These 10 questions are just a sampling of the type of querying that would begin to generate a narrative about the child's gender status, in terms of how they know themselves to be as boy, girl, or other, and how they "do" their gender. The same genre of queries would inform the therapist's direct interactions with the child, if the child is to be seen at all.

APPLES

Simply put, the apples are those children who often show up in the child gender research as the persisters. Typically, they demonstrate cross-gender identifications early in life and continue with these identifications into and beyond puberty. The term *cross-gender* is being used judiciously, in line with the common lexicon in the professional literature. From the child's point of view, however, this assignation of their behavior, thoughts, and feelings may be experienced as an affront. From their perspective, they have never "crossed over" at all. Instead, it is those around them who must cross over in their thinking and in coming to the realization that the child before them is not the gender that the adults assumed that child to be. So, one might hear the child say, "I have always been a girl. It's you all who have always gotten it wrong." These are the children who are often referred to as "consistent, persistent, and insistent" in their affirmed gender identities that do not match the sex assigned to them at birth. These are children who are also typically binary in their gender identity, adapting to the girl–boy dichotomy but not to the equation that sex assigned at birth equates with authentic gender. Their primary concern is not gender expression but gender identity, but it should be noted that their identity, particularly in early life, is often first communicated through gender expansive expressions.

One indicator of a child being an apple is that this child may typically say, "I *am* a ______ (boy, girl, other)" rather than "I wish I were a ______ (boy, girl, other)." The presence of this indicator should be qualified by the reality that some children as young as 3, or even as young as the beginning stages of expressive language development, will have already read the signals of the upset of the social environment when they defy social gender expectations. So, they learn to hedge their bets, so to speak, diluting or softening their gender assertions with statements such as, "Well, maybe sometimes I would like to be a ______" to avoid negative or aversive responses or to assuage their parents' anxieties. As the child gets older and increasingly cognizant of the attitudes and mores of the world around them, such dilutions can be expected to be even more in evidence for a child who is nonetheless an apple.

Many of these children will express body dysphoria at a very young age. They may be displeased or distraught about the genitalia they have, feeling it is a betrayal of the gender they know themselves to be and a marker that perhaps they can never be a "real" person of that gender. This dysphoria increases if the child receives messages that only people with vaginas can be girls and only people with penises can be boys. Yet even without those messages the young child may express frustration or anger that "God got it wrong and made me the wrong way" or "Why can't I go back into Mommy's tummy and come out the right way next time?" In their frustration or distress, some children may attempt to mutilate their genitals, and others, particularly those still traversing early stages of childhood in which magical thinking prevails, may insist that their vagina is actually a penis or believe that they can go to the pharmacy and purchase the genitalia of their choice in exchange for the one they do not want.

Their gender expressions are either gender expansive or sometimes very gender rigid, following strict social norms applied to the gender they know themselves to be rather than the gender everyone else assumes they are. In the latter case, their gender activities are often not just frivolous exercises of play. They are serious business with an important social message embedded. So, for example, a boy who knows he is a girl may sneak into his sister's room and take off with her favorite school dress, not her fairy princess costume. In donning the school dress, the child is trying to tell the world that she is a girl just like her sister; this is not just fantasy play. It should be noted that often the rigidity of the gender expressions among the apple cohort relaxes once the child is affirmed in their authentic gender, as the need to send out a clarion call, "Now do you see who I am," with every gender move is no longer needed.

In the context of nature, nurture, and culture being the three interweaving components of each child's individual gender self, for the apples, the nature threads appear to be quite strong. Whether it is genetics, prenatal environmental influences (e.g., the distribution of hormones through hormone receptors in the critical fetal months of sex formation), or some other biological factors, the narrative from parents of an apple is often the same: "I swear, we did not do anything to make this happen. Our child just came to us this way." We can reflect back on Lady Gaga's (2012) song, "Born This Way," as we bring the apples into focus. In sum, they are the youngest cohort of transgender people.

The indicators listed above are not requisites for a child to qualify as an apple but rather a set of guidelines to help get the child in focus. Often it is an ex post facto test that enables a clinician to fully recognize who the child is and to measure whether he or she was correct in the assessment. When allowed to socially transition to their affirmed gender, symptoms of anxiety, agitation, stress, and distress typically dissipate (but not necessarily disappear), replaced by increased confidence and psychological well-being. Reports from clinicians indicate that this transformation in psychological functioning following a full social transition to their authentic gender identity stands out as one of the most dramatic changes observed among children seeking psychological services for any kind of issue. Put another way, this youngest cohort of transgender people do well when given the opportunity to live in their authentic gender identity. Other research findings (Olson et al., 2015) have also shown that young apples who have had the opportunity to socially transition are doing equally well as a comparison group of same age nontransgender peers in several areas of psychological functioning. Further, the profile of the apple just outlined matches the findings of Steensma et al. (2013) when they returned to their early data on binary persisters and desisters and discovered that the persisters, at a young age, more likely indicated that they *were* the other gender rather than they wanted to *be* the other gender, showed early body dysphoria, and demonstrated an early history of cross-gender interests and activities. Whereas some doubt the ability of young children to know their own gender, and worry about prematurely constraining children into a new gender box before they have had the rest of their childhood to explore, both clinical observations and emerging research data indicate that allowing children to socially transition once their affirmed gender is in focus, a phenomenon that can occur as early as the preschool years, appears to be in the child's best interests. Assuming that the parents are accepting and supportive of the transition, this may be the best insurance policy against the psychological risk factors for a child chronically confronted with the dysphoria of being forced to live in a gender that is not their authentic one. It should be mentioned that in Steensma et al.'s (2013) reevaluation of the persister and desister data, evidence indicated that the persisters showed more intense and consistent gender dysphoria. This would make sense, especially if they were barred from socially transitioning to their authentic gender.

Can clinicians know with 100% accuracy that a young child who presents as an apple and desires a social transition, which might include name, pronoun, and gender marker change, will be stable and consistent in their transgender identity? The answer to that question is simple: No. The present WPATH *Standards of Care* cite a study by Steensma and Cohen-Kettenis (2011) in which three middle-school-age girls experienced stress when shifting from a masculine presentation to a more feminine presentation. It is unfortunate that this case was cited in the *Standards of Care* as a cautionary tale against early transitions, as (a) nothing indicates that these girls ever socially transitioned, only that they presented as masculine in their gender expressions earlier in childhood; and (b) the stress they experienced was a result of others' negative response to their shift to a more feminine presentation. Absent a rejecting social environment, no documented evidence to date suggests that a child's psychological well-being will suffer if they either traverse back to an earlier gender identity that had been discarded or move forward toward yet another one as they carve out their gender pathways. In the GAM, in which gender development is seen as a lifelong unfolding rather than fixed at an early age and in which pathology is perceived to lie more in the culture's repudiation of gender expansiveness, the major risk of social transitions for young apples is more likely in the society's discomfort with it than in the child's internal gender confusion or distress. With surrounding support and acceptance, both from parents and professionals, the apple should have a blooming future.

A last caveat regards developmental time lines for apples. Because the apple guidelines include a presentation of gender expansiveness early in childhood, a presentation that is "insistent, consistent, and persistent," it is misconstrued by parents and professionals alike that if a child's first assertion of a transgender identity shows up only much later, particularly in adolescence or beyond, it is not authentic. Often this will be presented in a clinical session with a parent expressing, "I swear to you, my child never showed even the slightest sign of cross-gender interests until now. He was not one of the kids like Jazz [Jennings, the transgender girl featured in her early childhood in the first Barbara Walters special (Goldberg, 2007) on transgender children, and now a teen author and renowned media spokesperson for transgender youth]. I think he's putting us on. This couldn't be real." Doing a gender affirmative assessment with this parent's child will hopefully reveal whether the youth's declarations of a gender identity are authentic, but let it be said that an apple can first show up at any time—age 2, 10, or 20—as each individual consolidates their authentic gender self over the course of their lives. Last, it is important that the onset of puberty is sometimes the first moment when the youth's sense of being an apple may surface, or more accurately, may erupt, often from the depths of unconscious repression or the layers of conscious suppression as the youth is confronted with a change in body that suddenly feels out of body in the context of an emergent self-realization of the gender they are rather than the one they have been living in.

ORANGES

Oranges include the group of children who are gender expansive in their gender presentations but do not repudiate the sex assigned to them at birth, finding it a fine fit as long as they are not policed in their gender expressions. These are children and youth who often fall under the category of "desisters" in the existent gender research. Many of these children will later discover their gay or queer sexual orientation identities, while others will grow to be cisgender gender nonconforming heterosexuals;

some may shed their gender nonconformity by adolescence; some will first discover it then. Because of the developmental track of gender formation criss-crossing the developmental track of sexual orientation identity formation, many "protogay" children find themselves exploring gender on the way to affirming their sexual orientation identities. For some of these children, the exploration of gender on the way to discovering their sexual orientation has cognitive roots. In a culture that is predominately heterosexist in its norms, young children have few opportunities to experience relationships between a male and a male or a female and a female. Even with the publication of books such as *King and King* (De Haan & Nijland, 2002), the dominant theme in the children's socialization will be kings and queens, princes and princesses. For a young boy with an awakening realization that he longs for the prince, he might fashion himself as the princess as the only way to fetch himself a prince. Thus, you might see this young boy donning a princess costume, imagining himself as the belle of the ball attracting the admiration of the prince, and telling his parents, "I wish I was a girl." As he grows older and discovers that men can love men and women can love women, he may discard his earlier cross-gender expressions as he realizes he does not have to change genders to partner with the gender he desires.

These, incidentally, are exactly the group of "effeminate" boys who have been historically captured in clinical and research programs (e.g., Green, 1987) to purge them of their cross-gender interests to avoid a "homosexual" outcome. These are also the children who get tagged as gender dysphoric early in childhood, mistakenly lumped in the same category as the apples but later identified as desisters, aka cisgender lesbian, gay, bisexual, or queer youth.

Again, not all oranges will be protogay; some simply revel in rebelling against societal gender norms and mix and match as they please. In either case, oranges do not tend to repudiate their bodies or show distress about the genitals they were born with. Instead, they may engage in fantasy play or ruminations about life in another body. For example, a little girl might pack her pajama bottoms with socks to have a bulge like her brother's, giggling all the while. A little boy may borrow his sister's ballet costume, stuff the bodice with socks, many socks, and prance through the house as the buxom ballerina, giggling all the while. If one investigates their play, one typically finds a jouissance in celebrating the delightful and transgressive expression of gender outside the binary gender boxes, rather than play as serious business and urgent communication about a gender self like the apples.

Returning to "I wish I was a girl," this is often the differentiating feature between the apple and the orange. Whereas the apple may declaratively state, "I am a ______," the orange will more likely say, "Sometimes I wish I were a ______," or "I want to be a ______ sometimes." This recalls the apple who may hedge their bets by choosing the same lexicon as the oranges to express their gender desires. The challenge for clinicians is to differentiate between the two: "I wish" as an authentic articulation and "I wish" as a defensive strategy. In either case, time will tell. In other words, with enough open and safe space for in-depth exploration in the child–clinician relationship, the genuine articulations typically surface: the orange stays firm with "I wish"; the apple is eventually able to express "I am." Parallel to this uncovering is the observation that the orange is occupied most centrally with gender expressions, whereas the apple is centrally occupied with gender identity, using gender expressions as a means of communication of the true gender identity as well as an authentic expression of how that child wants to "do" their gender.

In comparison with the apples, oranges do not need to transition to another gender identity, as they do not repudiate the gender identity matching the sex assigned at birth. Yet, in promoting gender health, it is ever necessary to open up a path to more expansive gender expressions and to challenge any social policing of those expressions. As one watches the oranges blossom, one observes a true medley of nature, nurture, and culture: nature, because like with the apples, these children appear to just come to the parents, rather than being molded by them; nurture, because the acquisition of their specific gender is established within the relational matrix of parent and child relations, teacher–child relations, and so forth; culture, because the norms of gender and therefore the challenges to those norms vary significantly from culture to culture. For example, in our culture the wearing of a skirt may serve as a strong statement for a little boy who is gender expansive and be considered transgressive; in another culture, no one would even take notice because skirts or long wraps are typically worn by males as normative gender garb.

FRUIT SALADS

Although "talking apples and oranges" was a critical response to the research reports differentiating persisters from desisters, it subsequently became apparent that another whole group of children were presenting themselves in gender creative fashion and needed to be identified. In line with the orchard metaphor, these are the fruit salads.

Children who qualify as fruit salads are those who are repositioning both their gender identities and their gender expressions. Typically, they are older at onset than the apples or oranges, but not necessarily. Those in the older cohort may identify themselves as agender, genderqueer, gender fluid, nonbinary, or any other assignation that signifies that they do not consolidate a gender self based on "either/or" but rather "all or any" (Goldner, 2011). In short, they are the gender weavers who make a tapestry of self, which is neither male nor female but their own creative understanding of gender, both in identities and expressions. These children are not beyond gender but immersed in all of it. Steeped in their own socialization within a binary gender model, professionals and parents alike may feel drawn to labeling these children in one of two boxes—male or female. Typically, if fortified with enough gender resilience, the children will resist. As one 9-year-old explained it, "Look, I'm a boy-girl. And that's all I can tell you about me right now."

Regarding their physical selves, their bodies can be cause for stress. In the context of a culture that equates penis with boy and vagina with girl, they struggle to be the boy with a penis who is also a girl, and so forth. If they have body dysphoria, it should be noted that clinical observation suggests that it is seldom to the extent of the body dysphoria witnessed in the apples. Instead, it is more of a conundrum, as the fruit salads come to embrace the gender middle grounds of "all and any." The fruit salads' body conundrums have also presented a challenge to gender affirmative providers, particularly those working in medical or interdisciplinary clinics where medical interventions—puberty blockers, hormones, surgeries—are potential provisions of care. If one is to abide by the gender affirmative rubric that gender does not come in two boxes but an infinite variety of possibilities, the youth who qualifies as a fruit salad may push for professional practices that abide by this rubric. They may ask for just a touch of testosterone, or a small dose of estrogen, or chest surgery but no other medical intervention as they strive toward consolidating a gender self that is uniquely theirs. Meeting the needs of young fruit salads is an area of gender care which, more than any other, requires practitioners to examine their own values, biases, discomforts, or countertransference reactions as youth push providers to expand beyond their training and sensibilities that would suggest gender only comes in two boxes.

In recent history, the number of children and youth presenting with this mélange of gender identity and gender expressions appears to have rapidly increased. One might think of these youth, the fruit salads, as the "flower children" of their generation, resonating strongly to the emergent social understandings, which appear to have gone viral, that gender exists beyond two boxes and that it may be a revolutionary rite of passage to question, explore, and create a mosaic of gender. In the 20th century Erikson (1963) identified the developmental stage of adolescence as one in which youth strive to consolidate their identities. Whereas adult sexual selves were included in his categories of exploration, gender was not, as in that historical period of Western psychology gender was considered bedrock rather than something to be reckoned with. In the 21st century, gender can now be considered one more identity category that youth consider ripe for exploration and questioning, rather than taken for granted. Thus, for many of the youth who present as fruit salads, particularly those in the stage of adolescence, it is helpful to think of them as "poetry in motion," taking full advantage of the stage of identity versus role confusion to fully and creatively plumb the depths of their gender selves. This can indeed create challenges or out-and-out headaches for providers who are experiencing the youth as moving targets rather than as poetry in motion. It is important to hold in mind, about the fruit salads, that the cultural component of their gender selves is in vibrant relief in influencing their questioning and explorations of "What's my gender?" The challenge for clinicians in working with fruit salads is to facilitate these youth living an authentic gender life without prematurely pushing them into one box or another, which might be a tendency stemming from one's own angst about not being able to answer the question—boy or girl?

Interventions for Apples, Oranges, and Fruit Salads

APPLES

Before the onset of puberty, the central intervention for young transgender children is social transitions—an allowance for the child to leave an ill-fitting gender behind and embrace an alternative gender identity that feels more authentic. A child will be a good candidate for a social transition if the below are true.

1. Other possibilities besides gender are ruled out as being at the core; specifically, if gender is discovered to be a symptom of some other underlying problem.
2. The central issue is determined to be gender identity, not gender expressions.
3. The child expresses need/desire to socially transition to another gender.
4. Parents can offer positive support for their child transitioning.

If all those criteria are met, a full social transition can be considered, either everywhere, or at least to begin, in more limited settings that are considered safe (this is particularly important for children who live in communities that are openly hostile or abusive to anyone who defies gender norms and in which the child would be subject to chronic maltreatment). In the latter situations, the ongoing community-based work, which should include the clinician's input, is to widen the circles of safety and acceptance for that child, so they can move toward full expression of themselves at all times.

Apples who arrive at the threshold of puberty should receive the option of puberty blockers and then later masculinizing or feminizing hormone therapy. Considerations of gender affirming surgeries are also possible for those apples well into adolescence. Because fertility options will be compromised for children who receive puberty blockers before going through puberty and then following up with hormone therapy, interventions will also involve counseling about alternative family building options for the apples. For those apples who have already gone through puberty before receiving medical interventions, counseling should include possibilities of gamete preservation before going through hormonal or surgical treatments.

ORANGES

In some ways, this is the easiest group of children to support. If the issue is not core gender identity but gender expressions, the role of the environment, including parents and mental health providers, is to carve out space and support for the child to perform their gender in a way that suits the child, rather than society. For the orange, no social gender transition, as defined above, is called for.

In the context of a social system that is not accepting of expansive gender expressions, an orange may need a safe therapeutic space to work out the stresses of going against the grain of social gender expectations in how they "do" their gender and in building gender resilience so that they can assert their gender selves with pride and confidence rather than fear and anxiety. It should be noted in this respect that much homophobic and transphobic bullying and harassment toward youth is based primarily on the individual's nonconforming gender presentations, rather than their identities—either gender or sexual orientation identity. In that regard, the orange—for example, the boy in a dress—may be at higher risk for maltreatment than the apple—for example, the transgender girl in a dress who presents like any other girl in her class (as long as she remains dressed). The orange, therefore, may need added supports, a factor often overlooked when compared to the more dramatic trajectory of the apple.

FRUIT SALADS

They are a mélange. Some may request or benefit from a gender transition but not necessarily a binary one. Others are fine with the sex assigned at birth but redefine what that means. Like the oranges, they may benefit from supportive psychological services or community support groups to support their unique and diverse gender consolidations and to offer them protective coating against a society that may be even more ill-equipped to accept them than it is the apples or oranges. Mental health professionals and medical professionals will need to join together to consider the possible medical interventions that will support a youth who is neither male nor female, either in gender identity, gender expressions, or both.

Case Study

Cameron was 5 years old, about to enter kindergarten. Cameron's parents had been struggling to decipher what Cameron had been telling them about Cameron's gender identity. Cameron was assigned male at birth. Cameron was the oldest of three children, with both a younger sister and a young brother. Cameron throughout preschool wore dresses over pants, bright colored beads, sparkly shoes, and painted nails. In preparation for kindergarten, Cameron's parents were anxious to pin down Cameron's gender so they could communicate to the kindergarten teacher how to best support Cameron. They would ask Cameron, daily, whether to use the pronoun *she* or *he* that day. Cameron would stonewall them, refusing to answer. Having had surgery at age 3 to correct a circumcision that had not been done properly, Cameron, postsurgery, had consistently insisted that he had nothing between his legs, neither penis nor vagina. Expansive gender expressions, however, preceded the surgery. Observing Cameron's gender expressions, Cameron's movements were very "boy-like," his attire more "girl-like," by cultural standards. Finally, in a meeting with a therapist, scheduled because of the parents' own concerns about whether they had a transgender child, Cameron, when queried about what pronoun they would like their kindergarten teacher to use (this teacher, who had been part of a gender training for educators, asked that of each child in the class), Cameron responded irately, "Just tell her to use 'Rainbow Kid.'" The reader is left to muse whether Cameron is an apple, an orange, a fruit salad, or a child whose gender issues are an indicator of an underlying psychological problem, in this case potential posttraumatic stress disorder subsequent to a surgical genital procedure.

Conclusion

Children at a young age, both cisgender and transgender, can definitively know their gender. The challenge for the adults is to decipher what they are trying to communicate. By differentiating gender identity from gender expressions and using the template of apples, oranges, and fruit salads, this complex task will hopefully become simpler. This can happen only if it is also held in mind that there are no set time lines—apples, oranges, and fruit salads can make themselves known at any point in their development—and that no child is permanently relegated to one of the three categories and not every gender expansive child will fit neatly into one of the three. Like gender itself, these categories flow and meld among one another.

References

American Psychiatric Association. (1994). *Diagnostic and statistical manual of mental disorders* (4th ed.). Washington, DC: Author.

American Psychiatric Association. (2013). *Diagnostic and statistical manual of mental disorders* (5th ed.). Washington, DC: Author.

Beemyn, G., & Rankin, S. (2011). *The lives of transgender people*. New York, NY: Columbia University Press.

De Haan, L., & Nijland, S. (2002). *King and king*. Berkeley, CA: Tricycle Press.

Ehrensaft, D. (2011). *Gender born, gender made*. New York, NY: The Experiment.

Ehrensaft, D. (2012). From gender identity disorder to gender identity creativity: True gender self child therapy. *Journal of Homosexuality, 59*, 337–356. http://dx.doi.org/10.1080/00918369.2012.653303

Ehrensaft, D. (2014). Found in transition: Our youngest transgender people. *Contemporary Psychoanalysis, 50*, 571–592. http://dx.doi.org/10.1080/00107530.2014.942591

Ehrensaft, D. (2016). *The gender creative child*. New York, NY: The Experiment.

Erikson, E. (1963). *Childhood and society*. New York, NY: Norton.

Goldberg, A. B. (Producer). (2007, April 27). *My secret self: A story of transgender children* [Television program]. Houston, TX: ABC News.

Goldner, V. (2011). Trans: Gender in free fall. *Psychoanalytic Dialogues, 21*, 159–171. https://doi.org/10.1080/10481885.2011.562836

Green, R. (1987). *The "sissy boy" syndrome and the development of homosexuality*. New Haven, CT: Yale University Press.

Lady Gaga. (2012). Born this way. On *Born this way* [CD]. New York, NY: House of Gaga.

Malpas, J. (2011). Between pink and blue: A multi-dimensional family approach to gender nonconforming children and their families. *Family Process, 50*, 453–470. http://dx.doi.org/10.1111/j.1545-5300.2011.01371.x

Olson, K. R., Durwood, L., DeMeules, M., & McLaughlin, K. A. (2016). Mental health of transgender children who are supported in their identities. *Pediatrics, 137*, 277–282. http://dx.doi.org/10.1542/peds.2015-3223

Olson, K. R., Key, A. C., & Eaton, N. R. (2015). Gender cognition in transgender children. *Psychological Science, 26*, 467–474. http://dx.doi.org/10.1177/0956797614568156

Robles, R., Fresán, A., Vega-Ramírez, H., Cruz-Islas, J., Rodríguez-Pérez, V., Domínguez-Martínez, T., & Reed, G. M. (2016). Removing transgender identity from the classification of mental disorders: A Mexican field study for *ICD–11*. *The Lancet, 3*, 850–859. http://dx.doi.org/10.1016/S2215-0366(16)30165-1

Steensma, T. D., Biemond, R., de Boer, F., & Cohen-Kettenis, P. T. (2011). Desisting and persisting gender dysphoria after childhood: A qualitative follow-up study. *Clinical Child Psychology and Psychiatry, 16,* 499–516. http://dx.doi.org/10.1177/1359104510378303

Steensma, T. D., & Cohen-Kettenis, P. T. (2011). Gender transitioning before puberty? *Archives of Sexual Behavior, 40,* 649–650. http://dx.doi.org/10.1007/s10508-011-9752-2

Steensma, T. D., McGuire, J. K., Kreukels, B. P., Beekman, A. J., & Cohen-Kettenis, P. T. (2013). Factors associated with desistence and persistence of childhood gender dysphoria: A quantitative follow-up study. *Journal of the American Academy of Child & Adolescent Psychiatry, 52,* 582–590. http://dx.doi.org/10.1016/j.jaac.2013.03.016

World Professional Association for Transgender Health. (2011). *Standards of care for the health of transsexual, transgender, and gender nonconforming people* (7th version). Retrieved from https://www.wpath.org/media/cms/Documents/Web%20Transfer/SOC/Standards%20of%20Care%20V7%20-%202011%20WPATH.pdf

Eb. (Ebony) Brown and Kobi Mar

Culturally Responsive Practice With Children of Color

4

The purpose of this chapter is to increase clinicians' consciousness about issues impacting transgender and gender expansive (TGE) children of color and deeply held beliefs about communities of color's acceptance of TGE children. Because of the lack of literature on TGE children of color, we relied on clinical experience, professional consensus, and reported experiences of TGE children of color. We present brief histories of TGE people in communities of color, introduce the concept of cultural splitting, and provide guidelines for clinical treatment and structural resources to affirm all dimensions of TGE children of color.

Effects of Colonization on Gender Identity, Roles, and Beliefs

African, Asian, and indigenous cultures of the Americas had a consistent pattern of gender diversity, pre-Christianity. Documentation of the *Bianxing* ("one who changes sex") in China, *Kathoey* (historically "ladyboy," although this definition is being replaced with "transgender woman") in Thailand, *Hijras* ("third sex") in India, and *Fa'afafine* ("third gender") in Samoa shows TGE

http://dx.doi.org/10.1037/0000095-004
The Gender Affirmative Model: An Interdisciplinary Approach to Supporting Transgender and Gender Expansive Children, C. Keo-Meier and D. Ehrensaft (Editors)
Copyright © 2018 by the American Psychological Association. All rights reserved

people held valued social roles, such as healers and spirit mediums (Chung & Singh, 2009). In 2011, Nepal was the first country in the world to allow people to register as third gender in their national census. India, Pakistan, and Bangladesh have also legally recognized people as third gender. History points to more than 50 African tribes with practices of gender diversity embedded in their societal structures (Roscoe & Murray, 2001). The *'yan daudu*, of the Hausa's in Sub-Saharan and West Africa, are "men" who take on feminine gender expression and consider themselves lesbians when partnered together. The Bala of southern Africa identify *kitesh* as a third gender, and the Bantu in northern Africa have acknowledged the mixed- and cross-gendered as healers (Roscoe & Murray, 2001). Precolonization representation of nonbinary genders was observed in indigenous communities of the Juchitán and in representation of Aztec and Mayan deities. The Muxes, a third gender, from the Zapotec people, were individuals assigned male at birth but who dressed in "female" clothing (Mirandé, 2014). The Muxes are still a recognized third gender category in Oaxaca, Mexico, and have an annual parade. The term *two-spirit* is applied in contemporary times to a person embodying both feminine and masculine spirits in American Indian, Alaskan Native, and Canadian First Nations communities (Balsam, Huang, Fieland, Simoni, & Walters, 2004).

Each of these communities was impacted by the role of Christian colonization and conversion campaigns in their language, social practice, and acceptance of nonbinary genders. The Christian (Catholic and Protestant) colonization of the Americas decimated indigenous populations and targeted nonbinary gender representation for the most horrific treatment. Explorers of Asia and Africa brought their Christian morals and aggressively challenged the presence of nonbinary genders on both continents. With 63% of the populations of Africa and 42% of Asia identifying as Christian, the remnants of forced conversion are reflected in the morality laws jeopardizing the safety of TGE people throughout both continents (Funk & Lugo, 2012; Hackett, Connor, Stonawski, & Skirbekk, 2015). Even today, debates over the term *two spirit* have emerged to encourage a departure from the use of Western terms to describe American Indian, Alaskan Native, and Canadian First Nations identities.

Globally, nonbinary genders have existed in racial/ethnic groups both precolonization and in current cultural traditions. The histories represented here are a starting place for clinicians to research culturally specific nonbinary genders relevant to their practice. Clinicians benefit from learning about culturally specific nonbinary gender identities to enhance their understanding of the impact of colonization on TGE children of color, their families, and communities, while also addressing the resilient presence of such gender diversity even in face of such colonial repression.

The Relationship Between Medical Treatment and Communities of Color

The *Diagnostic and Statistical Manual of Mental Disorders* (fifth ed.; *DSM–5*; American Psychiatric Association, 2013) definition of Gender Dysphoria guides social and physical transitions through the medical treatment system. This system presumes a

Western-medicalized conception of the transgender experience (Roen, 2001). However, TGE people of color experience barriers in accessing Western medicine to assist with their identity development. Some may choose to not access Western medicine in conjunction with their TGE identity development. Language barriers, fear of deportation, and intergenerational trauma experienced at the hands of doctors, nurses, and hospital administrators all create barriers for TGE youth of color and their families to access Western medical interventions for transition. TGE children of color and their families also come with a host of culturally specific medical, spiritual, and emotional practices which do not depend on the use of hormones and surgeries to be accepted in their gender identity. This acceptance was historically observed among TGE people of color, who may not have had access to medical intervention in previous centuries, such as the Kathoey, Muxe, and two spirit.

As with TGE adults of color, cultural constraints (e.g., the taboo of discussing sex, sexuality, and breaking gender roles for Asian Americans) also play a role in TGE children of color and their families accessing medical transition resources less frequently (Chung & Katayama, 1998; Wilkinson & Gomez, 2004). Class and economic access are also major factors to consider for TGE children of color to pursue Western medical transition options. As a result of the *DSM* and the World Professional Association for Transgender Health (2011) guidelines, TGE youth may be charged $60 to $200 per session to complete the assessment for a letter to attain gender affirmative medical services. Without insurance, gender affirmation surgeries can cost between $6,000 and $100,000; puberty blockers may range from $5,000 to $20,000 annually; and hormone treatment could be anywhere from $20 to $100 per month. When pursuing Western medical treatment, TGE youth of color may experience great anxiety due to these costs, which may burden their already economically disadvantaged caregivers. The combination of non-Western cultural practices for transition and barriers to accessing Western medicine requires a broader look at the meaning of gender transitions outside of the Western medical model in ways that support TGE youth of color.

Reducing Cultural Splitting for Transgender and Gender Expansive Children of Color

Race/ethnicity and gender identity are often held as two separate identity development processes resulting in a type of cultural splitting in which TGE children of color face the choice of identifying with their racial/ethnic group or White lesbian, gay, bisexual, transgender, and queer (LGBTQ) community (Parks, Hughes, & Matthews, 2004). For example, TGE youth of color are often told by White peers and adults that their family is "rejecting" them because the family is not following dominant cultural patterns of "acceptance" (e.g., joining PFLAG). *Cultural splitting,* in which a dominant social group sets apart a social group marginalized by the dominant group and imposes their own values upon the latter, is reinforced by White mainstream LGBTQ communities through media images portraying only White LGBTQ lives, a monolithic narrative of "coming out," taking on a White savior mentality when working with TGE children of color, and upholding the stereotype of communities of color as more transphobic than White communities. Like the general public, clinicians are affected by these dominant narratives, with the risk of producing cultural splitting through single-identity based interventions with TGE children of color, seeing the child only through the lens of gender.

Redefining Coming Out for Transgender and Gender Expansive Children of Color

The term *coming out* is commonly used to describe the path of an individual as they internally accept and publicly state their identity—most often sexual orientation (Zimman, 2009). Coming out for TGE children is divided into two discrete experiences: *declaration* (pretransition) and *disclosure* (posttransition; Zimman, 2009). For TGE children, declarations are often combined with a diverse set of social and physical transitions that can include change of gender pronouns, change of legal name, change of clothing and appearance, establishment of new friend groups, and so on (Zimman, 2009). TGE children are faced with the option of disclosure with every new grade level, new friend, and new out-of-school activity and anywhere their gender assignment, identity, and expression are questioned.

Equally important for TGE children of color is how coming out is viewed through the norms inside of race and culture. Comparative studies of coming out for LGB individuals found no significant difference in age of coming out to self or others between African American, Asian, Latino, and Caucasian participants (Grov, Bimbi, Nanin, & Parsons, 2006). In addition, studies of the coming out process for Black, Latino, and White youth showed no difference in age of reaching developmental and sexual milestones across race (Rosario, Schrimshaw, & Hunter, 2004). Studies of people of color coming out across ethnicities and age show a consistent theme in the role of intersectional identity development in the ways individuals view the impact of coming out as a person of color: People of color cite the importance of family connections and a sense of belonging within their racial/ethnic group as equally important, or more important, than their LGBT identity (Bowleg, Burkholder, Teti, & Craig, 2009; Clark, 2005; Li & Orleans, 2001; Loiacano, 1989).

People of color and TGE people tend to express negative reactions to coming out campaigns (Bowleg et al., 2009; Zimman, 2009), which often include messages admonishing those who do not come out and place value-based judgments on individuals and communities rejecting of the coming out process (Bowleg et al., 2009). These campaigns position coming out as a responsibility of LGBTQ people to reduce violent reactions to gender nonconforming and nonheterosexual sexual orientation identities (Bowleg et al., 2009). This monolithic version of coming out does not consider how the impact of racism and transphobia can create greater risk of psychological harm, physical violence, and social isolation for TGE children of color (Bowleg et al., 2009). Clinical interventions with TGE children of color must consider coming out models that foster positive multidimensional identity development, value culturally specific experiences of rejection and acceptance, respond to parents' fear of increased violence for their children, and promote a positive relationship with their racial/ethnic group.

TABLE 4.1

Cultural Values of Coming Out

Race/ethnicity	Value
African American/Black	Attributing stress of *coming out* to external forces (heterosexism, sexism, racism). Ties with family help to mediate impact of rejecting family members (Bowleg et al., 2009).
Asian	"Honor or disgrace, we share with each other"—rejection as a "disgrace" is mediated by the family's commitment to "togetherness." Rejecting family members can go through a "re-educating" process to prepare for the family to "come out" to community (Li & Orleans, 2001). The existence of multiple genders across continents influences "normalization" of TGE identities (Bockting & Cesaretti, 2001).
Latino	Motivated by education on the impact of rejection on transgender and gender expansive (TGE) children. For immigrant families, strong desire to see child "succeed" in the United States mediates rejecting behaviors.

The foundation to build new interventions begins with clinicians expanding their understanding of cultural values for coming out across race and ethnicity (see Table 4.1). For example, a clinician who is aware of the Asian American cultural value of "togetherness" would not evaluate parents of a TGE Chinese child as "rejecting" because the child has not declared their gender identity to the family. The clinician would be primed to look for places of acceptance that reflect "reeducation" or behavioral shift of family members, which in turn reflect an understanding of the child's gender identity (e.g., parents have been purchasing clothing in alignment with the child's gender identity).

White Saviors in Clinical Practice

The domination of White clinicians in the field requires an examination of the effects White privilege has on TGE children of color; in the United States, 89% of psychologists and 63% of counselors or social workers identify as White (U.S. Department of Health and Human Services, 2013). One effect of White privilege is the emergence of the White savior archetype among clinicians. A *White savior* is one who, through noblesse oblige, swoops in to elevate the lives of those "below" them. The core of this archetype is a belief in White culture and morality as superior to the cultures and moralities of communities of color (Ash, 2013; A. Brown, 2013). As an archetype, White saviorism is not limited to Caucasian/White therapists: The principles, based on belief, either explicit or implicit, in the superiority of the dominant culture, could be enacted by any clinician who holds a position of power (e.g., middle and upper class, heterosexual, cisgender, Christian) and by anyone who believes White culture is morally superior to the cultures of communities of color. In clinical practice with TGE children of color, the White savior archetype reinforces the stereotype of communities of color as more transphobic, often resulting in cultural splitting by favoring White culture as positive references for TGE children of color.

Critical race theory forces an examination of both the social constructs maintaining systems based on White privilege and power and the individual's role in maintaining those systems (Ortiz & Jani, 2010). Using critical race theory as a platform, clinicians can deconstruct their views of racism, definitions of morality, and the nature of their professional engagement with TGE children of color and their families. Views on racism within the White savior archetype include seeing racism as unintentional, passive, or unconscious and block clinicians from seeing how their practice with TGE children of color is influenced by all systems of oppression. Clinical approaches based in critical race theory create interventions that allow TGE children of color to feel connected to the positive aspects and strengths of their community to accept TGE identities. To examine the transition from a White savior archetype to a critical race theory approach with TGE children of color, consider the case of Elisabeth and Diamond:

> Elisabeth is a Caucasian therapist providing mental health services to children of color in a large urban area. Elisabeth began working with Diamond when Diamond was 11. Diamond is Latino and has lived intermittently between group homes and biological parents since they started to dress in gender expansive ways, choosing pronouns different from those associated with their sex assigned at birth, and changing their name. At age 14, Diamond requested that Elisabeth start doing family sessions with their parents to help support Diamond's transition back home on a full-time basis. Elisabeth struggles with the decision to begin family therapy because she feels like Diamond's parents will "never change" and "Latinos will never accept Diamond." Confirming that she is reacting to the request through the lens of White saviorism, Elisabeth expresses to her supervisors that it would be better for Diamond to be placed with a White queer family so Diamond can experience "acceptance." Diamond seeks out local LGBTQ organizations for support and finds multiple organizations that support TGE children of color and finds a service specifically designed to work with Latino families. Diamond brings the resources into therapy sessions and discusses their experience of acceptance among other Latino TGE youth and heteronormative adults. Using resources provided by Diamond, Elisabeth develops a consultation relationship with a Latino health care worker who has experience working with issues of sexual orientation and gender identity in Latino families. With the support of the health care worker from the service working with Latino families, Elisabeth develops a critical race theory approach and agrees to begin family therapy with the support of the Latino health care worker.

Challenging Stereotypes of Communities of Color

Historically, stories of TGE children and adults of color have been invisible in the media. This lack of representation has supported a narrative that TGE people of color are an anomaly within society as a whole and has reinforced their invisibility as a function of rejection from their racial/ethnic group. Between 2000 and 2015, visibility for TGE people of color was raised as a result of prominent TGE women of color coming out, television shows depicting the lives of TGE people of color, President Barack Obama's public acceptance of LGBTQ people, and even an article and video of an African American mother's acceptance of raising her TGE child published in the magazine *Cosmopolitan* (Barker, 2015). Although focused on adults, the National Transgender Discrimination Survey is the most comprehensive profile of TGE people across race, class, and education highlighting social needs and family acceptance (Grant, Mottet, & Tanis, 2011). In 2011, Black TGE people reported the highest rate (55%) of family resilience, and 65% of Latino respondents reported their relationships with family improved over time (Grant et al., 2011). Native Americans and Alaskan Native respondents (51%) report having improved relationships with their family after coming out; multiracial respondents (59%) represented the highest cultural group to report being out to their families (Grant et al., 2011). These statistics paint a picture of acceptance of TGE people of color that enables clinicians to encourage safe family contact and reaffirms the ability of families from various ethnic backgrounds to display affirming behaviors over time.

It is important for clinicians to validate TGE children of color's feelings of family rejection and the risk of negative health outcomes associated with family rejection, as well as to challenge stereotypes of communities of color created from the intersectionality of racial oppression and TGE phobia. Intersectionality pairs well with critical race theory by providing an avenue to explore identity in the context of structures of power and interdependent forms of oppression created by colonialism, imperialism, racism, homophobia/transphobia, patriarchy, and ableism (Hankivsky, 2014). Intersectionality means not reducing injustice to a single root but allowing the intersections of social location, relationships to power, and experience to guide mental health professionals in addressing oppression (Hankivsky, 2014). When faced with parental rejecting behaviors toward TGE children of color, clinicians should ask themselves, their clients, and their client's families, "How has racism impacted your community's view on TGE children?" versus locating rejection solely in that ethnic/racial group. For example, the rejecting behaviors shown to TGE African American/Black female children is stereotypically assigned to the impact of conservative social views of African Americans on issues of sexual orientation, gender identity, and expression. In contrast, applying a lens of intersectionality, the rejecting behavior would be better described as an impact of slavery from the use of forcible rape and systemic "feminization" of male slaves as tools of degradation, punishment, and power. By offering this reframing to rejecting family members, clinicians can refocus acceptance, helping parents address this intergenerational fear of homosexuality as a tool of oppression and rejecting behaviors toward the child.

Intersectionality and Critical Race Theory in Practice

Clinicians often lack a model of praxis to apply intersectionality and critical race theory to interventions with TGE children of color. The following praxis paradigm is built on clinical assessment and practice strategies with TGE children of color successful at reducing cultural splitting, White saviorism, and reinforcement of stereotypes. Creating a nonbiased framework of assessment for TGE children of color requires the following ideological shifts:

- *From coming out to being out.* Attuning to a child's behaviors—to their *becoming*—can offer subtle clues to gender diversity without requiring declarative statements of identity (Renold, 2000). The research base for evaluating levels of "outness" for youth of color as compared with their White counterparts reveals no substantial difference as measured by certainty, comfort, or self-acceptance of their identity (Rosario, Schrimshaw, & Hunter, 2004). People of color tend to engage in non-heterosexual sexual encounters before their White counterparts do (Grov et al., 2006) and develop friendships supportive of their identity predeclaration (Bowleg et al., 2009). For TGE children of color, honoring this becoming allows for greater flexibility in identity and expression and reduces the pathology often associated with gender diversity.
- *From single-identity development* to *intersectional identity development.* When working with TGE children of color, clinicians must reduce dependence on single-identity development models. Embracing intersectional identity development creates assessments that account for interactions between identities and enables the development of strategies to support healthy adjustment to paradoxes created by multiple identities (i.e., developing a positive self-image of their gender diversity while still living with caregivers who may reject them by, e.g., not using their chosen name).
- *From cultural splitting to cultural affirmation.* Clinicians must provide imagery, first person stories, mentors, and local agencies for TGE children of color to feel affirmed by members of their own cultural group. This requires intentional efforts on the part of clinicians to reach out and locate these resources.

Using Resilient Therapy to Support Intersectionality

Resilient therapy (RT) was created as a response to working with diverse groups of disadvantaged children within public mental health systems in Europe (Hart, Blincow, & Thomas, 2008). Its originators' objective was to create a therapeutic intervention reflective of the ability of clinicians to help young people build resilience amidst experiencing disadvantages (Hart et al., 2008). Included in the list of disadvantaged children are those who have characteristics that have historically led to prejudice and discrimination and those who have experiences of prejudice and discrimination, that is, TGE children of color. The foundation of RT is the ability of clinicians' self-reflection process, termed the *inequalities imagination*; RT provides a systematic way for clinicians to enhance awareness of their responsibility to challenge structural inequalities while addressing individual clients' needs (Hart, Hall, & Henwood, 2003). The development of the inequalities imagination sets a stage for clinicians to rehearse future behaviors and develop empathy for TGE children of color by using the clinician's imagination versus a countertransference experience with clients. The inequalities imagination is built from the clinician's desire for equality for TGE children of color, awareness of inequalities, learned skills to address inequalities, and motivation to action to reduce inequalities in their practice (Hart et al., 2008). Increasing cultural knowledge through respectful cultural encounters helps broaden the clinician's worldview to include the experiences of TGE children of color and analyze the success of interventions to reduce cultural splitting.

RT paired with the gender affirmative model (GAM) supports *resilient moves* for TGE children of color through the domains of belonging, basic needs, coping, core-self, and learning (Hart et al., 2008). These resilient moves are identified by the child during the therapeutic process through the use of Hart, Blincow, and Thomas's (2012) Resilient Framework (Children & Young People) table. RT encourages clinicians to conceptualize the domains as equally strategic in developing resilience. The framework is a tool for intervention that also helps clinicians complete a resilience-based assessment of the child and family unit. A similar framework has been developed for adults, thus supporting consistent assessment and interventions with children and their caregiver.

To support resilient moves, clinicians are encouraged to practice the four noble truths of accepting, conserving, committing, and enlisting (Hart et al., 2008):

- Fostering *acceptance* of the social context TGE children of color experience helps validate emotional responses and gives clients power over their reactions and ability to change. Acceptance is not complacency or condoning harmful things children experience; instead, it helps the child to make decisions by developing an understanding of how racism and transphobia impact their life.
- *Conserving* is the act of tracking positive changes occurring over time to support resilient moves. Finding systematic ways to reflect on progress with children and their caregivers provides motivation for continued work.
- *Commitment* comes in the form of the clinician's commitment to the client, the caregiver's commitment to the client, and the client's commitment to their own self. Clearly articulating these commitments throughout the therapeutic process promotes independence in the child while engaging adults as the safety net to support the child when there are setbacks.
- *By enlisting support*, the clinician, client and caregiver collectively address the complex needs faced by TGE children of color. Given the level of acceptance and rejection the child experiences at home, school and in the community, enlisting support from various resources will be crucial to building resilience for TGE children of color.

Synthesizing the Approach: Case Study

KJ is 15 years old, mixed race (Black and Caucasian), and resides with KJ's Caucasian mother. KJ was referred to school-based therapy because of cursing at teachers, getting into physical fights with peers, and poor academic performance. KJ stated he was willing to engage in therapy because he felt the clinician, a Black, gender-nonconforming, masculine-of-center-identified person, would "understand" him better than other therapists might. Within the first session, KJ declared his identity as female-to-male transgender. Using the RT framework, KJ identified four approaches to focus on and requested family sessions to help him "explain to his mother that he was not a tomboy." Through the use of critical race theory, intersectionality, and the GAM, the clinician supported KJ in articulating his need for gender and racial/ethnicity affirmation from his mother, peers, and school community. The clinician enlisted support for KJ and his mother by referring them to local LGBTQI2-S organization with Black transgender staff for social and leadership development programs. By the conclusion of therapy, KJ reduced the frequency of disruptive behavior at school, developed a mentor relationship with a Black TGE community member, initiated safe contact with his Black father, articulated his understanding of himself as a Black male living with a Caucasian family to his mother, and switched to using *he/his/him* pronouns in school and at home.

Structural Resources to Support Gender Diverse Children of Color

Clinicians require unique practice models that address the social and educational needs of TGE children of color whose experiences are often rooted in racism, homophobia, and transphobia. Over half of youth of color report experiencing discrimination on the basis of race or gender identity or expression (Kosciw, Greytak, Palmer, & Boesen, 2014). This discrimination leads to depression, anxiety, and increased dropout rates for TGE children of color. Therefore, clinical practice with this population must include an assessment of structural resources and strategies to help connect TGE children and families to those resources. The guidelines presented here are intended to help clinicians make informed choices when making referrals for structural resources: programs and activities designed to address the needs of clients across the five domains of the RT Framework—basic needs, belonging, learning, coping, and core self.

CULTURAL REPRESENTATION

Cultural representation, a visual mirroring of race/ethnicity, within a structural support for TGE children of color and their families, is a key element in making resources accessible to families. Although a surface-level assessment of cultural competence, cultural representation does provide an observable mirroring for children and families of color. An assessment of cultural representation includes identifying the race/ethnicity of the population served; number of staff representing the child's race/ethnicity; and inclusion of racial/ethnic images, celebrations, and cultural practices. To increase the probability of cultural representation, clinicians should ensure that resources can be accessed through the natural support systems of the child, for example, school, library, community center, afterschool program, summer camps, or religious institutions. The clinician's familiarity with cultural representation at TGE-specific services will increase safety for TGE children of color and their families.

LANGUAGE ACCESSIBILITY

One challenge for children or youth who have caregivers who speak a language other than English is finding TGE resources appropriate for their caregivers. Multilingual resources (e.g., pamphlets, websites, books, e-mail lists) and support groups for caregivers of TGE children can normalize caregivers' experience. Linguistically matched clinicians, along with the use of translators, create a safe space for caregivers to process their emotions related to their child's gender identity or expression, understand their child's needs, and connect to available resources (e.g., the *Supportive Families, Healthy Children Helping Families With Lesbian, Gay, Bisexual & Transgender Children* [Ryan, 2009] tool kit is provided in both English and Spanish).

MENTORSHIP

With limited visibility of positive experiences as a TGE person of color, facilitating mentorship relationships between TGE children and TGE adults of color nurtures positive identity development. Through this relationship, the child can learn from the experience of the adult, ask them questions related to navigating TGE identities within their racial/ethnic group, and experience validation as a TGE person of color. TGE children of color can also get guidance about culturally specific effects of hormones, medications, surgeries and non-Western methods of transitioning.

SAFE SPACES

Safe spaces for TGE children of color create opportunities for them to hear stories from other TGE children of color about navigating friends, romantic partners, schools, cultural values, families, and their spiritual homes. Examples of safe spaces for TGE children of color are support groups, conferences, workshops, art-based programs, and leadership camps. These affinity groups also create opportunities for TGE children of color to discuss racial aggressions experienced in TGE spaces, learn coping strategies to be able to create a stronger sense of self, and learn the history of TGE people of color and the resilience tools they have used to navigate racism and transphobia.

POSITIVE PEER SUPPORT

Affirming peer relationships are a commonly overlooked structural resource for TGE children of color. In a series of focus groups with youth of color on issues of sexual orientation, gender identity, and gender expression, peer support was highlighted as an essential component of positive gender identity development (E. Brown, 2015). Non-TGE participants also identified a need for more youth-friendly resources on gender diversity to help them be better allies to TGE children of color through the coming out process and counteract experiences of rejection (E. Brown, 2015). This youth voice should shape clinical practice by creating more opportunities for group services, enlisting child allies into the clinical process, and creating opportunities for non-TGE children to receive guidance on how to best support their TGE peers.

Conclusion

The impetus for this chapter was the lack of research on the effects of systemic oppression on clinical practice with TGE children of color. Christianity and colonization have impacted communities of color by reinforcing gender binary models and devaluing gender diversity. The legacy of this oppression has been a monolithic perception of TGE identities exclusive to the experiences of Caucasian/White TGE people and positions communities of color as only rejecting of TGE children. But increased visibility and study of TGE people in communities of color reveal more complex layers to the experiences of TGE children of color. Clinicians are challenged to create a praxis allowing for self-reflection on held beliefs about communities of color and acceptance of TGE children and their own perceptions of acceptance of TGE children in communities of color. Through embracing a critical race theory perspective and an intersectional analysis, clinicians can develop assessments and interventions aimed at reducing cultural splitting and reinforcing positive multidimensional identity development for TGE children of color. Equally important for TGE children of color is the clinician's efforts to connect them to safe spaces, positive peer support, and mentors reflecting the client's racial/ethnic culture.

The guidelines presented in this chapter require the investigation of cultural representation beyond what is available through brochures or online content. Clinicians must be in the practice of e-mailing, conducting in-person interviews, and researching virtual platforms to ensure TGE children of color are represented. Before working with a TGE child of color, the clinician must be prepared to engage in a redesign of their practice and a praxis of creating culturally responsive interventions that consider the intersections of race, gender identity, and expression. To create truly safe therapeutic spaces for TGE children of color, White/Caucasian clinicians must be mindful of the impact of White privilege within the therapeutic process, and gender normative clinicians of all races/ethnicities must be willing to deconstruct their transphobic ideologies. Most important, before working with TGE children of color, clinicians need to become familiar with this population's nuanced struggles and resilience, accurately assess their ability to truly support the child, and enlist TGE people of color through consultation to ensure TGE children of color are able to become thriving adults.

References

American Psychiatric Association. (2013). *Diagnostic and statistical manual of mental disorders* (5th ed.). Washington, DC: Author.

Ash, E. (2013). *Emotional responses to savior films: Concealing privilege or appealing to our better selves?* (Unpublished doctoral dissertation). The Pennsylvania State University, State College. Retrieved from https://etda.libraries.psu.edu/catalog/18966

Balsam, K. F., Huang, B., Fieland, K. C., Simoni, J. M., & Walters, K. L. (2004). Culture, trauma, and wellness: A comparison of heterosexual and lesbian, gay, bisexual, and two-spirit Native Americans [Special issue]. *Cultural Diversity & Ethnic Minority Psychology, 10,* 287–301. http://dx.doi.org/10.1037/1099-9809.10.3.287

Barker, E. (2015, October 12). What it's really like when your daughter becomes your son. *Cosmopolitan.* Retrieved from http://www.cosmopolitan.com/sex-love/news/a47585/what-its-really-like-when-your-daughter-becomes-your-son/

Bockting, W. O., & Cesaretti, C. (2001). Spirituality, transgender identity, and coming out. *Journal of Sex Education and Therapy, 26,* 291–300.

Bowleg, L., Burkholder, G., Teti, M., & Craig, M. L. (2009). The complexities of outness: Psychosocial predictors of coming out to others among Black lesbian and bisexual women. *Journal of LGBT Health Research, 4,* 153–166. http://dx.doi.org/10.1080/15574090903167422

Brown, A. (2013). Waiting for superwoman: White female teachers and the construction of the "neoliberal savior" in a New York City public school. *The Journal for Critical Education Policy Studies, 11,* 123–164.

Brown, E. (2015). *Leading together: Peer support for LGBTQI2-S children, youth, adults, and seniors.* Berkeley, CA: Pacific Center of Human Growth and Development.

Chung, Y. B., & Katayama, M. (1998). Ethnic and sexual identity development of Asian-American lesbian and gay adolescents. *Professional School Counseling, 1,* 21–25.

Chung, Y. B., & Singh, A. A. (2009). Lesbian, gay, bisexual, and transgender Asian Americans. In A. Alvarez & N. Tewari (Eds.), *Asian American psychology: Current perspectives* (pp. 233–246). New York, NY: Taylor & Francis.

Clark, C. (2005). Deconstructing "the down low"—People of color "coming out" and "being out" on campus: A conversation with Mark Brimhall-Vargas, Sivagami Subbaraman, and Robert Waters. *Multicultural Education, 13,* 46–59. Retrieved from http://eric.ed.gov/?id=EJ727808

Funk, C., & Lugo, L. (2012, July 19). *Asian Americans: A mosaic of faiths.* Retrieved http://www.pewforum.org/files/2012/07/Asian-Americans-religion-full-report.pdf

Grant, J. M., Mottet, L. A., & Tanis, J. (2011). *Injustice at Every Turn: A Report of the National Transgender Discrimination Survey.* Washington, DC: National Center for Transgender Equality.

Grov, C., Bimbi, D. S., Nanin, J. E., & Parsons, J. T. (2006). Race, ethnicity, gender, and generational factors associated with the coming-out process among gay, lesbian, and bisexual individuals. *Journal of Sex Research, 43,* 115–121. http://dx.doi.org/10.1080/00224490609552306

Hackett, C., Connor, P., Stonawski, M., & Skirbekk, V. (2015, April 2). *The future of world religions: Population growth projections, 2010–2050: Why Muslims are rising fastest and the unaffiliated are shrinking as a share of the world's population.* Retrieved from http://www.pewforum.org/files/2015/03/PF_15.04.02_ProjectionsFullReport.pdf

Hankivsky, O. (2014). *Intersectionality 101.* Retrieved from http://vawforum-cwr.ca/sites/default/files/attachments/intersectionallity_101.pdf

Hart, A., Blincow, D., & Thomas, H. (2008). Resilient therapy: Strategic therapeutic engagement with children in crisis. *Child Care in Practice, 14,* 131–145. http://dx.doi.org/10.1080/13575270701868744

Hart, A., Blincow, D., & Thomas, H. (2012, October). *What is resilient therapy and the resilience framework?* Retrieved from http://www.boingboing.org.uk/resilience/resilient-therapy-resilience-framework/

Hart, A., Hall, V., & Henwood, F. (2003). Helping health and social care professionals to develop an "inequalities imagination": A model for use in education and practice. *Journal of Advanced Nursing, 41,* 480–489. http://dx.doi.org/10.1046/j.1365-2648.2003.02555.x

Kosciw, J. G., Greytak, E. A., Palmer, N. A., & Boesen, M. J. (2014). *The 2013 National School Climate Survey: The experiences of lesbian, gay, bisexual and transgender youth in our nation's schools.* New York, NY: Gay, Lesbian & Straight Education Network.

Li, L., & Orleans, M. (2001). Coming out discourses of Asian American lesbians. *Sexuality & Culture, 5*(2), 57–78. http://dx.doi.org/10.1007/s12119-001-1018-z

Loiacano, D. K. (1989). Gay identity issues among Black Americans: Racism, homophobia, and the need for validation. *Journal of Counseling & Development, 68,* 21–25. http://dx.doi.org/10.1002/j.1556-6676.1989.tb02486.x

Mirandé, A. (2014). Transgender identity and acceptance in a global era: The Muxes of Juchitán. In J. Gelfer (Ed.), *Masculinities in a global era: International and cultural psychology* (pp. 247–263). New York, NY: Springer. http://dx.doi.org/10.1007/978-1-4614-6931-5_14

Ortiz, L., & Jani, J. (2010). Critical race theory: A transformational model for teaching diversity. *Journal of Social Work Education, 46,* 175–193. http://dx.doi.org/10.5175/JSWE.2010.200900070

Parks, C. A., Hughes, T. L., & Matthews, A. K. (2004). Race/ethnicity and sexual orientation: Intersecting identities. *Cultural Diversity and Ethnic Minority Psychology, 10,* 241–254. http://dx.doi.org/10.1037/1099-9809.10.3.241

Renold, E. (2000). "Coming out": Gender, (hetero) sexuality and the primary school. *Gender and Education, 12,* 309–326. http://dx.doi.org/10.1080/713668299

Roen, K. (2001). Transgender theory and embodiment: The risk of racial marginalization. *Journal of Gender Studies, 10,* 253–263. http://dx.doi.org/10.1080/09589230120086467

Rosario, M., Schrimshaw, E. W., & Hunter, J. (2004). Ethnic/racial differences in the coming-out process of lesbian, gay, and bisexual youths: A comparison of sexual identity development over time. *Cultural Diversity & Ethnic Minority Psychology, 10,* 215–228. http://dx.doi.org/10.1037/1099-9809.10.3.215

Roscoe, W., & Murray, S. O. (2001). *Boy-wives and female husbands: Studies of African homosexualities.* New York, NY: St. Martin.

Ryan, C. (2009). *Supportive families, healthy children helping families with lesbian, gay, bisexual and transgender children.* Retrieved from https://familyproject.sfsu.edu/sites/default/files/FAP_English%20Booklet_pst.pdf

U.S. Department of Health and Human Services. (2013). *The U.S. Health Workforce Chartbook*. Rockville, MD: Health Resources and Services Administration, National Center for Health Workforce Analysis, U.S. Department of Health and Human Services.

Wilkinson, W., & Gomez, P. (2004). *Assessing the needs of female-to-male transgender people of color and their partners*. Retrieved from http://www.ftmi.org

World Professional Association for Transgender Health. (2011). *Standards of care for the health of transsexual, transgender, and gender nonconforming people* (7th version). Retrieved from https://www.wpath.org/media/cms/Documents/Web%20Transfer/SOC/Standards%20of%20Care%20V7%20-%202011%20WPATH.pdf

Zimman, L. (2009). "The other kind of coming out": Transgender people and the coming out. *Gender and Language, 3*, 53–80. http://dx.doi.org/10.1558/genl.v3i1.53

Karisa Barrow and Demetry Apostle

5 Addressing Mental Health Conditions Often Experienced by Transgender and Gender Expansive Children

Psychologists and academics have long grappled with the meaning of gender and how social constructs influence its definition. Inflexible and outdated views of gender identity development continue to persist in the clinical community. Much is to be learned in the way of gender identity as a "web" of expression—that is, a compilation of nature, nurture, culture, and time (Ehrensaft, 2016). We emphasize that a person's gender expression and/or identity, in and of itself, is never pathological. However, transgender and gender expansive (TGE) children, in comparison with their peers, are more susceptible to developing mental health issues. Research shows that this vulnerability is more likely due to societal discrimination and rejection, as well as environmental trauma (Erickson-Schroth, 2014; Toomey, Ryan, Diaz, Card, & Russell, 2010) than to intrapsychic conditions. To best serve clients' needs while assessing, diagnosing, and providing interventions, it is essential to consider the mental health conditions that co-occur with diverse gender development.

It is common for TGE children who seek therapeutic intervention to present with psychological issues, which may include anxiety, social anxiety, depression, attention-deficit/hyperactivity disorder, eating disorders, enuresis, or other behavioral problems. They may also develop symptoms resulting from strained or abusive relationships in their home and/or school

http://dx.doi.org/10.1037/0000095-005
The Gender Affirmative Model: An Interdisciplinary Approach to Supporting Transgender and Gender Expansive Children, C. Keo-Meier and D. Ehrensaft (Editors)
Copyright © 2018 by the American Psychological Association. All rights reserved.

environment. Common misconceptions among mental health providers who have not received training in working with TGE children are that the child's expression of gender is due to parental pathology, a traumatic experience, or a psychotic delusion. In response to these misconceptions and in a milieu where parents are not uncommonly accused of "causing" their child's gender issues, parents will benefit from learning that they actually have little control over their child's internal gender identity (Ehrensaft, 2016). As for traumatic experiences, no evidence substantiates trauma as a direct or sole factor in gender expression or identity development. However, evidence does indicate that TGE children are more at risk for traumatic experiences because of their identity, because of familial or societal reactions (Roberts, Rosario, Corliss, Koenen, & Austin, 2012). Last, psychotic disorders are rarely present in TGE children (Donnelly-Boylen, 2016). If a delusion were to occur (i.e., a person believing they are the other gender while experiencing a psychotic episode), the gender affirmative model (GAM) would encourage providers to give space for the child to express their gender identity as experienced while simultaneously addressing presenting psychotic symptoms. It is important to note that dissecting the origins of a child's presentation is far less important than creating an affirming space.

Although GAM and affirming care in general have their critics, those of us who work directly with the population have seen its effectiveness in reducing distress related to gender dysphoria and resulting mental health symptoms. The GAM prescribes a more flexible approach to assessment and practice. Our work here represents an effort to provide informed guidance that will lead to the development of a comprehensive treatment model that meets the complex needs of gender diverse children living with mental health issues. The GAM posits that children should not be denied the opportunity to explore and embrace their identity, socially and/or medically if they are simultaneously being treated for other presenting problems. It also maintains that allowing gender exploration and expression socially and/or medically can reduce negative mental health symptoms, whereas withholding this opportunity often exacerbates negative mental health consequences (Ehrensaft, 2016; Wallien, Swaab, & Cohen-Kettenis, 2007).

In this chapter, we review the literature on psychological issues prevalent among TGE children and provide a critical analysis of previous nonaffirming treatment approaches. We illustrate relevant clinical cases that emphasize the benefits of the GAM approach to assessment, diagnosis, case formulation, and treatment interventions that take into account co-occurring issues.

Review of the Literature on Psychological Issues Among TGE Children and Adolescents

Although gender dysphoric symptoms are likely to wax and wane over time, to a large extent, the suffering of TGE children is not limited to the impact of these symptoms. We know from clinical experience that many transgender adults and youth experience other significant forms of psychological distress over the course of self-discovery and coming out, particularly before and during social and medical transition. Their parents also experience distress in reaction to these revelations and transitions. Yet, clinical literature and research on this topic are sparse. Nevertheless, research outcomes and clinical observations suggest that TGE children are at an increased risk for anxiety, depression, academic and behavioral problems, social isolation, eating disorders, substance abuse, self-harming behaviors, bullying, high-risk sexual practices (including higher risk of contracting HIV and other sexually transmitted infections), suicide attempts, and completed suicides when compared with their same-aged peers (Grossman & D'Augelli, 2007).

A study of youth at the Gender Management Services (GeMS) program in Boston found that nearly 44% of transgender youth were diagnosed with psychiatric conditions, such as anxiety-related disorders and severe mood disorders (Spack et al., 2012). Several studies lend further evidence to the ubiquity of co-occurring diagnoses among gender diverse youth. The estimates of children diagnosed with Gender Dysphoria (GD; previously gender identity disorder) having one or more co-occurring diagnoses ranges from 32% to 52% (de Vries, Doreleijers, Steensma, & Cohen-Kettenis, 2011; Wallien et al., 2007). These data likely reflect the experience of TGE children's internalizing negative messages and experiences of microaggressions in their social environment (Hendricks & Testa, 2012). As evident in U.S. society's recent discourse on the public's policing of bathroom use by transgender individuals, denial of TGE children's access to public accommodations, as well as experiences of hostility, can result in both clinical and medical conditions (e.g., enuresis and/or urinary tract infections from avoiding using the bathrooms at school). Although little research is available on these problems, trends in our practices tell us that some of these children avoid staying hydrated because of the anxiety and fears around using public restrooms.

Interweaving factors of internalized transphobia, as well as interpersonal, institutional, and cultural influences outlined in the gender minority stress model (Hendricks & Testa, 2012), help contextualize understanding of the oppression of TGE children and the resulting psychological suffering and symptomatology. The model suggests that the stress associated with stigma, prejudice, and discrimination increases rates of psychological distress. Unrelenting transphobic experiences lead to clinical symptomatology. In turn, TGE children develop defensive responses to being stigmatized. These responses can manifest in an external way in which a child may exhibit an exaggerated, obsessive concern with the stigmatized characteristic (e.g., hyperfeminization or hypermasculinization). The responses may also express themselves internally, in which self-denigration and identification with the aggressor (becoming a bully themselves) are present. Many theorists contend that the internalization process is inevitable because children are exposed to gender norms from birth and may adopt negative attitudes about their gender nonconforming and transgender self at an early age (Williamson, 2000). Among marginalized groups, emotional and psychological injuries are the direct results of minority stress, which elicits hypervigilance and anxious expectations of perceived threats. The need to continuously scan the environment for safety can be emotionally draining and exhausting. Higher levels of reported distress may typically manifest in depression, social anxiety, suicidal ideation, anxiety, mood disorders, and dysregulated behaviors (Lewis, Derlega, Griffin, & Krowinski, 2003; Meyer, 1995).

In that context, TGE children may isolate or become aggressive in response to perceived threats. These children are often misdiagnosed with oppositional or conduct disorders, when such behaviors are actually symptoms of distress in their social environment (Cook et al., 2005). For instance, if a child steals and lies, it may be to procure toys and articles of clothing that affirm their gender identity. In some cases in which a diagnosis of conduct disorder is given, the defensive response (identification with the aggressor) may subside when gender congruence is achieved.

Some youth, in an attempt to institute adaptive responses to the stress caused by transphobia, may engage in obsessive practices, fixated on "passing" with their identified gender through dress, mannerisms, and so forth. Some of those youth may find themselves straying into less adaptive and potentially self-injurious responses, such as cutting, extreme tucking or binding techniques, and genital mutilation (Donnelly-Boylen, 2016).

Untreated symptoms exacerbate mental health conditions and decrease functioning. Furthermore, psychological issues experienced by TGE children may become more problematic with the onset of puberty, especially if they experience dissonance from or a sense of "betrayal" by their changing body. This, coupled with experiences of social rejection, marginalization, and bullying, leads to significantly higher rates of suicidal thoughts, attempts, and completions when compared with the general population (Grossman & D'Augelli, 2007). The rates of self-harm ideation expressed by these youth are also high (Roberts, Rosario, Corliss, Koenen, & Austin, 2012). Herman, Haas, and Rodgers (2014) reported that by adulthood, 41% of self-identified TGE respondents had attempted suicide, and within this group, 57% had been rejected by their families and 78% had experienced physical or sexual harassment in school. Research by the Family Acceptance Project has shown that experiences of family rejection and trauma in gender and sexual orientation diverse children lead to adverse outcomes, severe mental health issues, acting out behaviors (e.g., high-risk sexual behavior and substance abuse), homelessness, and possibly suicide (Ryan, Huebner, Diaz, & Sanchez, 2009). Among the older youth, stress can lead to maladaptive coping strategies to modify the body (e.g., eating disorders) and in extreme cases, suicide (Reisner et al., 2015).

Autism Spectrum Disorder and Gender Diverse Children

Autism spectrum disorder (ASD) is now classified under the umbrella of pervasive developmental disorders (American Psychiatric Association [APA], 2013). Symptoms of ASD include difficulties in communication and social realms of functioning, repetitive behaviors, and restricted interests (APA, 2013). Clinical impressions as well as increasing empirical evidence point to an overrepresentation of ASD among TGE patients (Baird et al., 2006). In an article published in 2010, de Vries, Noens, Cohen-Kettenis, van Berckelaer-Onnes, and Doreleijers examined more than 200 children and adolescents presenting for treatment of gender dysphoria between 2004 and 2007. Their results indicated that the participants had a sevenfold higher incidence of ASD than did the general population (7.8% vs. 0.6%–1.0%).

Although an ASD diagnosis requires that symptoms be present in childhood, a diagnosis of GD does not (APA, 2013). Even so, features of both conditions are often present in childhood (de Vries et al., 2010). Both ASD and GD have no agreed-upon origin—and many hypotheses concerning their cause remain controversial—but the scientific community converges in their understanding that both are likely to stem from a multifactorial etiology, including genetic predisposition, exposure to intrauterine hormones, social environment, and the impact of other psychological phenomena (Jacobs, Rachlin, Erickson-Schroth, & Janssen, 2014; Strang et al., 2018).

Conceptual challenges exist in understanding the process of gender identity development in individuals with ASD, which inevitably impact clinical decisions. If gender identity formation is characterized as a normal developmental stage in childhood—in which various gender roles are experienced and gender stability and constancy are established—individuals with ASD who are understood to experience differing patterns of social development are likely to travel down a different developmental trajectory with respect to gender identity formation (Mukaddes, 2002). Accounting for these disparate developmental paths adds to the already difficult task of accurately assessing gender-related concerns in children and adolescents with ASD. Accordingly, it is important to differentiate to what degree gender dysphoria stems from the differences inherent in being a neurodiverse individual (a person who has an ASD) or differences associated with being a gender diverse individual or the combination of both (de Vries et al., 2010).

Abelson (1981) defined *gender identity* as "the developed ability of a child to categorize themselves either as a boy or a girl and the ability to recognize other children as being boys or girls" (p. 347). From his original study, Abelson concluded that gender identity development relied on cognition and developed in conjunction with mental age. He further hypothesized that some autistic children may not be picking up relevant cues and qualities that would support their ability to differentiate between boys and girls. It is noteworthy that this perspective on gender is based on a binary model. Studies have demonstrated a higher prevalence of ASD among TGE children than in the general population; therefore, appropriate screening and support for neurological conditions must be concurrent with addressing gender-related concerns. However, at the same time, children assessed to be on the autism spectrum should be recognized as able to conceptualize and articulate their authentic TGE selves, albeit following different pathways and cognitive and emotional consolidations than their neurotypical TGE peers (Ehrensaft, 2016).

Proper assessment, diagnosis, and treatment of gender-related concerns for individuals with ASD should not differ from neurotypical individuals, but the prevalence of gender-related concerns among individuals with ASD must be taken into account in the healthy exploration and development of their gender narrative. A common misstep made by parents and clinicians with children on the autism spectrum is to dismiss their claims of being TGE. This can lead to errors in diagnosis and treatment because their gender identity may be misperceived as just another short-lived obsessive interest.

Critique of Historical Perspectives

Historically, psychological models of development and clinical treatment have differed in their understanding of and recommendations for treatment concerning co-occurring psychological issues for TGE children and adolescents. We explore three of these approaches in this section: (a) traditional psychoanalytic models; (b) Coates and colleagues' (e.g., Coates, 1990; Coates, Friedman, & Wolfe, 1991) model of attachment disruptions and trauma; (c) Zucker, Wood, Singh, and Bradley's (e.g., 2012) model. We then focus on the GAM and its perspective on co-occurring psychological issues for TGE children and adolescents.

TRADITIONAL PSYCHOANALYSIS

Psychoanalytic theory aspires to provide a blueprint for developmental psychological norms. Freud postulated gender identity and sexuality as not necessarily biological but rather as internalized representations of the projections surrounding them, taking into account internal conflicts and unconscious experiences that motivate actions. Practitioners adopting this theory have mistakenly assessed gender diversity as a negative outcome predicated on an unresolved oedipal complex and a fixation at that psychosexual stage of development. In sum, gender diversity itself is perceived as a psychological condition coexisting alongside a pathological developmental delay. The causal factors in this psychological co-occurrence were considered to be the neuroses of mothers and fathers, but particularly mothers, in projecting their unconscious wishes and desires onto these children. No empirical evidence supports this paradigm, and the theory, when put into practice, has proved harmful to gender and sexually diverse children and families across many decades.

COATES

Coates and colleagues assert that an "atypical" trajectory of gender identity development is a process that mirrors severe disturbances among family members, focusing specifically on the mother and her relationship with her son (Coates, 1990). It claims that "cross-gender" behavior typically presents between 2 and 3 years of age. The presentation, considered pathological, presents as the result of a composite of complex variables: biology, child temperament, and traumatic experiences during the early years of child development (Coates et al., 1991). In general, it is posited that the child, in expressing cross-gender behaviors, desires, and identifications, has experienced either an attachment disruption with a primary love object, typically the mother, or an early developmental trauma. Thus, the child is left with a gender disorder and co-existing attachment issues and potential posttrauma syndromes. It should be noted that history taking with TGE children aggregately indicates no such evidence of attachment disruption or early trauma in the vast majority of these children.

ZUCKER

Beginning in the 1970s, a group of providers under the leadership of Kenneth Zucker at the Gender Identity Clinic at the Center for Addiction and Mental Health in Toronto, Ontario, Canada, presented the benefits of a particular form of "live in your own skin" treatment created for young children discouraging both gender expansive expression and transgender identity development in children (Hill, Rozanski, Carfagnini, & Willoughby, 2007). The group posited that parental psychopathology was correlated with symptoms of gender dysphoria in children. In these instances, the co-occurring psychological issues exist in the family members: gender dysphoria in the child and parental anxiety, or parental projection of their own needs onto the child (Zucker & Cohen-Kettenis, 2008). The clinic has since closed because of controversy around the treatment approach.

The Gender Affirmative Model

The GAM takes issue with each of these conceptualizations of co-occurring, indeed causative, psychological issues that appear alongside a child's deviation from traditional gender norms. Instead, in the GAM, co-occurring psychological issues among TGE children are handled in the following way:

1. following a clinical interview that considers a thorough developmental history, distress identified as related to gender dysphoria is addressed first;
2. following interventions to ease gender dysphoria or symptoms of distress, other symptomatic conditions (e.g., depression, anxiety, eating disturbances, interpersonal problems) are re-evaluated and addressed;
3. parents are not pathologized in the face of their child's gender diversity but are offered support; and
4. further clinical investigation is definitely considered when a child's gender expression and/or identification may potentially be the symbolic representation of a psychological problem, for example, perceived cultural advantage (a girl who wants to play on the boys' baseball team), a response to trauma (identification with or flight from the aggressor), or a solution to a non–gender-related life problem (e.g., a boy who feels lonely and concludes that girls have better luck making friends, ergo, become a girl to have friends).

Social transitions have been found to address co-occurring psychological issues. A *social transition* occurs once a child's gender identity is determined to be consistent, insistent, and persistent. Following social transition, it has been observed that a child's co-occurring psychological issues, such as social anxiety or compromised frustration tolerance, may subside (Olson, Durwood, DeMeules, & McLaughlin, 2016). If, on the other hand, the symptoms do not decrease, or if they increase, other clinical symptomatology should be evaluated.

Gender affirming practitioners are called upon to balance their understanding of a child's variables of gender identity and gender expression with an assessment of other non–gender-related psychological issues that might either be causative, coexisting, or at an outgrowth of the child's gender status. This can result in a highly complicated clinical picture. The priority is to alleviate a child's suffering, identify their true gender self in the context of other psychological issues that may be occurring, and help the child along the developmental trajectory that will lead to self-determination and fulfill their potential alongside their peers.

Contemporary psychoanalytic teaching and its progressive interpretation of gender development have proved helpful in this task. Internal conflicts with the relational world for TGE children can lead to symptomatic behaviors and mental health issues. Symptomatic difficulties can be lessened by naming repressed thoughts and feelings, as well as by easing the tensions between the patient's unconscious wishes and social expectations. In turn, this will enable them to connect with their true gender self.

A review of the literature emphasizes that many TGE children and adolescents urgently need accurate psychological assessment, diagnosis, and therapeutic support because they are at great risk for distress stemming from sociocultural rejection and isolation. Addressing children's symptoms of gender dysphoria with a comprehensive diagnostic assessment coupled with attuned and appropriate mental health interventions can help mitigate emerging psychological distress. In our practices, we have observed that following the lead of the child within a GAM framework results in a remarkable decrease in emotional and behavioral instability, as well as improved interpersonal relationships with family and friends. In fact, clinical symptoms seem to subside once children receive affirmative care. It is imperative that a concerted effort be made to recognize the differences between symptoms associated with gender dysphoria and symptoms related to other psychological issues, as well as the interaction between them. It is our hope that strengthening the accuracy of assessment and diagnostic practices will lead to more competent care practices and improvements in a child's global functioning. Clinical evidence of these treatment gains will be provided in the following section on cases.

Clinical Implications and Treatment

CASE STUDY ONE

Enrique is a 9-year-old, biracial self-identified transgender boy, assigned female at birth, who began insistently and consistently stating he was a boy from the age of 3. Enrique lives with his mother, who separated from and divorced Enrique's father when Enrique was 3 years old. His father has remained active in his life. The relationship between his parents has been and remains quite acrimonious, with his father's lack of support for Enrique's gender identity and expression being just one of the many flashpoints between the parents. Enrique's parents would frequently argue in front of him. The difficulty between Enrique's parents has led to several family court interventions over the years, including court involvement instigated by Enrique's mother, which led to Enrique's social gender transition at school at age 7. While Enrique previously struggled in school socially and academically, his transition to going to school as a boy at a new school went well, as shown by increased interest in academics and sports. His mother considered his overall adjustment and emotional growth since socially transitioning at school nothing less than remarkable.

From the start of his masculine gender expression and insistency, Enrique's father made it clear that he does not consider his child's gender expansive behavior acceptable, given his religious beliefs. He often refuses to use Enrique's chosen name, instead referring to the child using Enrique's given name. Since his father's remarriage to a religiously conservative woman 1 year ago, Enrique is experiencing increased levels of distress and anxiety after weekend visitations at his father's home. Aggravating Enrique's stress levels, Enrique's father and stepmother have been taking him to a conservative church where they refer to Enrique as Rita and use *she/her/hers* pronouns when referring to him with others.

Subsequently, Enrique began acting out in school and at home. He consistently refused to go to school. The elevated level of anxiety and distress led his mother to seek ongoing supportive therapy and medication assessment. After a 3-day weekend visit with his father, Enrique began arguing with his mother. He retreated to the bathroom threatening to kill himself. His distraught mother was able to talk him down from the emotional meltdown but not before he had his mother promise him that he no longer needed to spend weekends at his father's home. Enrique's mother, upon the advice from his therapist, sought a change in custody arrangement requiring supervised visitations. Enrique frequently expressed that he loves his father and that his relationship with his father is important to him, but the lack of support of his gender identity was overwhelming. Two months after his suicidal threat, clearly defined expectations were mandated to guide Enrique's father and stepmother's behavior toward supporting his gender identity during supervised visits. Since then, Enrique's distress has subsided and concerns for self-harm have abated.

CASE STUDY 2

Roberta is an inquisitive, 11-year-old, transgender girl, assigned male at birth to Hispanic and Eastern European parents. Roberta was diagnosed at age 7 with ASD. Although the diagnosis was not a complete surprise to her parents, they readily made adjustments in the care and services needed to assist her in school, as well as manage their expectations and hopes for her future. They have been struggling with Roberta's relatively recent talk that "he" was in fact a girl. Roberta became increasingly distressed in proceeding months, leading her parents to seek treatment for her.

The parents reported that Roberta began to show early stages of puberty at age 10. At that time, she had become increasingly agitated and depressed. The progress she had been making in her special education classes in school was declining, and during that time, Roberta, then living as Robert, began to insist she was a girl and wanted to be called Roberta. Accustomed to their child's rich fantasy life filled with Pokémon stories, superheroes, and anime characters, Roberta's parents initially went along with calling her Roberta, believing this was just a phase.

It was only when they brought their child for an annual physical exam that they realized something more was transpiring. Roberta, then Robert, kept insisting to the doctor that she was uncomfortable with the changes happening "down there" and asked when she was going to grow breasts like the other girls in her school. During this same period, Roberta's parents received a call from the school counselor reporting that Roberta was involved in an altercation with several boys after she had come out of the girls' bathroom.

Roberta was brought to a gender specialist for assessment and therapy. The initial clinical testing verified her high levels of distress. In the clinical interview, Roberta spoke of how she always thought she was a girl from an early age, contradicting her parents' report of her gender history. Using a rainbow-colored abacus with male/masculine markings on one pole and female/feminine on the opposite pole, Roberta was asked to move as many rings in the direction she thinks is appropriate. Roberta responded to the question about the gender she was assigned at birth by immediately moving the entire row to the male end. When asked what gender she felt inside or thought of herself as, she moved the entire row of rings to the female end. In response to how she thinks people see her gender now, she moved the rings to the female end.

Early on in the assessment work, Roberta completed the House–Tree–Person projective test (Buck, 1948), drawing a very detailed picture of a female with rounded features and developed breasts, who was holding her arms behind her back. Roberta was very proud of her picture but could not say who the drawing depicted or describe what the girl was doing in the picture, likely in alignment with her autism diagnosis.

Roberta's seemingly late "coming out" as female, although perplexing to her parents, is not an unusual occurrence for individuals on the autism spectrum, who often do not develop a fuller sense of their gender identity until puberty. In Roberta's case, her assertion of a female gender identity came upon the heels of the onset of early puberty and the increasing discomfort and dissonance with her secondary sex characteristics, which began to appear.

It was quite apparent that Roberta met the criteria for ASD early on in treatment. Her fixations and preoccupation with action figures, Pokémon, and anime could be quite intense. Even after opening up about the discomfort she was experiencing with not having breasts and the feelings she had being around girls in school, she would quickly retreat into talk about her limited interests, a recurring pattern whenever an area of discomfort would arise. Without taking into account Roberta's patterns of thinking and feeling, her silences or redirection of conversations could have been mistakenly attributed to ambivalence about being transgender. Yet, when approached with direct non–open-ended questions, Roberta expressed an unwavering female gender identity and a longing to transition from male to female.

Helping Roberta better articulate her self-knowledge of her gender to others was a key component of her transition process. Given her own limited theory of mind, a common feature of autism, Roberta's understanding of her identity as female was accompanied by the assumption that others would of course come to that same understanding. Her outer appearance is still visibly masculine with a budding Adam's apple and signs of facial hair. Similar to many other autistic youth who develop their own idiosyncratic mosaic of gender, free from the bondage of social cueing and social mores, her gender is her gender, no matter how she looks, and it confuses her that no one else would see it the same way. With that in mind, Roberta will need assistance so that she can appreciate that others would will to gradually come to terms with her new identity, including her family members and peers. Putting into place consistent supports for both Roberta and her parents will be integral to a successful transition for Roberta that keeps both her autism and her gender dysphoria in mind as coexisting psychological experiences.

CASE STUDY 3

Colin is a 14-year-old, nonbinary, Asian youth who was assigned female at birth. He is on the transmasculine spectrum, and he has identified with being more male since latency and uses *he/him/his* pronouns. He struggles with his gender identification; disordered eating; self-regulation; anxiety; and obsessive thoughts, including fears about his hips becoming too shapely because of his erratic eating patterns. Early assessments concluded that he does not meet criteria for an eating disorder; however, therapeutic interventions were employed to address his relationship with food and attempt to control his physical features. Colin is also notably anxious and has fears of having panic attacks, which started when he was in the sixth grade.

Colin stated that he has always has felt different and did not fit in or feel a sense of belonging with girls. Reflecting on his gender narrative growing up, he found that his parents were permissive of his interests of video gaming and stereotypical male sports. He recounted that for a short time during elementary school he tried tirelessly to adopt the sense of femininity modeled by his sister, Becky, by wearing dresses and growing his hair long. With the onset of puberty came menstruation, which in turn led to an increase in feelings of depression and anxiety in part due to a sense of betrayal from his body. His relationship with his mother became strained. Daily routines resulted in yelling matches, which were uncharacteristic of their relationship. His gender dysphoric states were in full force.

Although most of his school friends were supportive, they were seemingly dismissive of the endurance of Colin's gender identity and reacted as if it were a "phase." Subsequently, Colin suffered from obsessive thoughts and beliefs about his body, for example, "I hate my voice; it's what gives me away." He then experienced gender dysphoria specific to his breasts, voice, and hips, and he wondered aloud about being asexual. In reaction to intrusive thoughts related to body dysphoria, Colin compulsively picks his skin and checks his appearance in the mirror.

Eventually, his sensitivity to criticism and rejection by others led to near functional and psychological collapse. Colin was referred to a child psychiatrist and prescribed an antidepressant medication. Colin's depressive episodes and obsessive behaviors served as a defense against his body dysphoria and misgendered experiences. It is noteworthy that his first treating psychiatrist diagnosed him with bipolar disorder, yet he does not have a family history of this, nor had he demonstrated manic, impulsive, or grandiose symptoms. Unfortunately, that psychiatrist did not follow up to collaborate with Colin's treating therapist of 2 years. In working with complex cases with coexisting psychological issues, collaborative teamwork is essential. Since Colin has started taking medication, his severe anxiety and depressive symptoms have improved significantly, leading to increased ability to develop and utilize coping skills that lead to greater self-reliance and esteem. It is clear that the misattunement between Colin's interpersonal interactions and his internal sense of his gender self-exacerbated his gender dysphoria, which also led to the development of more significant symptomatology, such as obsessive–compulsive behaviors and moderate to severe depression and anxiety symptoms.

Conclusion

TGE children may present with mental health conditions secondary to, as well as those unrelated to, the experience of gender dysphoria. These conditions, at times, are related to internal turmoil, stemming from perhaps both biological and adverse social influences. When this is the case, symptoms may be intensified or convoluted by moderate to severe experiences of gender dysphoria. The success of any treatment with these vibrant children depends on gender informed and affirming assessments, as well as thoughtfulness around intervention to safeguard their resilience and alleviate their suffering. Often their treatment requires a team approach. No gender identity or expression is in and of it itself pathological, yet an unsupportive environment, whether at home or school, can have adverse effects and be detrimental. It is imperative that TGE children are diagnosed from a culturally informed and gender affirmative position, while considering the possibility of co-occurring psychological issues that may run alongside, be an aftermath, or in rare occasions be the primary issue causing the child's presented gender stress. In all cases, providing pathways that support gender identity and expression will likely alleviate many symptoms, even though many other symptoms may be present.

References

Abelson, A. G. (1981). The development of gender identity in the autistic child. *Child: Care, Health and Development, 7,* 347–356. http://dx.doi.org/10.1111/j.1365-2214.1981.tb00851.x

American Psychiatric Association. (2013). *Diagnostic and statistical manual of mental disorders* (5th ed.). Washington, DC: Author.

Baird, G., Simonoff, E., Pickles, A., Chandler, S., Loucas, T., Meldrum, D., & Charman, T. (2006). Prevalence of disorders of the autism spectrum in a population cohort of children in South Thames: The Special Needs and Autism Project (SNAP). *The Lancet, 368,* 210–215. http://dx.doi.org/10.1016/S0140-6736(06)69041-7

Buck, J. N. (1948). The House–Tree–Person technique: A qualitative and quantitative scoring manual. *Journal of Clinical Psychology, 4,* 317–396. http://dx.doi.org/10.1002/1097-4679(194810)4:4<317::AID-JCLP2270040402>3.0.CO;2-6

Coates, S. (1990). Ontogenesis of boyhood gender identity disorder. *The Journal of the American Academy of Psychoanalysis, 18,* 414–438. http://dx.doi.org/10.1521/jaap.1.1990.18.3.414

Coates, S., Friedman, R. C., & Wolfe, S. (1991). The etiology of boyhood gender identity disorder: A model for integrating temperament, development, and psychodynamics. *Psychoanalytic Dialogues, 1,* 481–523. http://dx.doi.org/10.1080/10481889109538916

Cook, A., Spinazzola, J., Ford, J., Lanktree, C., Blaustein, M., Cloitre, M., . . . van der Kolk, B. (2005). Complex trauma in children and adolescents. *Psychiatric Annals, 35,* 390–398. http://dx.doi.org/10.3928/00485713-20050501-05

de Vries, A. L. C., Doreleijers, T. A. H., Steensma, T. D., & Cohen-Kettenis, P. T. (2011). Psychiatric comorbidity in gender dysphoric adolescents. *Journal of Child Psychology and Psychiatry, 52,* 1195–1202. http://dx.doi.org/10.1111/j.1469-7610.2011.02426.x

de Vries, A. L. C., Noens, I. L., Cohen-Kettenis, P. T., van Berckelaer-Onnes, I. A., & Doreleijers, T. A. (2010). Autism spectrum disorders in gender dysphoric children and adolescents. *Journal of Autism and Developmental Disorders, 40,* 930–936. http://dx.doi.org/10.1007/s10803-010-0935-9

Donnelly-Boylen, K. (2016). Gender dysphoria, serious mental illness, and genital self-mutilation: A case report. *Journal of Gay & Lesbian Mental Health, 20,* 376–381. http://dx.doi.org/10.1080/19359705.2016.1209395

Ehrensaft, D. (2016). *The gender creative child.* New York, NY: The Experiment.

Erickson-Schroth, L. (Ed.). (2014). *Trans bodies, trans selves: A resource for the transgender community.* New York, NY: Oxford University Press.

Grossman, A. H., & D'Augelli, A. R. (2007). Transgender youth and life-threatening behaviors. *Suicide and Life-Threatening Behavior, 37,* 527–537.

Hendricks, M. L., & Testa, R. J. (2012). A conceptual framework for clinical work with transgender and gender nonconforming clients: An adaptation of the minority stress model. *Professional Psychology: Research and Practice, 43,* 460–467. http://dx.doi.org/10.1037/a0029597

Herman, J. L., Haas, A. P., & Rodgers, P. L. (2014). *Suicide attempts among transgender and gender nonconforming adults.* Los Angeles, CA: The Williams Institute, UCLA School of Law. Retrieved from https://williamsinstitute.law.ucla.edu/wp-content/uploads/AFSP-Williams-Suicide-Report-Final.pdf

Hill, D. B., Rozanski, C., Carfagnini, J., & Willoughby, B. (2007). Gender identity disorders in childhood and adolescence: A critical inquiry. *International Journal of Sexual Health, 19,* 57–75.

Jacobs, L. A., Rachlin, K., Erickson-Schroth, L., & Janssen, A. (2014). Gender dysphoria and co-occurring autism spectrum disorders: Review, case examples, and treatment considerations. *LGBT Health, 1,* 277–282. http://dx.doi.org/10.1089/lgbt.2013.0045

Lewis, R. J., Derlega, V. J., Griffin, J. L., & Krowinski, A. C. (2003). Stressors for gay men and lesbians: Life stress, gay-related stress, stigma consciousness, and depressive symptoms. *Journal of Social and Clinical Psychology, 22,* 716–729. https://doi.org/10.1521/jscp.22.6.716.22932

Meyer, I. H. (1995). Minority stress and mental health in gay men. *Journal of Health and Social Behavior, 36,* 38–56.

Mukaddes, N. M. (2002). Gender identity problems in autistic children. *Child: Care, Health and Development, 28,* 529–532. http://dx.doi.org/10.1046/j.1365-2214.2002.00301.x

Olson, K. R., Durwood, L., DeMeules, M., & McLaughlin, K. A. (2016). Mental health of transgender children who are supported in their identities. *Pediatrics, 137,* 277–282. http://dx.doi.org/10.1542/peds.2015-3223

Reisner, S. L., Vetters, R., Leclerc, M., Zaslow, S., Wolfrum, S., Shumer, D., & Mimiaga, M. J. (2015). Mental health of transgender youth in care at an adolescent urban community health center: A matched retrospective cohort study. *Journal of Adolescent Health, 56,* 274–279. http://dx.doi.org/10.1016/j.jadohealth.2014.10.264

Roberts, A. L., Rosario, M., Corliss, H. L., Koenen, K. C., & Austin, S. B. (2012). Childhood gender nonconformity: A risk indicator for childhood abuse and posttraumatic stress in youth. *Pediatrics, 129,* 410–417. http://dx.doi.org/10.1542/peds.2011-1804

Ryan, C., Huebner, D., Diaz, R. M., & Sanchez, J. (2009). Family rejection as a predictor of negative health outcomes in white and Latino lesbian, gay, and bisexual young adults. *Pediatrics, 123,* 346–352. http://dx.doi.org/10.1542/peds.2007-3524

Spack, N. P., Edwards-Leeper, L., Feldman, H. A., Leibowitz, S., Mandel, F., Diamond, D. A., & Vance, S. R. (2012). Children and adolescents with gender identity disorder referred to a pediatric medical center. *Pediatrics, 129,* 418–425. http://dx.doi.org/10.1542/peds.2011-0907

Strang, J. F., Meagher, H., Kenworthy, L., de Vries, A. L. C., Menvielle, E., Leibowitz, S., . . . Anthony, L. G. (2018). Initial clinical guidelines for co-occurring autism spectrum disorder and Gender Dysphoria or incongruence in adolescents. *Journal of Clinical Child and Adolescent Psychology, 47,* 105–115. http://dx.doi.org/10.1080/15374416.2016.1228462

Toomey, R. B., Ryan, C., Diaz, R. M., Card, N. A., & Russell, S. T. (2010). Gender-nonconforming lesbian, gay, bisexual, and transgender youth: School victimization and young adult psychosocial adjustment. *Developmental Psychology, 46,* 1580–1589. http://dx.doi.org/10.1037/a0020705

Wallien, M. S. C., Swaab, H., & Cohen-Kettenis, P. (2007). Psychiatric comorbidity among children with gender identity disorder. *Journal of the American Academy of Child & Adolescent Psychiatry, 46,* 1307–1314. http://dx.doi.org/10.1097/chi.0b013e3181373848

Williamson, I. R. (2000). Internalized homophobia and health issues affecting lesbians and gay men. *Health Education Research, 15,* 97–107. http://dx.doi.org/10.1093/her/15.1.97

Zucker, K. J., & Cohen-Kettenis, P. T. (2008). Gender identity disorder in children and adolescents. In D. L. Rowland & L. Incrocci (Eds.), *Handbook of sexual and gender identity disorders* (pp. 376–422). Hoboken, NJ: Wiley. http://dx.doi.org/10.1002/9781118269978.ch13

Zucker, K. J., Wood, H., Singh, D., & Bradley, S. J. (2012). A developmental, biopsychosocial model for the treatment of children with gender identity disorder. *Journal of Homosexuality, 59,* 369–397. http://dx.doi.org/10.1080/00918369.2012.653309

Amy Tishelman and AndreAs Neumann-Mascis

Gender-Related Trauma

6

Alex is 22 years old, White, and identifies as genderqueer, using *he/him/his* pronouns. Alex described having been gender expansive from a very early age. Alex also described memories that begin in kindergarten and continue to the present of being verbally abused and bullied, physically threatened and assaulted, rejected by family and isolated from peer companionship, only finding a supportive community when he was old enough to move away from home. Two things are striking about his trauma experience. First, the traumas that Alex describes come from peers and adults, and occurred across contexts and developmental phases. These traumas are filled with passive observers who did nothing to stop the aggressions, and are nearly universally justified by identifying the problem as Alex's general gender nonconforming presentation. Second, when, in the intake materials he is asked if there had ever been abuse, Alex said no. When asked about this later, Alex said simply, "So that was just because of how I look, how I am," absorbing and accepting the transphobic trope that "he asked for it."

Alice is a 35-year-old African American transgender woman coming into therapy to deal with symptoms of anxiety and depression that emerged after she lost her job as a programmer. Some facts indicated that the layoff was discriminatory. Alice had received positive performance reviews while presenting as male. After transition, she received feedback that she was "unprofessional."

http://dx.doi.org/10.1037/0000095-006
The Gender Affirmative Model: An Interdisciplinary Approach to Supporting Transgender and Gender Expansive Children, C. Keo-Meier and D. Ehrensaft (Editors)
Copyright © 2018 by the American Psychological Association. All rights reserved.

Eventually, she also acknowledged experiencing transphobic sexual harassment at work, but she minimized both the impact on her and the culpability of her colleagues. In the course of treatment, Alice also described having been beaten regularly by one or both parents. This history emerged only after she made a joke about a wooden spoon having been broken on her back as an adolescent. When asked about the abuse she shrugged and said, "They just really, really did not want a faggot."

Peggy is a 46-year-old White transgender woman who reported that she did not particularly want psychotherapy but did want access to hormones. In the course of the intake interview, she described engaging in contact sports growing up, going into construction work, and working on a lobster boat as an adult. She related that both her mother and father made critical and at times demeaning remarks, threatened her, and engaged in physical abuse. She admitted that the reasons for abuse were hard to understand, but ultimately she realized that they were focused on her failure to perform masculinity and that how she walked or carried herself, her tone of voice, and her expression of emotion could all elicit aggressive or abusive responses.

Perspectives on Child and Adolescent Trauma

Although all of the people in these cases are adults, their childhood histories illustrate the complex, often chronic, singularly profound adversities experienced by many transgender youth. Transgender and gender expansive (TGE) youth are often raised in a milieu of rejection, psychological abuse, and isolation, all because of an aspect of self that is immutable—gender identity. Research, self-report, years of developmental psychopathology investigation, and common sense contribute to the conclusion that transgender youth may experience chronically traumatizing conditions, with a high risk of trauma being underrecognized and untreated. Studies indicate that transgender youth experience high rates of depression, anxiety, self-harm, and suicide attempts but that these psychiatric issues are rarely interpreted through a trauma lens (e.g., Reisner, Vetters, et al., 2015; Reisner et al., 2016). Thus far, research directly examining adverse childhood experiences in TGE youth consistently indicates a high risk of significant adversities. Not only do youth struggle with isolation and passive indifference, but they also often experience deliberately inflicted interpersonal violence and trauma. For instance, Roberts, Rosario, Corliss, Koenen, and Austin (2012) examined youth who were gender nonconforming before age 11 and concluded that gender nonconformity poses significant risks for sexual, physical, and psychological abuse, and for lifetime probable posttraumatic stress disorder (PTSD). Reisner et al. (2016) examined 412 transgender adults, who reported both everyday discrimination experiences and PTSD symptoms. The most frequently reported reason for discrimination was gender identity and/or expression, with higher everyday discrimination and a higher rate of attributed reasons for discrimination, independently associated with symptoms of PTSD. Others have found similar results, sadly, suggesting that adversities encountered by TGE children, starting in early childhood, are often multiple and significant (e.g., Reisner, Greytak, Parsons, & Ybarra, 2015).

Potentially traumatizing experiences for TGE youth of every age are pervasive and informed by institutionalized, interpersonal, and internalized transphobia. Traumatic adversity in childhood is often chronic, occurs across important settings (e.g., home, school, community), risks impacting all essential areas of function for youth, and yet can be misidentified as a host of other conditions, including attentional disorders, oppositional/disruptive disorders, learning disabilities, and an array of other syndromes and diagnoses.

At this juncture, a critical accumulation of developmental literature strongly indicates the extreme costs of certain forms of stress on children's development and adaptation. Shonkoff et al. (2012) discussed the relevance to development of data from a myriad of disciplines, including "neuroscience, molecular biology, genomics, developmental psychology, epidemiology, sociology, and economics" (p. e232). Their biodevelopmental framework illustrates the profound effects that early trauma can have on a child's development, at times shattering a youth's well-being and creating a circumstance of continuing stress, associated with many later life morbidities and sometimes early mortality. This framework highlights the potentially long-lasting and toxic influence of early adversity, noting that many "adult diseases should be viewed as developmental disorders that begin early in life and that persistent health disparities associated with poverty, discrimination, or maltreatment could be reduced by the alleviation of toxic stress in childhood" (Shonkoff et al., 2012, p. e232). Similarly, a series of influential studies illuminates the profound long-term risks associated with significant trauma and stress during critical periods of early development (e.g., Centers for Disease Control and Prevention, n.d.; Felitti et al., 1998), concluding that as childhood adversities increase, risks for endangering behaviors, medical disease, and mental health challenges become significantly greater. In other words, not only is the immediate quality of life diminished for gender diverse youth, but their childhood suffering is associated with risks of stress and challenges in numerous areas across the lifespan, with a higher possibility of earlier mortality than same-age peers.

Trauma emanating in childhood differs from traumatic experiences first encountered as an adult. Potential pervasive effects of trauma on children affect many domains of important functioning (Cook et al., 2005; Tishelman, Haney, Greenwald O'Brien, & Blaustein, 2010). Any trauma is unfortunate and holds extreme risks. However, individuals who first experience trauma as adults often have had the opportunity to develop secure relationships, positive self-esteem, academic and professional skills, and trust, and perhaps most important, they may have a vision of what life can be like in the absence of trauma, as well as having the cognitive capacities and confidence often associated with effective coping and resilience. Trauma in childhood, on the other hand, often starts in the family, violating a basic sense of trust, and can go on to be pervasive and chronic. As a result, the world is never experienced from the vantage point of safety, gratification, self-value, hope, and love, with the opportunity for sensitive adult guidance. Cook et al. (2005) identified seven areas of risk for children who experience complex trauma impairments in attachment, physiology (e.g., neurobiological impacts hindering emotion regulation in response to stress), affect regulation, dissociation, behavioral regulation, cognition, and self-concept. Cook et al. described the dual nature of these problems, which include "children's exposure to multiple traumatic events and the impact of this exposure on immediate and long-term outcomes" (p. 4). Four interacting and overlapping domains of functioning often impacted by trauma in a school setting include self-regulation, physical function, relationships, and academics (Tishelman et al., 2010). These domains can be extrapolated to all settings in a child's life.

Notably, in childhood many of the manifestations of trauma can be misconstrued as falling under the domain of another *Diagnostic and Statistical Manual of Mental Disorders* diagnosis. As an example, a dissociating child may be perceived as inattentive, and be evaluated for attention-deficit/hyperactivity disorder (ADHD), without sensitivity to the underlying distress that child may be enduring. This can potentially lead to mismanagement and even improper administration of medication for ADHD, while the trauma is left unidentified, profound, and untreated. As another example, to avoid an untenable and inhospitable environment, a child may act out in school to be placed outside of the classroom, be put in detention, or be suspended or expelled, thereby being labeled with oppositional defiant disorder (ODD) or conduct disorder, without a closer understanding of the child's deep unhappiness and loneliness and their associated causes emanating from a singular or chronic trauma. TGE children are strong candidates for falling into this category of overlooked trauma and subsequent misdiagnoses and management.

Consider the case of Leslie, assigned male at birth, and currently a 12-year-old child identifying as both male and female, using *they/them/their* pronouns. Leslie has flowing long blond hair and is consistently teased at school, called in a taunting way a "he/she" and pushed and shoved while teachers are not looking. Leslie had no history of aggression in school before this year but recently threw all the papers and other materials off the desk of several classmates, an act that seemed unprovoked to Leslie's teacher. In addition, Leslie recently started to forcefully resist going to gym class, arguing with teachers, sitting on the floor, and refusing to move. Although a strong student intellectually, Leslie has been falling behind classmates academically, with frequent absences. The teacher reports that Leslie seems to have attention issues, completing work sheets only partially, and spending much of class staring out of the window. The teacher reported to Leslie's parents at a recent conference that Leslie needs an evaluation for ADHD, and possible co-occurring ODD.

If a school-based evaluation focuses primarily on Leslie's school behaviors, in the absence of the context of Leslie's victimization related to their gender, it is very possible that interventions will be inadequate and even inappropriate, such as using behavior management reward techniques for attending to class work and compliance, paired with medication for ADHD. Instead, a trauma-informed focus would understand Leslie's behavioral and emotional responses as reactions to the toxic stress of bullying and rejection, and would provide a very different treatment plan. This treatment would first have to differ conceptually from one that assumes that mental illness (e.g., ADHD, ODD) stemming from within Leslie is creating havoc at school and detrimentally impacting classmates and adults. Instead, an initial reframing from a trauma perspective would recognize the direction of the problem, originating in a destructive environment impinging upon Leslie's well-being and creating an expectable distress reaction, given the circumstances of threat to their welfare. Any treatment would need to start with creating safety across environments. This would entail developing a trauma and gender sensitive milieu at Leslie's school, with zero tolerance for bullying of any kind. If that is not possible, alternatives would need to be explored, including changing schools or, in the unfortunate circumstance of no other options, home-schooling Leslie. Fortunately, school-related experiences like Leslie's have not gone unnoticed by gender affirmative practitioners. Groups have been working with schools to reduce or eliminate trauma and strengthen supportive environments for TGE youth. For example, the organization Gender Spectrum has developed a website with a wealth of information relevant to reducing trauma in school settings (https://www.genderspectrum.org/).

The ultimate implication of a developmental model of trauma is that transgender youth, who are likely targets of abusive behaviors, are at risk for long-term mental health and physical health struggles enduring through adulthood (Reisner et al., 2016). These challenges are not due to gender identity per se but to the extreme stress youth endure because of attachment disruptions, isolation, and persecution within a transphobic cultural context. Masten and Cicchetti (2010) invoked the term *developmental cascades* to refer to the cumulative effects of developmental experiences on a child's life. We have often witnessed such a negatively valanced cascade in the trauma histories of TGE people. The situations of Leslie, Alex, Alice, and Peggy illuminate the all-too-common victimization experiences of these individuals. Transgender youth journey through a self and gender exploration that can be powerful and confusing, often while simultaneously responding to relationship disruption and rejection, accompanied by lack of safety, loneliness, and isolation.

In short, trauma research and the accompanying developmental framework suggest that therapeutic intervention can ameliorate the effects of prior adverse experiences. In such a framework, development is shaped and sometimes constrained by prior experience. In addition, and unfortunately, adversity often begets adversity. As an example, child maltreatment is associated with significantly aberrant parent–child attachment, or disorganized attachment, which then predicts a host of other childhood vulnerabilities, including peer relationship disruption and poor social skills. For a child already at risk for social ostracism because of gender differences, the lack of opportunity to develop adequate social skills can only exponentially increase risks. Poor peer relationships, in turn, predict school absence and school dropout, regardless of cognitive ability.

But negative mental health outcomes for transgender youth are far from inevitable. In a positive environmental context, TGE youth have the potential to be resilient, comfortable with themselves, and enjoy healthy relationships. Research indicates that both family and peer acceptance are critical factors related to resilience in transgender youth, facilitating positive mental health (e.g., de Vries, Steensma, Cohen-Kettenis, VanderLaan, & Zucker 2015). Olson, Durwood, DeMeules, and McLaughlin (2016) demonstrated that transgender youth who have socially transitioned to living as their affirmed gender, with family support, are often perceived by their parents as well-adjusted and without the mental health struggles that have been demonstrated in many transgender youth in the past. Recent research also reflects the concept that "outness," or living in the world as one's asserted identity, can mitigate the negative effects of a minority identity for lesbian, gay, bisexual, and transgender (LGBT) youth and foster resilience, although substituting disclosure for secrecy also precipitates an increased risk for victimization (e.g., Kosciw, Palmer, & Kull, 2015).

Historical Perspective

The legacy of institutionalized ambivalence toward and abuse of TGE people is profound. It has resulted in a population that has been raised with both internalized and normalized experiences of chronic abuse. Not only has this population lost access to informed trauma care, but clinical knowledge regarding TGE-informed trauma treatment, as well as gender affirmative treatment, is only now emerging.

Although we have entered a time of greater awareness and some increased acceptance of transgender people (Case & Meier, 2014; Glicksman, 2013), it is also true that on an institutionalized, community, social, and interpersonal level, gender nonconformity has historically been met with what is too often a form of sanctioned "correction" (Toomey, Card, & Casper, 2014). This has, for TGE people, been vividly true within the medical and mental health communities (Grant et al., 2011). The evolution in mental health from an understanding of gender diversity as a psychological limitation at best and psychosis at worst, to a current paradigm (in some places) of a valid and meaningful identity, does not reflect a change in known etiology or even a significant change in psychiatric knowledge but instead reflects a change in social understandings away from bias and toward acceptance (Glicksman, 2013). Newer research, as noted above, and clinical experience would suggest that as bias diminishes and gender diversity is viewed through a lens of expected human variance, traumatic responses will lessen.

The beginning of that change within mental health can be credited in no small part to Benjamin (1969), a German physician and sexologist. As early as the 1950s, he began to revolutionize the field by positing that care for transgender people was available if mental health professionals validated and responded to the needs of the felt sense of self. Benjamin believed that the etiology of gender variance was physiological and not psychological in nature and was therefore not impacted by a psychiatric intervention. At the same time, Benjamin both acknowledged and expressed some of the moralistic attitudes toward transgender people that determined their access to care and relief.

For some TGE youth, mental health symptoms arise not only because of victimization from others, which can include the negative attitudes of providers as well as result from the anxiety and sometimes trauma of being perceived in the world as a gender other than one's felt gender. In this case, treating mental health symptoms may be futile if that youth's transgender status is not recognized. The acknowledgment of being transgender as a valid identity has, only in recent years, facilitated access to the framework of trauma through which transgender individuals can understand and name experiences. The ability to name an experience as traumatic and not poor behavior or a failure of character is one important aspect of healing. It properly externalizes the roots of the child's negative experiences while providing a protective barrier against internalizing behaviors, which include a sense of oneself as bad or deficient. With TGE youth, it is imperative for adults across settings to recognize and be sensitive to the trauma of their children, students, or patients, and thus be able to interpret a child's behavior through a "trauma lens" and with empathy rather than dismissal (Tishelman et al., 2010), as noted in the example of Leslie.

Ecological Factors

Kaufman and Tishelman (see Chapter 11, this volume) discuss an ecological perspective as it impacts a child's life. According to this framework, children are influenced by biological and autobiographical/historical factors, as well as family, school, culture, and community spheres that touch their lives. Youth who start off life in an insensitive or rejecting family are more likely to emerge into the larger world of school and community with atypical and sometimes disturbing ways of perceiving and behaving, which causes risk to snowball, as suggested by the above discussion. Environments can vary regarding risk, with some experiences replicating and/or amplifying traumatizing circumstances and other factors buffering children from harm. It is important to note that not only is a developmental perspective critical for understanding the experiences of lesbian, gay, bisexual, transgender, queer or questioning, and intersex (LGBTQI) populations, but a multidimensional and multigenerational perspective is also warranted (D'Augelli, 2012). The hope is that, as with LGBTQI adults, the trajectory of social and cultural change regarding transgender youth will be toward acceptance and normalization, leading to better outcomes and lower levels of trauma risk.

Gender Minority Stress Model

The trauma endured by TGE youth is among the most compelling illustrations of the ways in which conceptions of illness and health are tied to sociocultural context. This context was articulated by Hendricks and Testa's (2012) adaptation of the minority stress model to TGE youth. They pointed to the chronic stress of navigating a transphobic, cisnormative environment, including (a) anticipating a transphobic response, (b) experiencing a traumatic event, (c) confronting barriers to resources, and (d) internalizing transphobia into a negative self-assessment. The researchers pointed out that the last of these, a negative self-assessment, can have a devastating impact on one's life. Having internalized a phobic response to one's own self has a significant effect on the psychological resources available to mitigate the impact of external stressors.

Microaggressions

The term *microaggression* refers to the ways in which institutionalized, systemic oppression, expressed through daily interpersonal interactions, creates the psychological context of chronic traumatization (Hill, Lau, & Sue, 2010; Sue, 2010). This work has meaningful implications for the growing understanding of the impact of transphobia on children and youth who are gender diverse. Chang and Chung (2015) identified a number of themes of microaggressions toward TGE individuals, including misuse of identity language; exoticization; denial of identity or experience; endorsement of gender normative, binary roles or behaviors; physical threat or harassment; being antagonized or rejected by family members. These microaggressions occur across institutions and settings, including restrooms, health care, the workplace, and the legal system. Although Chang and Chung focused on the experiences of adults, it is not difficult to extrapolate these themes to TGE children and youth. The general expectation and reinforcement of gender normative behaviors and interests is present for children and most frequently actively enforced by adults and peers alike.

Trauma Treatment

Researchers now understand that gender diverse youth and adults experience trauma profoundly and disproportionately (Reisner et al., 2016). The field is only beginning to understand the needs and challenges of treatment that is knowledgeable about both gender and trauma, as well as developmentally sensitive. It is evident that institutionalized and interpersonal transphobia can create and extenuate trauma for transgender youth. Overcoming barriers to informed and safe care is only the beginning. Transgender youth and families often live in fear of the institutions that define their psychosocial environment (see Chapter 10, this volume). As illustrated in the case examples, being raised in a rejecting environment, absent ordinary protections, creates profound psychosocial vulnerability. This kind of chronic stress has a substantial impact on trauma recovery.

Stigma can lead to a state of chronic stress that can increase vulnerability to trauma, but enhanced social support can compensate for this (Budge, Katz-Wise, Tebbe, Howard, Schneider, & Rodriguez, 2013). A meaningful response to trauma for TGE youth must first recognize the possibility that a child may be traumatized simply by virtue of being in the world as a transgender youth, but it must also assess the secondary traumatic experiences that often can co-occur, including significant abuse and everyday microaggressions. Several sensitive and moving case studies of psychotherapeutic treatment approaches with transgender youth have been published. For instance, Ehrensaft (2010) published the account of her developmental approach to treatment of a TGE child of mixed heritage (Mexican/American). A gender affirmative model of treatment for preadolescent youth has also been proposed through a gender affirmative framework (Ehrensaft, 2014; Hidalgo et al., 2013). Malpas (2011) illustrated a family approach to working with TGE youth. Nevertheless, few publications have highlighted treatment of TGE youth using a trauma treatment model or integrating a trauma perspective into the complexities of mental health care. Minshew (2015) presented a case study of a transgender adolescent treated from a trauma perspective, with sensitivity to this youth's gender status and associated stressors. However, trauma treatment models for younger children often diverge in significant ways from treatments of older adolescents and adults. Young children reside within ecological contexts and often have little control or choice regarding fundamental aspects of their world, such as culture, community, and school. In addition, gender diversity may be a novel concept for their parents and others close to them, elevating the risk of disbelief, denial, and/or rejection. A unique experience of TGE children of color—who are both racial and gender minorities—is that although they typically share their racial minority status with their parents, they generally do not also have gender minority status in common with them. The TGE children of color who experience rejection from their own parents face a unique form of trauma. Joanna Fields, a Black transgender woman who has since passed away, shared memories of her childhood on the playground at school during her keynote presentation at a Transgender Day of Remembrance gathering in Texas. She said that if any of the kids called her a racial slur, she knew she could tell her parents and receive understanding, support, encouragement, and racial empowerment: "They told me that they had been called that same thing before, told me it wasn't my fault, and that my Blackness is beautiful. They offered to come talk to the teacher." However, she stated that if those same kids called her name for being perceived to be "too effeminate," their response would not be the same: "They told me that maybe I should not act that way anymore and the kids would stop calling me that," effectively blaming her for the other children's cruelty. Effective models of care for traumatized youth may need to integrate these contexts into treatment. Creating safety across environments is a critical step for any effective approach to treating traumatized youth, which may involve advocacy with schools.

The National Child Traumatic Stress Network (n.d.) published a list of empirically supported treatments and promising approaches to treating trauma in youth, reflecting a consistent model of integrating families and other social systems surrounding the child into treatment. In addition, psychodynamic approaches have also been developed to treat chronic and complex trauma in children (Heineman, 1998). Perhaps the approach to trauma treatment for children most often cited involves trauma-focused cognitive behavior therapy (TF-CBT; see http://tfcbt.musc.edu). This short-term approach employs skills training, psychoeducation, and a trauma narrative. Other approaches, such as the attachment, self-regulation, and competency (ARC) model (Blaustein & Kinniburgh, 2010) and the trauma systems therapy approach (Saxe, Ellis, & Kaplow, 2006) integrate an ecological systems framework and a flexible approach, which may be helpful for transgender youth struggling to manage in difficult or even hostile school and community settings. Trauma systems therapy was specifically designed to address social and environmental factors impacting children ages 6 to 19. For younger children, Parent–Child Interaction Therapy emphasizes improving the quality of the parent–child relationship. None of these interventions has been adapted specifically to meet the needs of traumatized transgender youth. Austin and Craig (2015) published an adaptation of cognitive behavioral therapy for adults, called transgender affirmative cognitive–behavior therapy (TA-CBT), providing a useful model of how CBT might be modified to specifically meet the needs of TGE youth who have experienced trauma. They focus on components of CBT, such as psychoeducation, problematic thinking styles, social support, and preventing suicidality, with specific examples of applications for transgender adults. With regard to TGE youth, novel approaches could similarly apply adaptations of known approaches to integrate trauma assessment and treatment approaches informed by a deep knowledge of developmental issues associated with growing up as a TGE youth. As just one example, imagine if Leslie and their family became involved in TF-CBT. Such an intervention could involve psychoeducation and normalization regarding gender diversity, for both Leslie and Leslie's family, help Leslie identify emotional reactions and feelings when exposed to overt and more covert macro- and microaggressions, assist Leslie in examining their own thoughts about gender as well as possible internalization of negative beliefs about their own gender diversity inculcated by others, and facilitate Leslie's developing and processing a trauma narrative related to their traumatic victimization.

Importantly, no mental health treatment should assume trauma in TGE youth, but at the same time treatment should take into account the possibility that it is there. Approaches to care should address the specific needs of the youth and family requesting intervention, and should therefore include a careful assessment including a screening for trauma. As with any youth, care should be taken to ensure safety across settings and to advocate and advise as appropriate to create safety. In the most unfortunate situations, child protection agencies may need to be contacted when maltreatment is occurring, with the caveat that filing a mandated report of abuse suspicion does not always immediately create safety for a child and may engender another set of stressors. In fact, placement in an unsupportive (i.e., nonaffirmative) foster home, which sometimes follows a report to a child protection agency, can compound trauma, rather than be ameliorative.

Case Study

BACKGROUND

Chris is an 11-year-old Hispanic transgender girl who was recently removed from public school in the inner city following chronic taunting and physical aggression, and placed in a therapeutic day school environment for LGBTQI youth. Chris is currently residing in a therapeutic foster care situation, after running away from home a year ago in response to physical and verbal abuse from her biological parents. Chris was raised as a boy, but for many years asserted a female identity, to the dismay of her parents and extended family, for whom it was profoundly important to have a son and inconceivable that their child could be transgender and repudiate their maleness.

Starting at a young age, Chris gravitated toward "girlie" types of toys, such as Barbie dolls and dress-up in princess clothes, often arguing with her sister, 2 years older, because she preferred her sister's toys and clothes, even after redirection and punishment from her parents. Chris presented as a boy when she first started kindergarten, where she excelled academically and displayed an outgoing and fun-loving personality. However, Chris soon started to be perceived as "different" by classmates, as she preferred to play with girls and displayed other very "female" choices. For instance, when asked to bring favorite toys to school, Chris brought her sister's portable pink princess house with dolls and was widely ridiculed. By the end of first grade, Chris's initially upbeat and optimistic style had been replaced by a more withdrawn and somber demeanor. Notably, although not all classmates and teachers were overtly hostile, almost all were confused by Chris, and peers often asked her whether she was a boy or a girl, whereas teachers would seem perplexed and make statements such as, "Why are you reading that book? That's a *girl's* book!" Chris was relentlessly ridiculed by her father at home for being a "sissy"—soon the ridicule escalated to beatings for wearing items such as her sister's underwear. Although not physically abusive, Chris's mother regularly admonished Chris and forbade her to "act like a girl." By third grade, Chris stopped completing homework, and often stared listlessly into space when she was asked to engage in academic work at school. On a number of occasions, Chris lashed out at classmates and had crying meltdowns at school, from her teachers' perspective seemingly without provocation. Often Chris would ask to go to the nurse's office, complaining of headaches or stomachaches. Doctor visits suggested no biological cause for these symptoms, and Chris was considered to be feigning illness to get out of class. Her teachers called her parents several times suggesting that mental health treatment might be helpful for Chris, without response. At school, Chris attended a social skills group and visited with the school social worker once a week, where she was typically subdued and guarded. By the time Chris ran away from home at age 10, she was considered a disturbed and difficult child, in need of academic remediation despite considerable intellectual potential.

MENTAL HEALTH

Chris was placed with foster parents who had their own biological transgender son and were supportive of Chris. Residing with an accepting family and attending school in a community of acceptance for TGE youth was the first exposure that Chris had to enduring safety. It was a thankful novelty for Chris to have contact with people who embraced her gender presentation as part of a welcome diversity, as opposed to a "sickness" that should be thwarted or punished, or at its least be perceived as a stigmatized oddity. Following placement, Chris showed positive changes almost immediately: Her aggression diminished, and she demonstrated interest in attending school without her long-standing dread of recess, gym, and lunch. However, weekly visits with her parents in a supervised setting triggered reminders of her complex and chronic traumatic experiences under their care, paired with a sense of loss and attachment disruption. These visits often concluded with Chris becoming more withdrawn and refusing to eat. She also experienced frequent vivid nightmares, yelling out and crying in her sleep; she avoided going to sleep for this reason and was frequently fatigued. In addition, Chris continued to balk at using school bathrooms, as she associated bathrooms with extreme forms of bullying, and would sometimes become physically sick if she needed to use the bathroom at school, even within her current context of safety. The teacher would notice Chris staring into space often, as if she were not even in the room; it was very difficult to get her to refocus her attention during these episodes. These represented periods of dissociation, common in traumatized children. Chris often refused to go on school trips and avoided unfamiliar settings, people, and contexts, exhibiting extreme emotional dysregulation if teachers or peers tried to persuade her to participate. She was slow to trust others, and upon initially meeting new people would often look down and refuse eye contact. At times, new acquaintances presumed that Chris was a high-functioning autistic child, although this was untrue.

As described, Chris's symptoms appeared to be consistent with a traumatic reaction to a life of chronic adversity, relationship disruption, and gender confusion as her self-identity was repeatedly negated by others. Although in a safe network at present, Chris had experienced the world as dismissive and dangerous up until that point. From a trauma lens, she was exhibiting symptoms of fear and avoidance, reexperiencing (nightmares), and mood extremes from which she had difficulty emerging. Her lapses at school were related to episodes of dissociation, when either her own cognitions or environmental traumatic reminders became overwhelming. She also had a long history of experiencing people and contexts as unsafe and had never experienced a secure attachment or sensitive and loving caregiving before moving to her current therapeutic foster care situation. She continued to have extreme anxiety when exposed to new people or novel and untested situations. Before she first ran away, she would frequently make statements such as, "I hate myself," or other statements suggesting self-loathing. Such overt verbalizations diminished after she was placed in a supportive care environment, although upon questioning Chris would admit she did not like herself and felt unlovable.

A trauma-informed approach to mental health treatment should help Chris understand her reactions in light of her life history, develop positive coping skills, and engage in a process of self-acceptance. Without the newly created network of school and home safety, a trauma-sensitive approach to care would be unlikely to succeed. However, in the context of support, and most likely through a gradual process, Chris should be able to develop a relationship of trust with a therapist, and eventually with peers and her foster family. She will need an intervention that acknowledges and helps her explore issues of gender with acceptance and without judgmental persecution, including her desire for possible gender affirming medical intervention (e.g., puberty blockers) as she approaches puberty. She can be helped to develop a perspective on the unwarranted physical and emotional victimization and the microaggressions she endured in her daily life, as well as her emotional, behavioral, and cognitive responses to these experiences, including self-defeating negative self-beliefs. Therapy should help her develop positive stress management and coping skills that will engender confidence in her ability to navigate future challenges as well as help her learn to challenge herself to face feared situations (e.g., school bathrooms). Her foster family can participate in some of these interventions, acquiring a perspective that promotes an understanding of Chris through a lens of empathy. If possible, Chris's biological parents can work toward an empathetic understanding of their daughter as well, and toward building a positive alliance, involving a recognition of their detrimental contribution to Chris's unhappiness and current mental health struggles. The history suggests that relationship repair may be fraught and difficult. Chris's therapist, optimally, would be able to use a developmental understanding aligned with a gender- and trauma-informed approach to care, while ensuring that important people and settings in Chris's life continue to be safe and supportive, encouraging positive and adaptive change.

Conclusion

Although an understanding of TGE-informed trauma care reflects a painful history for children, it seems that society is evolving to be more accepting of these children. The possibilities created by shared cultural change and rapidly growing knowledge mean that cultivating care for transgender youth has entered a vital and enriching period. It is imperative that all mental health assessments and interventions for TGE youth incorporate a developmental perspective on trauma and use an ecological model. TGE youth need to live in and attend school in safety and trauma-sensitive environments to reach their full potential, and mental health approaches need to recognize, validate, and treat trauma in children. All practitioners who evaluate and treat TGE children and adolescents must take a proactive approach to developing competencies in this assessment with this population, and reach out for training and supervision as necessary. Practitioners can draw upon the rich and growing clinical research and literature on trauma in children and integrate it with their knowledge of gender development, thus providing services for youth that will stall and rectify detrimental developmental trajectories. Newer research has demonstrated that misery and gender diversity are not necessary partners. For instance, mental health measures of fully socially transitioned prepubescent children have shown that they appear to be as well-adjusted as cisgender peers, aside from some slightly elevated anxiety (e.g., Durwood, McLaughlin, & Olson, 2017; Olson, Durwood, DeMeules, & McLaughlin, 2016). Psychological perspectives from many frameworks can be brought to the service of creating happy and hopeful lives for transgender youth, who need the same love, acceptance, and support as any child. Aspirationally, over time gender identity and gender expression will be just one characteristic about a child, to be explored rather than pathologized, an exploration that will be free from trauma.

References

Austin, A., & Craig, S. L. (2015). Transgender affirmative cognitive behavioral therapy: Clinical considerations and applications. *Professional Psychology: Research and Practice, 46*, 21–29. http://dx.doi.org/10.1037/a0038642

Benjamin, H. (1969). Newer aspects of the transsexual phenomenon. *Journal of Sex Research, 5*, 135–141. http://dx.doi.org/10.1080/00224496909550610

Blaustein, M., & Kinniburgh, K. (2010). *Treating traumatic stress in children and adolescents: How to foster resilience through attachment, self-regulation, and competency.* New York, NY: Guilford Press.

Budge, S. L., Katz-Wise, S., Tebbe, E. N., Howard, K. A. S., Schneider, C. L., & Rodriguez, A. (2013). Transgender emotional and coping processes: Facilitative and avoidant coping throughout gender transitioning. *The Counseling Psychologist, 41*, 601–647. http://dx.doi.org/10.1177/0011000011432753

Case, K., & Meier, S. C. (2014). Developing allies to transgender and gender nonconforming youth: Training for counselors and educators. *Journal of LGBT Youth, 11*, 62–82. http://dx.doi.org/10.1080/19361653.2014.840764

Centers for Disease Control and Prevention. (n.d.). *Adverse childhood experiences.* Retrieved from https://www.cdc.gov/violenceprevention/acestudy/

Chang, T. K., & Chung, Y. B. (2015). Transgender microaggressions: Complexity of the heterogeneity of transgender identities. *Journal of LGBT Issues in Counseling, 9*, 217–234. http://dx.doi.org/10.1080/15538605.2015.1068146

Cook, A., Spinazzola, J., Ford, J., Lanktree, C., Blaustein, M., Cloitre, M., . . . van der Kolk, B. (2005). Complex trauma in children and adolescents. *Psychiatric Annals, 35*, 390–398. http://dx.doi.org/10.3928/00485713-20050501-05

D'Augelli, A. R. (2012). Restoring lives: Developmental research on sexual orientation. *Human Development, 55*, 1–3. http://dx.doi.org/10.1159/000336251

de Vries, A. L. C., Steensma, T. D., Cohen-Kettenis, P. T., VanderLaan, D. P., & Zucker, K. J. (2015). Poor peer relations predict parent- and self-reported behavioral and emotional problems of adolescents with gender dysphoria: A cross-national, cross-clinic comparative analysis. *European Child & Adolescent Psychiatry 25*, 579–588. https://doi.org/10.1007/s00787-015-0764-7

Durwood, L., McLaughlin, K. A., & Olson, K. R. (2017). Mental health and self-worth in socially transitioned transgender youth. *Journal of the American Academy of Child & Adolescent Psychiatry, 56*, 116–123.e2. http://dx.doi.org/10.1016/j.jaac.2016.10.016

Ehrensaft, D. (2010). "I'm a Prius": A child case of a gender/ethnic hybrid. *Journal of Gay & Lesbian Mental Health, 15*, 46–57. http://dx.doi.org/10.1080/19359705.2011.530571

Ehrensaft, D. (2014). Found in transition: Our littlest transgender people. *Contemporary Psychoanalysis, 50*, 571–592. http://dx.doi.org/10.1080/00107530.2014.942591

Felitti, V. J., Anda, R. F., Nordenberg, D., Williamson, D. F., Spitz, A. M., Edwards, V., . . . Marks, J. S. (1998). Relationship of childhood abuse and household dysfunction to many of the leading causes of death in adults: The Adverse Childhood Experiences (ACE) Study. *American Journal of Preventive Medicine, 14*, 245–258. http://dx.doi.org/10.1016/S0749-3797(98)00017-8

Glicksman, E. (2013, April). Transgender today. *Monitor on Psychology, 44*(4), 36. Retrieved from http://www.apa.org/monitor/2013/04/transgender.aspx

Grant, J. M., Mottet, L. A., Tanis, J., Harrison, J., Herman, J. L., & Keisling, M. (2011). *Injustice at every turn: A report of the National Transgender Discrimination Survey.* Washington, DC: National Center for Transgender Equality and National Gay and Lesbian Task Force.

Heineman, T. (1998). *The abused child: Psychodynamic understanding and treatment.* New York, NY: Guilford.

Hendricks, M. L., & Testa, R. J. (2012). A conceptual framework for clinical work with transgender and gender nonconforming clients: An adaptation of the minority stress model. *Professional Psychology: Research and Practice, 43,* 460–467. http://dx.doi.org/10.1037/a0029597

Hidalgo, M. A., Ehrensaft, D., Tishelman, A. C., Clark, L. F., Garofalo, R., Rosenthal, S. M., Spack, N. P., & Olson, J. (2013). The gender affirmative model: What we know and what we aim to learn. *Human Development, 56,* 285–290. http://dx.doi.org/10.1159/000355235

Hill, J. S., Lau, M. Y., & Sue, D. W. (2010). Integrating trauma psychology and cultural psychology: Indigenous perspectives on theory, research, and practice. *Traumatology, 16,* 39–47. http://dx.doi.org/10.1177/1534765610388303

Kosciw, J. G., Palmer, N. A., & Kull, R. M. (2015). Reflecting resiliency: Openness about sexual orientation and/or gender identity and its relationship to well-being and educational outcomes for LGBT students. *American Journal of Community Psychology, 55,* 167–178. http://dx.doi.org/10.1007/s10464-014-9642-6

Malpas, J. (2011). Between pink and blue: A multi-dimensional family approach to gender nonconforming children and their families. *Family Process, 50,* 453–470. http://dx.doi.org/10.1111/j.1545-5300.2011.01371.x

Masten, A. S., & Cicchetti, D. (2010). Developmental cascades. *Development and Psychopathology, 22,* 491–495. http://dx.doi.org/10.1017/S0954579410000222

Minshew, R. (2015). Lost in place: An adolescent case of gender fluidity and secondary trauma. *Journal of Gay & Lesbian Mental Health, 19,* 201–208. http://dx.doi.org/10.1080/19359705.2014.997910

National Child Traumatic Stress Network. (n.d.). *National Child Traumatic Stress Network empirically supported treatments and promising practices.* Retrieved from http://nctsn.org/training-guidelines

Olson, K. R., Durwood, L., DeMeules, M., & McLaughlin, K. A. (2016). Mental health of transgender children who are supported in their identities. *Pediatrics, 137,* 277–282. http://dx.doi.org/10.1542/peds.2015-3223

Reisner, S. L., Greytak, E. A., Parsons, J. T., & Ybarra, M. L. (2015). Gender minority social stress in adolescence: Disparities in adolescent bullying and substance use by gender identity. *Journal of Sex Research, 52,* 243–256. http://dx.doi.org/10.1080/00224499.2014.886321

Reisner, S. L., Vetters, R., Leclerc, M., Zaslow, S., Wolfrum, S., Shumer, D., & Mimiaga, M. J. (2015). Mental health of transgender youth in care at an adolescent urban community health center: A matched retrospective cohort study. *Journal of Adolescent Health, 56,* 274–279. http://dx.doi.org/10.1016/j.jadohealth.2014.10.264

Reisner, S. L., White Hughto, J. M., Gamarel, K. E., Keuroghlian, A. S., Mizock, L., & Pachankis, J. E. (2016). Discriminatory experiences associated with posttraumatic stress disorder symptoms among transgender adults. *Journal of Counseling Psychology, 63,* 509–519. http://dx.doi.org/10.1037/cou0000143

Roberts, A. L., Rosario, M., Corliss, H. L., Koenen, K. C., & Austin, S. B. (2012). Childhood gender nonconformity: A risk indicator for childhood abuse and posttraumatic stress in youth. *Pediatrics, 129,* 410–417. http://dx.doi.org/10.1542/peds.2011-1804

Saxe, G. N., Ellis, B. H., & Kaplow, J. (2006). *Collaborative care for traumatized children and teens: A trauma systems therapy approach.* New York, NY: Guilford Press.

Shonkoff, J. P., Garner, A. S., The Committee on Psychosocial Aspects of Child and Family Health, Committee on Early Childhood, Adoption, and Dependent Care, and Section on Developmental and Behavioral Pediatrics, Siegel, B. S., Dobbins, M. I., Earls, M. F., . . . Wood, D. L. (2012). The lifelong effects of early childhood adversity and toxic stress. *Pediatrics, 129,* 232–246. http://dx.doi.org/10.1542/peds.2011-2663

Sue, D. W. (Ed.). (2010). *Microaggressions and marginality: Manifestation, dynamics, and impact.* New York, NY: Wiley.

Tishelman, A. C., Haney, P., Greenwald O'Brien, J., & Blaustein, M. (2010). A framework for school-based psychological evaluations: Utilizing a "trauma lens." *Journal of Child and Adolescent Trauma, 3,* 279–302.

Toomey, R. B., Card, N. A., & Casper, D. M. (2014). Peers' perceptions of gender nonconformity: Associations with overt and relational peer victimization and aggression in early adolescence. *The Journal of Early Adolescence, 34,* 463–485. http://dx.doi.org/10.1177/0272431613495446

Dianne Berg and Laura Edwards-Leeper

Child and Family Assessment 7

With the influx of transgender and gender expansive (TGE) children and their families seeking support, understanding, and guidance in the past decade in the United States, the roles of mental health professionals (MHPs) in this process have come to the forefront of many discussions. To be affirming, MHPs need to appreciate what a child declares about their gender while simultaneously remaining cognizant of general child developmental theories and research as well as the more specific research on gender identity in gender diverse children (Edwards-Leeper, Leibowitz, & Sangganjanavanich, 2016). This information can help guide the affirming and supportive therapy MHPs provide, along with the assessments offered. This chapter focuses on the latter. Although the chapter title above is brief, to approach this uniquely complex client population in the most affirming way, a better title might be: "If you want to know a child's gender, ask in multiple ways, from multiple perspectives, over multiple time frames, and make sure that while you are asking, you are mindful of the incredible implicit and explicit pressure the gender binary asserts on the child, parent(s), and you as the MHP."

The field is still very much debating, developing, and defining what constitutes a gender affirmative model (GAM) and this holds true for the role of assessment within the GAM. Although the initial assessment is often

http://dx.doi.org/10.1037/0000095-007
The Gender Affirmative Model: An Interdisciplinary Approach to Supporting Transgender and Gender Expansive Children, C. Keo-Meier and D. Ehrensaft (Editors)
Copyright © 2018 by the American Psychological Association. All rights reserved.

helpful in determining a potential treatment trajectory, it typically does so with minimal established rapport between the clinician and the child/family. Thus, the assessment is only the starting point of a well-balanced and thoughtful application of available research and clinical knowledge in the field.

In this chapter, we first review the literature and discuss the current assessment protocols, with an emphasis on the extent to which various parent and child assessment measures align with the underlying tenets of the developing GAM. We also offer suggestions for how to move assessment beyond its historical focus on the gender dysphoria diagnosis and toward practices that can begin to tease apart gender expression from gender identity, while taking into account the influence of the gender binary for both the child and parent(s). We explain a way to do this by incorporating the concepts of gender fluidity, gender literacy, and gender resiliency. It is important to note that the assessment described in this chapter is intended for prepubescent children, not adolescents.

Approaches to Assessment in the Literature

The literature points to various clinical and theoretical viewpoints on the assessment of TGE children (Drescher & Byne, 2013). Some clinicians endorse the use of a multi-informant (child/parent/teacher), multimodal (psychological instruments, child observations, clinical interviews) approach (de Vries & Cohen-Kettenis, 2012; Zucker, Wood, Singh, & Bradley, 2012). In addition to discussing the importance of determining whether *Diagnostic and Statistical Manual of Mental Disorders* (*DSM*; e.g., fifth ed. [*DSM–5*], American Psychiatric Association, 2013) criteria are met, de Vries and Cohen-Kettenis (2012) argued that the following should be evaluated: child's cognitive level, psychosocial functioning, and school performance, as well as family functioning and the role that the child's gender nonconformity and/or gender dysphoria has on the family functioning. In addition to the above, Zucker et al. (2012) noted the importance of assessing how the parents have made sense of their child's gender development, how they responded to the child's gender expansiveness before the assessment, and the parental goals. Ehrensaft (2012) stressed the importance of listening to the child and providing a safe holding environment for the child over time so they will feel comfortable revealing their "true gender self" (p. 47). Her assessment focuses on the importance of differentiating children who consistently identify as a different gender (i.e., gender identity) from those who are simply exploring gender expression. Menvielle (2012) described the use of an "extended initial interview" (p. 70) in which both child and parent(s) are interviewed together and separately. Menvielle asked parents to bring "medical and school records, drawings, writings, journals, and photos" (p. 70) to help contribute to an understanding of the child. Last, both Zucker et al. (2012) and Menvielle (2012) discussed the importance of helping the parent prepare the child for the assessment, including offering parental "scripts" for how to present the idea to the child.

Purposes of Assessment in a Gender Affirming Model of Care

From the literature reviewed above, the following are typical reasons an assessment might be useful: (a) to discern whether a child meets the *DSM–5* criteria for Gender Dysphoria; (b) to rule out whether gender struggles are an authentic expression of the child's "true gender self" rather than a response to a drastic change in the child's life, such as a serious illness in the family, adoption, abuse (life events that are traumatic for the child), or influences within the family system that reinforce the child adopting a compensatory identity; (c) to differentiate whether a child is grappling with gender identity, gender expression, or a combination thereof; and (d) to determine whether co-occurring psychiatric/mental health or behavioral concerns are present and the extent to which these exacerbate the gender issues or are a result of them. In addition, an assessment that comes from a GAM will also do the following: (a) question the extent to which the use of the *DSM–5* diagnostic framework is going to be helpful (i.e., in securing insurance coverage) versus harmful (i.e., unnecessarily pathologizing gender diversity); (b) if decided that it is in the best interest of the child to use the *DSM* framework, discern the degree to which the *DSM–5* criteria are met because of gender dysphoria rather than gender expansiveness; (c) assess the degree to which both the child and parent(s) are struggling with gender-related stigma and discrimination; (d) determine the extent to which both the child and parent(s) could benefit from supportive interventions designed to build positive body awareness (Key, 2014), resiliency, and gender literacy; (e) incorporate measures that account for more complexity, including nonbinary gender identities and/or presentations (e.g., gender fluidity); and (f) consider the empirical research to date and recognize that the outcome does not lead to prescriptive treatment approaches. Because current assessment protocols have tended to conflate sexual orientation with gender identity, and because it is not possible to know what the sexual orientation of a child will be, it is important to clearly state that in a GAM, the purpose of the assessment is not to make determinations about the child's future gender identity or sexual orientation.

Gender Affirmative Assessment

To discuss aspects of a gender affirmative assessment, we must first evaluate in what ways the original protocols (see Exhibit 7.1) capture what is needed in a GAM and in what ways they require adaption.

Less Might Be More

Historically, lengthy protocols have been used in the gender assessment process, even with young children. The sheer number of tasks, the amount of time spent in clinical interviews, and the types of instruments used in these protocols point to two issues.

EXHIBIT 7.1

Test Battery for Children Younger Than 12 With Gender Dysphoria

Specific Instruments for Children Under 6

- Gender labeling task (Leinbach & Fagot, 1986)
- Gender constancy task (Slaby & Frey, 1975), which consisting of subtasks regarding:
  - Gender labeling
  - Gender stability
  - Gender consistency
- Toy preference (photographs)
- Playmate preference (photographs)

Specific Instruments for all Children Under 12

- Gender Preference Interview (see Exhibit 7.2.)
- Gender Identity Interview (Zucker & Bradley, 1995)
- Gender Role Questionnaire (Ijntema & Cohen-Kettenis, unpublished)
- Play and Games questionnaire (adapted from the Child Game Participation questionnaire, Bates & Bentler, 1973)
- Play observation (except for "mature" 11- to 12-year-olds; Rekers &Yates, 1976; Zucker, Bradley, Doering, & Lozinsky, 1985)
- Draw-a-Person test (Rekers, Rosen, & Morey, 1990)

General Instruments for Children Under 12

- IQ test
- Sentence Completion Test for Children Under 7
- Kinetic Family Drawing Test (Burns & Kaufman, 1972)
- Self-perception profile (Veerman, Straathof, Treffers, Van den Bergh, & ten Brink, 1997)

Specific Instruments for Parents for Children Under 6

- Preschool Attributes Inventory (PAI; Golombok & Rusk, 1994)
- Child Behavior and Attitude questionnaire (Bates et. al., 1973; modified by Meyer-Bahlburg, Sandberg, Dolezal, & Yager, 1994)
- Gender identity questionnaire (Elisabeth & Green, 1984, modified by Zucker & Bradley, 1995)

General Instrument for Parents

- Developmental History Questionnaire (unpublished)
- Child Behavior Checklist (CBCL; Achenbach & Edelbrock, 1983)

General Instruments for Teachers

- Teacher version of the CBCL (TRF, Achenbach & Edelbrock, 1986a)
- School Questionnaire (unpublished)

Clinical Assessment Protocol

Interview schedule	Approximate duration
Telephone intake interview	0.5–1.5 hours
Family interview	3 hours
Individual interviews with parents	2–5 hours/parent
Psychological testing of the child	4 hours
Individual interview with child	1 hours
Feedback session	1–2 hours

Note. Canada has universal health care coverage. When a child is seen in a hospital setting, the Canadian health care plan covers the entire cost. A psychiatrist bills the health care system directly for all face-to-face contact. Psychologists who work in a hospital setting are paid an hourly rate, but do not bill the health care plan. For child psychiatrists in private practice, they also bill the health care plan for all face-to-face contact. Psychologists in private practice operate on a fee-for-service basis. Clients pay the psychologist directly. If they have private health insurance, at least some of the costs are covered by the individual health care plan.

EXHIBIT 7.1 (*Continued*)

Test Battery for Children Younger Than 12 With Gender Dysphoria

Psychological Testing Protocol and Parent-Completed Questionnaires

Test/task/questionnaire	Comment/reference
Child measures	
IQ test	WPPSI-III or WISC-IV
Quality of attachment (mother-child observation)	Used with children 3–6 years of age. Cassidy and Marvin (1992)
Feelings, Attitudes, and Behaviors Scale for Children	Used with children 6–10 years of age. Beitchman (1996)
Youth Self-Report Form	Used with children 11–12 years of age. Achenbach and Edelbrock (1986b)
Rorschach	Zucker, Lozinski, Bradley, & Doering (1992)
Draw-a-Person test	Zucker, Finegan, Doering, & Bradley (1983)
Free play task	Zucker, Doering, Bradley, & Finegan (1982)
Playmate and Play Style Preferences Structured Interview	Fridell, Owen-Anderson, Johnson, Bradley, & Zucker (2006)
Color preference task	Chiu et al. (2006)
Gender Identity Interview for Children	Wallien et al. (2009) and Zucker et al. (1993)
Parent/teacher measures	
Separation anxiety interview schedule	Used for boys only. Zucker, Bradley, & Lowry Sullivan (1996)
Child Behavior Checklist	Achenbach & Edelbrock (1983)
Teacher's Report Form	Achenbach & Edelbrock (1986a)
Temperament questionnaire	Zucker & Bradley (1995)
Games Inventory	Bates & Bentler (1973)
Gender Identity Questionnaire for Children	Johnson et al. (2004)
Symptom Checklist–90	Derogatis (1983)
Dyadic Adjustment Scale	Spanier (1976)
Recalled Childhood Gender Identity/Gender Role Questionnaire	Zucker et al. (2006)

Note. We no longer use the two-gender constancy assessment reported on by Zucker et al. (1999). The Children's Depression Inventory is used on an ad hoc basis.

First, they appear to be research protocols rather than clinical protocols; second, the protocols give the perception of a fundamental assumption of pathology—that something has gone wrong with the child's gender development and functioning, and the purpose of the assessment is to decipher what went wrong so it can be fixed. For instance, what purpose is served by comprehensively measuring cognitive functioning unless there is reason to believe that children with gender issues are more likely to exhibit cognitive deficits? Certainly, it is prudent to ensure that the gender issues are not a result of cognitive impairment, but the clinical interview with the parent and child will likely provide the information needed to determine whether further evaluation in this area is warranted. Likewise, if a goal of the assessment is to clarify whether co-occurring psychiatric/mental health or behavioral concerns of which the parents are not already aware are present, completing a semistructured clinical interview and using a well-researched screening tool such as the Child Behavioral Checklist (CBCL; Achenbach & Edelbrock, 1983) should suffice. When using established psychological screening instruments that have been normed by sex assigned at birth (male/female), it may be worthwhile to score the form using both male and female norms. This may provide additional information about the psychological profile of the child that can help in case conceptualization. However, it is our experience that the scores are rarely much different when comparing an individual child's male versus female results, unlike in testing with transgender adults (Keo-Meier & Fitzgerald, 2017); thus, the added benefit of taking this approach is uncertain. Most important, if mental health concerns are present, the assessment should focus on the extent to which they exacerbate the gender concerns and/or are a function of the gender dysphoria felt by the child as well as the extent to which they are a function of the harassment, stigma, and the range of microaggressions that children who do not conform to the gender binary endure. An adaptation for children of the Gender Minority Stress and Resilience measure (Testa, Habarth, Peta, Balsam, & Bockting, 2015) currently developed for adults would be very helpful in this regard. Also, mounting research shows a correlation between gender identity issues and autism spectrum disorders (de Vries, Noens, Cohen-Kettenis, van Berckelaer-Onnes, & Doreleijers, 2010). Most clinicians do not recommend entirely discounting a child's struggles with gender dysphoria because of the presence of an autism spectrum disorder. However, because of this added layer of complexity, as with any child who has signs of developmental or cognitive impairment, it is wise to include screening instruments and ideally collaborate with autism spectrum specialists or neuropsychologists as part of the assessment process (see also Chapter 6). To summarize, although it is important to place the gender struggles within the broader context of the child's psychological, social, and family functioning, the use of screening instruments when appropriate is preferred over requiring extensive evaluation instruments of every child, as the latter may be unnecessary.

During the therapeutic process, the use of play can be very helpful in building rapport and providing useful insights into a child's gender conceptualization and struggles. However, we question whether it is necessary during assessment to spend considerable time observing the play of the child as outlined in the original protocols, where the play observation appears to be focused on determining the extent of gender expansiveness (i.e., whether the child plays with what would be considered, from a stereotypical binary perspective, "boy toys" or "girls toys"). This focus on gender expansiveness is discussed in the next section, as it is not particularly relevant in an assessment of gender identity and dysphoria. Also, it is unclear how much more information this type of play observation provides beyond what could be ascertained from the clinical interview with the parent(s) and child. Thus, this aspect of the original protocols seems not only to be redundant but also may suggest to the child that their play choices are to be scrutinized. Although other types of play techniques, such as the use of a sand tray (Ehrensaft, 2016), have been discussed as possible assessment tools, no standardized protocols have been put forth to date.

Last, many of the measures in the original protocols are based on theories of gender development that not only pathologize noncisgender experience but also pathologize and do not recognize nonbinary experience. Thus, the measures have an underlying assumption that the child falls neatly into the gender binary, leaving little space to understand children who fall somewhere in the middle or outside two gender poles altogether.

Discerning Gender Dysphoria From Gender Expansiveness

In an ideal world, an assessment would clearly discern children who are gender dysphoric and/or whose gender identity does not match that assigned at birth from children who are gender expansive (i.e., assessing both gender identity and gender expression, respectively). Because more and more researchers believe that by making this distinction, they will be better able to predict which children will ultimately identify as transgender in adolescence and which will not, the necessity and ability to make this differentiation is being discussed with increased frequency among providers and researchers in the field (see Chapter 3, this volume). Perhaps more important than future trajectory, however, is the likelihood that the type of support needed may be different for children who have gender identity concerns than for those who are gender expansive. Menvielle (2012) asserted that gender expansive children tend to benefit from discussions and interventions that open up possibilities for all the different ways to be a boy or a girl. Alternatively, for those children who are assessed to be gender dysphoric and possibly transgender, the interventions of choice may include partial or complete early social transition as well as options for medical interventions in early puberty. Fortunately, the changes made from the *DSM–IV* to the *DSM–5* diagnostic criteria should be very beneficial in this discernment process. Specifically, it is no longer possible to meet the *DSM–5* diagnosis of Gender Dysphoria through only gender expansive behavior; now there must be at least some indication of discomfort with one's gender, determined by Criteria 1, which reads, "a strong desire to be of the other gender or an insistence that one is the other gender (or some alternative gender) different from one's assigned gender" (*DSM–5*, p. 452). Of course, clinical judgment still must be used regarding what constitutes "a strong desire" and what constitutes an "insistence," as well as whether this desire or insistence is a solution to social stressors (e.g., teasing, bullying) related to gender expansiveness. Whereas Criteria 7 and/or 8, which address the issue of body dysphoria, are likely to be very meaningful, Criteria 2 through 6 are reminiscent of *DSM–IV* criteria, involving cultural norms of gender expression, and thus are not likely to aid in this discernment process.

Although substantial controversy has arisen around the Dutch research (Steensma, Biemond, de Boer, & Cohen-Kettenis, 2011; Steensma, McGuire, Kreukels, Beekman, & Cohen-Kettenis, 2013) because of its cautions around early social transition, this research points to certain factors that may help distinguish which children will likely continue to experience dysphoria in adolescence from those less likely to do so. The

2011 small qualitative study found that before age 10, distinguishing factors predicting persistence were the child having a "conviction" rather than just a "wish" or "desire" to be a gender other than their assigned gender, body dysphoria, and a very early history of gender expansiveness. By ages 10 to 13, however, the differences became more pronounced, suggesting that an assessment at these ages should include a focus on (a) how the child is responding to gendered changes in their social environment, (b) anticipation of and/or actual physical changes during puberty, and (c) the meaning the child makes of experiences related to falling in love and discovering sexual orientation (Steensma et al., 2011). The 2013 quantitative study confirmed the importance of the above distinction between "conviction" and "wish/desire." However, the bigger sample size and quantitative methods also determined that factors such as age at referral, intensity of gender expansiveness, and level of social transition were differentially predictive depending on assigned sex. Thus, Steensma et al. (2013) suggested that recommendations for how to best support may need to be developed separately for gender diverse children who were assigned female versus male.

It is unfortunate that the instruments in the original protocols, similar to the *DSM–IV* criteria, not only conflate the components of gender identity and gender expression but also do not directly assess the above foci found to be empirically important. In the next section, we review these instruments. Please refer to Exhibit 7.1 for a listing of the instruments used in the original protocols as well as Exhibit 7.2, which denotes how items from these instruments tend to measure certain domains.

GENDER-SPECIFIC PARENT MEASURES

The Gender Identity Questionnaire (Johnson et al., 2004; Zucker & Bradley, 1995) is a Likert-type scale completed by parents. Of the 16 questions, only four (Items 13–16) examine aspects of what would now be considered gender dysphoria. Of the remaining 12 questions, nine are clearly about gender expression (Items 1, 2, 3, 4, 7, 8, 10, 22, 12) and a few are difficult to categorize (those about imitation and role playing). Likewise, in The Core Behavioral Features of GID in Childhood (Zucker, 1992), two of the seven questions pertain to gender dysphoria by asking about identity statements (although conflate "conviction" with "wish") and anatomic dysphoria, and the other five focus on gender expression.

GENDER-SPECIFIC CHILD MEASURES

The Gender Identity Interview for Children (Zucker et al., 1993) is a semistructured interview completed with the child. Some of the questions (Items 1, 2, 11, and to a certain extent, 3 and 4) give some indication of the child's conviction, whereas Items 8 and 9 measure confusion and Items 5, 6, and 7 focus on desire/want.

The Gender Preference Interview (Cohen-Kettenis & Pfäfflin, 2003) also overtly focuses on aspects of gender role/expression (Items 1–9, 12, 17). Although these questions may be helpful to build rapport, they do not directly aid in the process of discerning gender dysphoria from gender expansiveness. Updating the interview to

EXHIBIT 7.2

Measures of gender dysphoria

Gender Identity

Parent Questions

Gender Identity Questionnaire—Boy Version
(Zucker & Bradley, 1995; Johnson et al., 2004)

13. He states the wish to be a girl or a woman
14. He states that he is a girl or a woman
15. He talks about not liking his sexual anatomy (private parts)
16. He talks about liking his sexual anatomy (private parts)

Behavioral Features of Gender Identity in Childhood (Zucker, 1992)

1. Identity Statements
   Child frequently/occasionally/rarely/never states the <u>wish</u> to be of the opposite sex or that he/she <u>is</u> a member of the opposite sex (e.g., "I want to be a girl, I am a girl," or "I want to grow up to be a Mommy, not a Daddy").
2. Anatomic Dysphoria
   Child frequently/occasionally/rarely/never states a dislike of his or her sexual anatomy (e.g., "I don't like my penis"; "I want a penis, not a vagina") or demonstrates this behaviorally (e.g., in a boy, sitting to urinate to simulate having female genitalia; in a girl, standing to urinate to simulate having male genitalia).

Child Questions

Gender Identity Interview for Children—Boy Version (Zucker et al., 1993)

1. Are you a boy or a girl?
2. Are you a (opposite of first response)?
3. Do you ever think that you really are a girl?

If YES, say: Tell me more about that. (Probe until satisfied.)

1. When you grow up, will you be a Mommy or a Daddy?
2. Could you ever grow up to be a (opposite of first response)?

Gender Preference Interview (Cohen-Kettenis & Pfäfflin, 2003)

1. If you look in the mirror, are there any parts of you that you are happy with?
2. If you look in the mirror, are there any parts of you that you are unhappy with? What is wrong with these parts of you?
3. If I were a fairy and I could change you with my magic wand, what parts of you do you want me to change?
4. If my magic stick could fulfill your greatest wish, what would that be?
5. Suppose you weren't born yet, and I, the fairy, asked you whether you would like to become a girl or a boy, what would you choose?

Gender Nonconformity/Gender Expression/Role

Parent Questions

Gender Identity Questionnaire—Boy Version
(Zucker & Bradley, 1995; Johnson et al., 2004)

17. His favorite playmates are
    a. Always boys (5)
    b. Usually boys (4)

(*continues*)

EXHIBIT 7.2 (*Continued*)

Measures of gender dysphoria

---

c. Boys and girls equally (3)
d. Usually girls (2)
e. Always girls (1)
f. Does not play with other children

18. He plays with girl-type dolls, such as "Barbie"
    a. As a favorite toy (1)
    b. Frequently (2)
    c. Once-in-a-while (3)
    d. Rarely (4)
    e. Never (5)

19. He plays with boy-type dolls, such as "G.I. Joe" or "Ken"
    a. As a favorite toy (5)
    b. Frequently (4)
    c. Once-in-a-while (3)
    d. Rarely (2)
    e. Never (1)

20. He experiments with cosmetics (makeup) and jewelry
    a. As a favorite activity (1)
    b. Frequently (2)
    c. Once-in-a-while (3)
    d. Rarely (4)
    e. Never (5)

Behavioral Features of Gender Identity in Childhood (Zucker, 1992)

3. *Toy and Role Play*
    - Child prefers to play with toys and to engage in roles stereotypically associated with the opposite sex (e.g., in boys, a preference for female dolls, such as Barbie or Bratz, role play as a female, emulation of female superheroes; drawings invariably are of women. In girls, a preference for male dolls, such as GI Joe or male Transformers, role play as a male, emulation of male superheroes; drawings invariably are of men).
    - Child plays with toys and engages in roles that are both stereotypically masculine and feminine.
    - Child avoids toys and roles that are stereotypically associated with his or her sex but does not engage in toy or role play associated with the opposite sex.
    - Child prefers neutral activities (e.g., drawing, making music) and does not engage in either same-sex or cross-sex toy or role play.
    - Child prefers to play with toys and to engage in roles stereotypically associated with own sex.
4. *Cross-Dressing*
    - Child frequently cross-dresses (e.g., in boys, use of mother's clothes, such as dresses, high-heeled shoes, jewelry, and makeup; simulation of long hair with towels; preference for a female swimsuit. In girls, refusal to wear culturally typical feminine clothing and use of clothing, such as boys' pants and shirts, to simulate a masculine appearance; often desire hair to be very short, in accordance with masculine convention; preference for a male swimsuit).
    - Child occasionally cross-dresses.
    - Child rarely cross-dresses.
    - Child never cross-dresses.

EXHIBIT 7.2 (*Continued*)

Measures of gender dysphoria

5. *Peer Relations*
   - Child prefers to play with opposite-sex peers.
   - Child is a loner or is rejected.
   - Plays with both same-sex and opposite-sex peers.
   - Child prefers to play with same-sex peers.
6. *Mannerisms*
   - Child frequently displays motoric movements and speech characteristics that are associated with the opposite sex, either in "natural" or "exaggerated" form (e.g., in boys, this includes hand movements, hip control, elevated pitch and lisp; in girls, this includes low voice projection).
   - Child occasionally displays motoric movements and speech characteristics that are associated with the opposite sex, either in "natural" or "exaggerated" form.
   - Child rarely displays motoric movements and speech characteristics that are associated with the opposite sex, either in "natural" or "exaggerated" form.
   - Child never displays motoric movements and speech characteristics that are associated with the opposite sex, either in "natural" or "exaggerated" form.
7. *Rough-and-Tumble Play*
   - In boys, there is an aversion to rough-and-tumble play or participation in group sports, such as hockey, football, and soccer. There is often a concern regarding physical injury. In girls, there is a strong attraction to rough-and-tumble play and group sports, particularly with boys.
   - In boys, there is no interest in rough-and-tumble play or participation in group sports, but the accompanying fear is not present.
   - In boys, there is an interest in rough-and-tumble play or participation in group sports. In girls, such interests are not dependent on a male peer group, but, rather, are expressed in more typical ways (e.g., mixed-sex teams, all-girls teams).

Gender Confusion

Child Questions

Gender Identity Interview for Children—Boy Version (Zucker et al., 1993)

1. In your mind, do you ever get mixed up and you're not really sure if you are a boy or a girl?
2. If YES, say: Tell me more about that. (Probe until satisfied.)
3. Do you ever feel more like a girl than a boy?
4. If YES, say: Tell me more about that. (Probe until satisfied.)

Desire/Want

Child Questions

Gender Identity Interview for Children—Boy Version (Zucker et al., 1993)

1. Are there any good things about being a boy?
2. If YES, say: Tell me some of the good things about being a boy. (Probe for a maximum of three responses.)
3. Do you think it is better to be a boy or a girl? (Probe for a maximum of three responses.)
4. In your mind, do you ever think that you would like to be a girl?
5. If YES, ask: Can you tell me why? (Probe for a maximum of three responses.)

(continues)

EXHIBIT 7.2 (*Continued*)

Measures of gender dysphoria

Gender Development Theory (Gender Binary, Outdated)

Child questions

Gender Preference Interview (Cohen-Kettenis & Pfäfflin, 2003)

1. Are there any people you admire a lot?
2. Do you want to marry when you are grown up? Any idea who will be the lucky person?
3. Are you already in love with someone? Can you tell me more about him/her?
4. Is someone in love with you?
5. When you are grown up, do you want to have children? How many? Boys or girls?

Note. Data from Cohen-Kettenis and Pfäfflin (2003); Johnson et al. (2004); Zucker (1992); and Zucker et al. (1993).

include questions that encompass current digitally relevant information such as avatars used in computer gaming would be fruitful. Question 10 and questions 13 through 16 all appear to be based on an outdated view of gender development theory that assumes gender is a binary construct and that veering from the majority (cisgender and heterosexual) is undesirable at best, pathological at worst.

It is interesting that despite the fact that these questions are outdated and based on assumptions that are now being questioned, in our work with these instruments over time, we have found that they can yield useful information. For instance, to the question "When you are grown up, do you want to have children?" a 6-year-old who was assigned male at birth reported they would like to have children, elaborating that "I would have at least two, one each, that way the boy could like girl stuff and the girl could like boy stuff." Also, they spontaneously shared, "Boy bodies can't have babies. I am kind of sad about that, but I can still be a parent." These comments not only provide a window into the child's view of the gender binary (on the one hand they believe there is "girl stuff" and "boy stuff," but on the other hand they do not think that the binary should be limiting). Further the child is demonstrating aspects of both gender literacy (see the next section for a definition) by having some understanding of sexual anatomy and function (part of the component of biological sex) and resiliency through their ability to weather the disappointment of not being able to carry and birth a baby.

On this interview schedule, the questions that have the most potential for discerning those children whose gender identity may not be congruent with gender assignment from those who are gender expansive, are Questions 18 through 22, the *mirror* and the *fairy* questions (see Exhibit 7.2). These questions provide an avenue to determine whether the child is experiencing body dysphoria by asking about how they feel when looking in a mirror, as well as what aspects of self the child would change if magically able to do so. To specifically assess genital dysphoria, one useful adaptation is to append the mirror questions with the words "while naked." It has been our experience that this addition will often reveal genital dysphoria if it has not been revealed before. Another activity that can be useful is what we call the *body awareness activity*. Much like the mirror questions, the body awareness activity is fun for the child in that the clinician uses their "magic wand" to "wave over" the child's body, stopping at any number of locations on the body (need to do enough that the child perceives the scan to be about their whole body rather than just the "culturally gendered" aspects of their body, i.e., genitals, hair length, fingernails, breast/chest) and asks the child whether they like or do not like this aspect. For those parts that the child likes, a follow-up question could be, "What do you like about that?" For those aspects that the child does not like, a follow-up question could be, "How would you like it to be different?"

In summary, assessment instruments for children need to be developed that explicitly capture body dysphoria and focus much more on the extent to which there is a sense of conviction versus a wish or desire to be a gender other than that matching the sex assigned at birth. Until more refined measurement tools are created, the original measures, when critically examined and adapted appropriately, can provide useful information for the assessment process.

Gender Literacy and Body Awareness

A GAM assesses the concepts of gender literacy and body awareness. Gender literacy, as presented in the Gender Affirmative Lifespan Approach (GALA; Berg et al., 2016), involves knowledge and understanding that on some level, within Western culture, people live in a world that is designed around a gender binary. This binary asserts rules around how people are supposed to think about themselves, what interests they are supposed to have, what they are supposed to wear, and so on. A child who is "gender literate" is not only able to name these "rules" but is also aware of the discrimination and stigma that can occur when one does not adhere to them. A child who is gender literate externalizes rather than internalizes these rules and by doing so is able to determine the extent to which they "buy into" them and allow the rules to dictate how they perceive their true gender self and their expression of that self. Berg et al. (2016) asserted that gender literacy is an important building block of resiliency; once children can name that they are inherently comfortable with themselves regardless of whether they follow the gender rules, the potential for shame is greatly decreased and resiliency is built. Within GALA, gender literacy is also about understanding the distinctions between birth-assigned sex, gender identity, gender expression, and sexual orientation, as well as one's subjective experience of each of these components. In becoming more gender literate, children begin to understand that their body parts do not define their true gender selves (even though this is what determined their initial sex assignment), and that what makes them a "real girl" or a "real boy" is how they think and feel.

Body awareness is another important component to explore when assessing children. Key (2014) wrote about the importance of body awareness for TGE children, explaining that many of these youth experience a negative relationship with all or parts of their bodies. This may include feeling betrayed by one's body because it is incongruent with how one feels, a feeling that is both shaped and reinforced by the cultural trope that penis = boy, and vagina = girl. As a result, Key postulated that TGE children may have difficulty experiencing body awareness; this, therefore, should be a key component of a gender assessment, with significant treatment implications.

With these concepts in mind, the assessment process in a GAM focuses on the extent to which the parents and child are equipped to cope with and challenge the pressures of the gender binary, including how much they have internalized the messages this binary asserts. Additionally, determining a child's degree of gender literacy and body awareness is important, as is exploring other areas of strength and resiliency in the child and family unit.

Projective Instruments

As noted in the original protocols (see Exhibit 7.1), projective psychological tests are listed (i.e., Rorschach, Sentence Completion Test for Children, Kinetic Family Drawing, and Draw-A-Person [DAP]). Children assigned male at birth diagnosed with Gender Identity Disorder (GID; the *DSM* diagnosis at that time) were more likely than controls to first draw their asserted gender on the DAP instrument (Green, Fuller, & Rutley, 1972; Skilbeck, Bentler, & Bates, 1975; Zucker, Finegan, Doering, & Bradley, 1983), and to make this drawing taller (Zucker et al., 1983) and more detailed (Skilbeck et al., 1975) than the drawing of the assigned gender. These are important elements to assess when using the DAP with a child, providing self-reflections of the child's affirmed gender and the saliency of that self-image. In addition, the DAP activity can also be an avenue to gain information about the child's level of gender literacy. Because we have found the DAP to be the most useful projective test in a gender assessment, we focus our discussion on it.

Although this projective test has been used in many ways, using the DAP in a gender assessment involves asking the child to draw a picture of a whole person. To discourage drawing stick figures as a means of avoiding the task, the assessor can also add that it can be any kind of person but not a stick or cartoon figure. If the child asks questions, noncommittal answers are given. After finishing the drawing, the child is asked to identify the gender of the person and then asked to make a second drawing, specifying it to be the other gender (e.g., if child identifies the first drawing as a "girl," the assessor asks that their second drawing be a "boy"). Alternatively, a beyond-the-binary approach would be to ask the child after they have completed the first drawing, "Does this child have a gender?" and then saying, "Now draw a child of a different gender." Once the two drawings are completed, it is very informative to go back and have a conversation with the child about the drawings. Responding to a few simple prompts such as, "Tell me about your drawings" and "You said this one was a girl, can you tell me what about your drawing makes it a girl?" the child will begin to articulate what goes into their understanding of gender. To put it another way, the extent to which the child uses what used to be called sex role stereotypes to articulate gender (hair length, clothing, activities; i.e., gender expression) will likely become apparent. Additionally, the child can be asked to tell a story about their drawing once completed. Specifically asking about the thoughts and feelings of the person drawn can shed light on the child's internalized feelings related to their own gender identity. The same procedure can be followed with the second DAP drawing. It can be enlightening to compare the thoughts, feelings, and stories the child describes between the two drawings. Sometimes children will resist drawing the second person, and their stories, thoughts, and feelings that correspond with this picture, if drawn, are more negative.

The DAP activity can also be used to evaluate the child's knowledge and comfort about bodies and possibly their own body awareness. Once the topics described above are being discussed, it is possible to shift to the question "When a baby is born, why do we call some babies boys and some babies girls?" How the child answers may be one indicator of the level of their gender literacy—do they know that most people believe that private parts determine the assigned sex, and do they know assigned sex and gender expression are not the same as gender identity? This discussion may also illuminate the child's comfort with and understanding of words related to their gendered anatomy, an important component of body awareness.

Last, from the DAP activity it is easy to move toward a discussion designed to assess the child's understanding of, comfort with, and expectations about, puberty. Just as children have varying degrees of comfort and knowledge about primary sex characteristics, they have varying degrees of awareness of the differences in secondary sex characteristics. Saying something like, "If we grew your drawing of the girl up to be a woman, what would change? How are adult bodies different from child bodies?" Often the child will use their family members to discuss this question. Additionally, to assess whether the child believes that bodies can change from one gender to another, the question "Could this girl's body change to a male body when she gets older?" could be asked, followed with "How?" Thus, any magical thinking the child may have, along with the child's awareness about body altering interventions available for transgender individuals, is assessed.

Beyond the Binary

As mentioned before, the original assessment protocols are very binary in their underlying philosophy and the manner in which questions are worded. Thus, until instruments are developed that move beyond the binary, the clinician must be creative to introduce nonbinary options, as discussed earlier with the DAP. One way to do this is through the introduction of spectrums or continuums. A tool that may be used is the child-friendly Genderbread Person (http://itspronouncedmetrosexual.com/2015/03/the-genderbread-person-v3). The Genderbread figure is presented with various parts of its anatomy labeled—the dotted line around the body for expression, the brain for identity, the area between the legs for sex, and the heart for attractions, introducing to the child the components of assigned sex, gender identity, gender expression, and sexual orientation. By assessing the child's understanding of this diagram, information about the child's level of gender literacy is gained. Once these components are introduced, a further discussion about understanding gender identity and expression on a continuum can occur. This can be done by drawing a continuum line corresponding to each of these components (i.e., for the expression line, one might label the ends as "girly girl" and "super boy" or some variation of the language that the child introduces) and then asking the child to place themselves on the continuum for each component. Each of these placements can be followed up with the prompt "Can you tell me why you put yourself there?" while pointing to their position on the line. In this way, the tool provides a range of options that includes identification with the binary (if the child picks the ends of a given spectrum) but also positions beyond the binary.

Incidentally, the Genderbread Person has also proven useful to assess other concepts discussed earlier that are relevant in the GAM. One example is body awareness. Because the "assigned sex" component for the Genderbread Person is drawn between the legs, it provides another avenue to discuss the child's knowledge and comfort/discomfort with genitals and the distinction between genitals, sex assigned at birth, and asserted gender identity. Similarly, the heart symbolizing sexual orientation (attraction), enables the MHP to discuss this component of one's identity. When giving the range of options on the continuum of attraction, the extent to which the child has already internalized heteronormative and homophobic beliefs often becomes obvious relatively quickly.

Parent Involvement in the Assessment

Children are not independent beings and do not live in isolation, so it goes without saying that every effort should be made to involve parent(s) or legal guardian(s) in any mental health assessment or treatment process, including those that address issues related to gender identity. Involving parents is essential for a number of reasons, including the following: (a) to obtain an accurate diagnostic picture and gender history; (b) to more fully understand the family dynamics (both immediate and extended), particularly as related to the child's gender identity and expression; (c) to ascertain the parents' level of support or rejection of the child's gender expansive behaviors, expression, and/or identity; (d) to assess the extent to which the parents may be struggling to understand and appreciate their child's gender and the extent to which they adhere to more traditional, binary and cisnormative notions about gender and to heteronormative beliefs about sexual orientation; (e) to assess discrepancies between what the child desires in terms of how they want to assert their gender identity versus what the parents perceive and feel is most appropriate, including social transition steps; and (f) to develop therapeutic rapport and acknowledge the parents as experts in their child's care as well as a critical part of the assessment team.

Parent Goals in Seeking Assessment

It is probably safe to say that as recently as 10 years ago, most children exhibiting gender expansive behaviors and gender dysphoria were not seen by mental health or medical providers either because they learned to hide this aspect of themselves or because their parents were too confused or ashamed and as a result "dealt" with the issue secretly within the privacy of their home. During this era, the children seen were likely those exhibiting more noticeable gender expansiveness and/or severe dysphoria, and it was not unusual for parents to seek professional assistance to "fix" their child, with a goal toward being comfortable with their assigned sex and the concordant social expectations for the gender matching that assignment.

As the GAM has gained momentum, parents now have implicit permission to seek services without shame and with a new consideration that their child's behavior and identity may not be pathological, but merely a normal variation of human diversity. Some providers and a range of parent-led support groups are now advocating for children to be supported in their asserted gender identity, often including early social transition, without the involvement of an MHP. On the one hand, not automatically including the services of an MHP highlights a positive shift in societal acceptance; on the other hand, because of the stigma that still exists and because the pressures of the gender binary can be so insidiously negative, assessment and consultation with a gender specialist trained in child development can be very helpful when such significant decisions concerning a child's gender are being considered.

Parents who do seek consultation from an MHP are typically hoping to achieve one or more of the following goals: (a) a better understanding of their child's developing gender identity, expressions, and/or sexual orientation; (b) discernment about whether their child is gender expansive, as described previously, or more severely gender dysphoric; (c) prediction regarding their child's future gender identity and sexual orientation; (d) assistance with sharing this aspect of their child's gender identity or expressions with extended family members, schools, religious institutions, neighbors, and friends and soliciting support from those entities; (e) support related to feelings of grief and loss the parents may be experiencing related to their child's true gender self; (f) assistance in determining whether a social transition is in the child's best interest; and (g) documentation of the child's early gender identity to help facilitate potential future medical interventions. Additionally, it is important to note that some parents seek services in the hopes of "fixing" their child; in other words, helping their child feel more comfortable with their assigned sex. Although the GAM does include assisting children in exploring their gender identity and learning about multiple ways to be a boy, a girl, or somewhere in between, the approach does not "help" a child try to be someone they feel they are not. The latter approach promotes a sense of shame (Wallace & Russell, 2013) and is not in line with the GAM. Thus, although the assessment process would proceed similarly in these types of cases of gender exploration in which the parents might desire a "cure," explicit discussions with the parents are needed about how and why the recommended treatment approach is gender affirming. Parents would then be in an informed position to decide whether to continue care after the assessment.

Complicating Factors in the Assessment Process

It is fortunate that many children who present for a gender assessment have supportive parents and are not hindered in their development by complicating factors. However, as with any child, much that occurs during this developmental period is out of their control and dictated by the adults in their life. Thus, because of the continued social stigma related to transgender individuals, these complicating factors are often exacerbated.

Specifically, parents who differ from each other in their understanding and acceptance of their child experience additional stress when dealing with gender-related issues. In some cases, this can result in one parent hiding information from the other (e.g., clothing and toys that are not stereotypical of the child's assigned sex) and only allowing the child to play and dress as their true gender self when the nonsupportive parent is not home. In other cases, the difficulty in parents agreeing with how to address the gender issue may result in separation or divorce. The resulting impact on the child in these situations can be guilt inducing and psychologically damaging, particularly if they perceive their gender identity to be the root cause of the family discord (see Chapter 10).

Families who adhere to more traditional views on gender, sometimes because of cultural or religious factors, also experience added stress. Parents who want to support their child but feel conflicted about doing so due to the incongruence between gender acceptance and their long-held values, beliefs, and traditions about appropriate gender behavior may feel unsettled. In some cases, parents ultimately choose to support their child, but this does not happen without very real consequences. Some cases of families from certain religious denominations have been excommunicated or rejected from the faith when the parents chose to support their gender creative child. Oftentimes, these families have extended family members who may also feel unable to maintain the relationship with the child's immediate family if they believe the parents' supportive behaviors are sinful, irresponsible, or even abusive.

Finally, parents often struggle with the need to tolerate the ambiguity of their child's developing gender identity, to be able to remain suspended in a state of not knowing. As a result, we have sometimes observed parents push for an early social transition of their child, largely because it would ease their own discomfort with either having a child who does not fall neatly in the male or female gender box or a child whose gender is still evolving rather than firmly set. Additionally, with the increased media attention and common use of the phrase *transgender children*, many parents unfamiliar with the existing research misinterpret their child's gender expansive expression and behavior interests as being indicative of a transgender identity, when in fact it may be more related to the child's developing sexual orientation or simply an aspect of their gender fluidity or their gender solidification process. The importance of working with parents around this issue, even during the assessment, cannot be overstated, as a premature social transition, in the ostensible name of parental acceptance, could result in the encouragement of an inauthentic rather than authentic gender self. Even using the term *transgender* to describe prepubescent children who exhibit a consistent, insistent, and persistent identity that is incongruent with their assigned gender, whether gender dysphoria is present or not, should be done with caution, as attaching this label to children who are still early in their developmental gender journey presumes a certain long-term trajectory that simply cannot be predicted for an individual child in the absence of more rigorous longitudinal research. We have no doubt that parents proceed in either promoting a social transition or endorsing a transgender label for their child in an effort to be supportive and affirming of their child, but without consultation with an objective, gender-trained mental health provider to provide guidance, education, and support, such actions inadvertently put the child at risk for potential psychological harm.

Case Study

Justin (Caucasian, 8.5 years old, assigned male at birth) and Justin's mother presented to the clinic reporting, "Justin has been telling me that he is a girl since he could talk." Mother wanted Justin to know that "he is not the only person who feels like this" and "to have support." Mother reported that Justin's "obsession with gender" has decreased over time.

In general, Mother described Justin as a happy child, without concerns about him medically or mental healthwise, and Justin does well academically, socially, and behaviorally at school. On the CBCL, mother's ratings on all competency and syndrome scales were well within the normative range. Justin has a good support system, naming grandparents, a dance teacher, and several friends as important.

Mother's report on the Behavioral Features of Gender Identity in Childhood and the Gender Identity Questionnaire, along with information from the clinical interview yielded the following:

- *Identity statements:* During ages 3 to 5, Justin was very matter of fact in their statements of "I'm a girl." Currently, Justin uses the terminology "half boy/half girl," as a self-descriptor.
- *Anatomic dysphoria:* Other than once at age 5 when Justin said, "I want to cut off my penis," Justin does not state a dislike of sexual anatomy or demonstrate this behaviorally. When younger, Justin believed they would grow up to have breasts. Mother reports that following conversations to the contrary, "He was sad about the reality but now knows this is not the case."
- *Gender expansiveness:* Justin gravitates toward clothing stereotypically considered as girls', including always wearing a swimsuit top with swim trunks. Justin exhibits a strong preference for engaging in play that is stereotypically associated with girls. In imaginative play, Justin will often take the role of girl or woman (e.g., being a female singer in pretend play with friends). Mother reports Justin prefers to play with girls and occasionally displays mannerisms and speech characteristics stereotypically associated with girls. Last, Justin is not interested in rough and tumble play but has no fear associated with this.

With regard to the first drawing on the DAP task, Justin did not specify whether the drawing was a boy or girl but eventually chose girl because "today is a girl day based on pattern." Justin then referenced that he alternates girl/boy every other day as a way to deal with the "are you a girl or a boy question" that peers often ask Justin. Justin then added longer hair with barrettes and some butterflies on the T-shirt signifying these as "girl." Justin's second drawing was slightly smaller than the first but similar in level of detail. In the discussion following, Justin referenced the shorter hair and having "looser straight-across sleeves" on the T-shirt as why the drawing was a boy. Justin differentiated T-shirts with "tighter angled sleeves" as being more "girly." In further discussions about societal beliefs/attitudes in terms of gender, Justin gave examples like "blue is a boy's color, boys play football, and girls do gymnastics" but also added, "but I think anyone should be able to wear anything."

The semistructured interview questions in the Gender Identity Interview for Children pertaining to conviction and wish/desire yielded either ambivalence or comments such as, "I am a boy, but wish I could be a girl." Justin would then follow this with some sort of qualification such as, "But it doesn't matter cause not a big difference so I don't really care." In response to the questions about identity confusion, Justin answered, "I am a boy" but then provided a detailed timeline stating,

> I really felt like a boy but then I started feeling like a girl and thought I was. Then, I got an American Girl doll so I was more "girly," and next I was "just girl," and now I am "between girl and middle" with closer to "middle" because I really like superheroes.

Anatomical dysphoria was assessed in several different ways. Most directly, the mirror questions on the Gender Preference Interview yielded only that Justin wanted a longer hair style. When extending the mirror question to "being naked," Justin shared that the only difference between girls and boys "really is their private parts." This enabled a direct question about how Justin felt about their private parts to which Justin replied, "It's okay, it doesn't bother me." Justin answered the magic wand question with "Get rid of birthmark, different haircut, and have a pet snake." On the final question on the Gender Preference Interview, which asks what the child would have liked to been born as, Justin said, "I asked God for me to be a girl and he didn't give me that. I once got angry but now I am okay with it."

Conclusion

This chapter provided an overview of the overarching areas to assess when working with TGE children and their parents, along with a discussion of ways in which to utilize the available measures in a way that fits within a GAM. A holistic assessment not only attempts to understand a child's gender identity and expressions, including whether gender dysphoria is present, but also attends to levels of gender resilience and gender literacy in both the child and parent(s), as well as gathering information about the child's body awareness. A holistic assessment in a GAM concludes with discussions with parents about (a) the fluidity of gender expression and identity in childhood; (b) the importance of increasing a child's gender literacy and resiliency so they are able to navigate a culture that does not readily embrace gender diversity; (c) the pros and cons of, as well as the appropriate motivations for, initiating a partial or complete social transition and if doing so, the need to provide space for potential change over time; and (d) the role that therapy can play in accomplishing the above.

Although a need clearly exists for improved measures and a deeper understanding of the various developmental trajectories for gender diverse children, the research to date, coupled with the clinical expertise of those engaging in this work, can shed light on recommendations for best practices. Although gender diverse expressions, behaviors, and identities are not pathological, an assessment by a qualified MHP who is also a gender specialist is a critical component of the GAM.

References

Achenbach, T. M., & Edelbrock, C. S. (1983). *Manual for the Child Behavior Checklist and revised profile*. Burlington: Department of Psychiatry, University of Vermont.

Achenbach, T. M., & Edelbrock, C. S. (1986a). *Manual for the Teacher's Report Form and Teacher Version of the Child Behavior Profile*. Burlington: Department of Psychiatry, University of Vermont.

Achenbach, T. M., & Edelbrock, C. S. (1986b). *Manual for the Youth Self-Report and Profile*. Burlington: Department of Psychiatry, University of Vermont.

American Psychiatric Association. (2013). *Diagnostic and statistical manual of mental disorders* (5th ed.). Washington, DC: Author.

Bates, J. E., & Bentler, P. M., (1973). Play activities of normal and effeminate boys. *Developmental Psychology, 9*, 20–27.

Bates, J. E., Bentler, P. M., & Thompson, S. K. (1973). Measurement of deviant gender behaviour in boys. *Child Development, 44*, 591–598.

Beitchman, J. H. (1996). *FAB: Feelings, Attitudes and Behaviors Scale for Children*. Toronto, Ontario, Canada: Multi-Health Systems.

Berg, D., Spencer, K., Becker-Warner, R., Vencill, J., McGuire, J. K., & Catalpa, J. (2016, June). *The gender affirmative lifespan approach: Promoting positive identity by increasing gender literacy, moving beyond the binary, building resiliency, and developing pleasure-based sexuality.* Symposium conducted at the World Professional Association for Transgender Health Conference, Amsterdam, the Netherlands.

Burns, R. C., & Kaufman, S. H. (1972). *Actions, styles and symbols in Kinetic Family Drawing (K-F-D): An interpretative manual.* New York, NY: Brunner and Mazer.

Cassidy, J., & Marvin, R. S. (1992). *Attachment organization in three- and four-year-olds.* Unpublished manual, University of Virginia at Charlottesville.

Chiu, S. W., Gervan, S., Fairbrother, C., Johnson, L. L., Owen-Anderson, A. F. H., Bradley, S. J., & Zucker, K. J. (2006). Sex-dimorphic color preference in children with gender identity disorder: A comparison to clinical and community controls. *Sex Roles, 55*, 385–395.

Cohen-Kettenis, P. T., & Pfäfflin, F. (2003). *Transgenderism and intersexuality in childhood and adolescence: Vol. 46. Making choices*. London, England: Sage.

de Vries, A. L., & Cohen-Kettenis, P. T. (2012). Clinical management of gender dysphoria in children and adolescents: The Dutch approach. *Journal of Homosexuality, 59*, 301–320. http://dx.doi.org/10.1080/00918369.2012.653300

de Vries, A. L., Noens, I. L., Cohen-Kettenis, P. T., van Berckelaer-Onnes, I. A., & Doreleijers, T. A. (2010). Autism spectrum disorders in gender dysphoric children and adolescents. *Journal of Autism and Developmental Disorders, 40,* 930–936. http://dx.doi.org/10.1007/s10803-010-0935-9

Derogatis, L. (1983). *SCL-90: Administration, scoring and procedures manual for the revised version.* Baltimore, MD: Clinical Psychometric Research.

Drescher, J., & Byne, W. (2013). *Treating transgender children and adolescents: An interdisciplinary discussion.* New York, NY: Routledge.

Edwards-Leeper, L., Leibowitz, S., & Sangganjanavanich, V. F. (2016). Affirmative practice with transgender and gender nonconforming youth: Expanding the model. *Psychology of Sexual Orientation and Gender Diversity, 3,* 165–172. http://dx.doi.org/10.1037/sgd0000167

Ehrensaft, D. (2012). From gender identity disorder to gender identity creativity: True gender self child therapy. *Journal of Homosexuality, 59,* 337–356. http://dx.doi.org/10.1080/00918369.2012.653303

Ehrensaft, D. (2016). *The gender creative child: Pathways for nurturing and supporting children who live outside gender boxes.* New York, NY: The Experiment, LLC.

Elisabeth, P. H., & Green, R. (1984). Childhood sex role behaviors: Similarities and differences in twins. *Acta Geneticae Medicae et Gemellologiae, 33,* 173–179.

Fridell, S. R., Owen-Anderson, A., Johnson, L. L., Bradley, S. J., & Zucker, K. J. (2006). The Playmate and Play Style Preferences Structured Interview: A comparison of children with gender identity disorder and controls. *Archives of Sexual Behavior, 35,* 729–737.

Golombok, S., & Rust, J. (1994). The pre-school activities inventory: A standardized assessment of gender role in children. *Psychological Assessment, 5,* 131–136.

Green, R., Fuller, M., & Rutley, B. (1972). It-Scale for Children and Draw-a-Person test: 30 feminine vs. 25 masculine boys. *Journal of Personality Assessment, 36,* 349–352. http://dx.doi.org/10.1080/00223891.1972.10119770

Johnson, L. L., Bradley, S. J., Birkenfeld-Adams, A. S., Kuksis, M. A., Maing, D. M., Mitchell, J. N., & Zucker, K. J. (2004). A parent-report gender identity questionnaire for children. *Archives of Sexual Behavior, 33,* 105–116. http://dx.doi.org/10.1023/B:ASEB.0000014325.68094.f3

Keo-Meier, C. L., & Fitzgerald, K. M. (2017). Affirmative psychological testing and neurocognitive assessment with transgender adults. *Psychiatric Clinics of North America, 40,* 51–64. http://dx.doi.org/10.1016/j.psc.2016.10.011

Key, A. (2014). Children. In L. Erickson-Schroth (Ed.), *Trans bodies, trans selves: A resource for the transgender community* (pp. 409–445). New York, NY: Oxford University Press.

Leinbach, M. D., & Fagot, B. I. (1986). Acquisition of gender labelling: A test for toddlers. *Sex Roles, 15,* 655–666.

Menvielle, E. (2012). A comprehensive program for children with gender variant behaviors and gender identity disorders. *Journal of Homosexuality, 59,* 357–368. http://dx.doi.org/10.1080/00918369.2012.653305

Meyer-Bahlburg, H. F. L., Sandberg, D. E., Dolezal, C. L., & Yager, T. J. (1994). Gender-related assessment of childhood play. *Journal of Abnormal Child Psychology, 22,* 643–660.

Rekers, G. A., Rosen, A. C., & Morey, S. M. (1990). Projective test findings for boys with gender disturbance: Draw-a-Person test, It-Scale, and Make-a-Picture-Story test. *Perceptual and Motor Skills, 71*, 771–779.

Rekers, G. A., & Yates, C. E. (1976). Sex-typed play in feminoid boys versus normal boys and girls. *Journal of Abnormal Child Psychology, 4*, 1–8.

Skilbeck, W. M., Bentler, P. M., & Bates, J. E. (1975). Human figure drawings of gender-problem and school-problem boys. *Journal of Abnormal Child Psychology, 3*, 191–199. http://dx.doi.org/10.1007/BF00916750

Slaby, R. G., & Frey, K. S. (1975). Development of gender constancy and selective attention to same-sex models. *Child Development, 52*, 849–856.

Spanier, G. B. (1976). Measuring dyadic adjustment: new scales for assessing the quality of marriage and similar dyads. *Journal of Marriage and the Family, 38*, 15–28.

Steensma, T. D., Biemond, R., de Boer, F., & Cohen-Kettenis, P. T. (2011). Desisting and persisting gender dysphoria after childhood: A qualitative follow-up study. *Clinical Child Psychology and Psychiatry, 16*, 499–516. http://dx.doi.org/10.1177/1359104510378303

Steensma, T. D., McGuire, J. K., Kreukels, B. P., Beekman, A. J., & Cohen-Kettenis, P. T. (2013). Factors associated with desistence and persistence of childhood gender dysphoria: A quantitative follow-up study. *Journal of the American Academy of Child & Adolescent Psychiatry, 52*, 582–590. http://dx.doi.org/10.1016/j.jaac.2013.03.016

Testa, R. J., Habarth, J., Peta, J., Balsam, K., & Bockting, W. (2015). Development of the Gender Minority Stress and Resilience Measure. *Psychology of Sexual Orientation and Gender Diversity, 2*, 65–77. http://dx.doi.org/10.1037/sgd0000081

Veerman, J. W., Straathof, M. A. E., Treffers, P. D. A., Van den Bergh, B. R. H., & ten Brink, L. T. (1997). *De Competentiebelevingsschaal voor kindern, CBSK: Handleiding* [The Competence Perception Scale for Children (CBSK): Handbook]. Lisse: Swetz & Zeitlinger.

Wallace, R., & Russell, H. (2013). Attachment and shame in gender-nonconforming children and their families: Toward a theoretical framework for evaluating clinical interventions. *International Journal of Transgenderism, 14*, 113–126. http://dx.doi.org/10.1080/15532739.2013.824845

Wallien, M. S. C., Quilty, L. C., Steensma, T. D., Singh, D., Lambert, S. L., Leroux, A., . . . Zucker, K. J. (2009). Cross-national replication of the Gender Identity Interview for Children. *Journal of Personality Assessment, 91*, 545–552.

Zucker, K. J. (1992). Gender identity disorder. In S. R. Hooper, G. W. Hynd, & R. E. Mattison (Eds.), *Child psychopathology: Diagnostic criteria and clinical assessment* (pp. 305–342). Hillsdale, NJ: Erlbaum.

Zucker, K. J., & Bradley, S. J. (1995). *Gender identity disorder and psychosexual problems in children and adolescents*. New York, NY: Guilford Press.

Zucker, K. J., Bradley, S. J., Doering, R. W., & Lozinsky, J. A. (1985). Sex-typed behaviour in cross-gender identified children: Stability and change at a one-year follow-up. *Journal of the American Academy of Child Psychiatry, 24*, 710–719.

Zucker, K. J., Bradley, S. J., Kuksis, M., Pecore, K., Birkenfeld-Aams, A., Doering, R. W., . . . Wild, J. (1999). Gender constancy judgments in children with gender identity disorder: Evidence for a developmental lag. *Archives of Sexual Behavior, 28*, 475–502.

Zucker, K. J., Bradley, S. J., & Lowry Sullivan, C. B. (1996). Traits of separation anxiety in boys with gender identity disorder. *Journal of the American Academy of Child and Adolescent Psychiatry, 35*, 791–798.

Zucker, K. J., Bradley, S. J., Sullivan, C. B., Kuksis, M., Birkenfeld-Adams, A., & Mitchell, J. N., (1993). A gender identity interview for children. *Journal of Personality Assessment, 61*, 443–456. http://dx.doi.org/10.1207/s15327752jpa6103_2

Zucker, K. J., Doering, R. W., Bradley, S. J., & Finegan, J. K. (1982). Sex-typed play in gender-disturbed children: a comparison to sibling and psychiatric controls. *Archives of Sexual Behavior, 11*, 309–321.

Zucker, K. J., Finegan, J. A., Doering, R. W., & Bradley, S. J. (1983). Human figure drawings of gender-problem children: A comparison to sibling, psychiatric, and normal controls. *Journal of Abnormal Child Psychology, 11*, 287–298. http://dx.doi.org/10.1007/BF00912092

Zucker, K. J., Lozinski, J. A., Bradley, S. J., & Doering, R. W. (1992). Sex-typed responses in the Rorschach protocols of children with gender identity disorder. *Journal of Personality Assessment, 58*, 295–310.

Zucker, K. J., Mitchell, J. N., Bradley, S. J., Tkachuk, J., Cantor, J. M., & Allin, S. M. (2006). The Recalled Childhood Gender Identity/Gender Role Questionnaire: Psychometric properties. *Sex Roles, 54*, 469–483.

Zucker, K. J., Wood, H., Singh, D., & Bradley, S. J. (2012). A developmental, biopsychosocial model for the treatment of children with gender identity disorder. *Journal of Homosexuality, 59*, 369–397. http://dx.doi.org/10.1080/00918369.2012.653309

Deb Coolhart

Helping Families Move From Distress to Attunement

8

Although the numbers of families that are able to respond to their child's gender diverse identity and/or expressions with acceptance or at least tolerance (Malpas, 2011) has increased, for many families, these responses are accompanied by varying levels of distress. It is common for parents to wrestle with difficult feelings, such as fear for their child's safety, disappointment, anxiety, embarrassment, blame, confusion, anger, concern, denial, self-blame, and shame (Lev, 2004; Malpas, 2011). Parents may also experience direct loss, where they feel like they are losing their child, or ambiguous loss, where the loss is indistinct and confusing (Boss, 1999), both of which can lead to a grieving process.

When a family seeks the assistance of a clinician because of distress about their child's gender diverse identity or expressions, it can be a delicate balance to support both the child and the parents, as well as the siblings. The stance of a gender affirmative clinician is that a transgender and gender expansive (TGE) child should be helped to live and express gender in ways that are most comfortable for the child (Hidalgo et al., 2013). Often, gender expressions that are most comfortable for the child are not comfortable for the family, and in fact, cause distress for the family. Therefore, clinicians must find ways to support and validate parents' emotional processes while simultaneously creating safety and support for the child.

http://dx.doi.org/10.1037/0000095-008
The Gender Affirmative Model: An Interdisciplinary Approach to Supporting Transgender and Gender Expansive Children, C. Keo-Meier and D. Ehrensaft (Editors)
Copyright © 2018 by the American Psychological Association. All rights reserved.

As clinicians work with families in distress, it is important to keep in mind that these families are in a process that usually shifts and changes over time. In other words, when families begin therapy struggling with a child's gender, often where they begin emotionally is not where they end up eventually. Although it is assumed in the gender affirmative model that each parent wants the best for their child, that intent may be undermined by their actual interactions with their TGE child. In that context, the goal of therapy is to help families reach an increased level of attunement to their child. The term *attunement* implies reaching a level of harmony, understanding, and peace with their child's gender self. This moves beyond the idea of tolerating or accepting the presence of gender diversity as though it is a problem that will not go away. Rather, in reaching attunement, families recognize that gender diversity is a normal variation of humanity and the challenges that families face are due to society's inability to embrace these natural variations. This chapter aims to provide strategies for creating balance between support for parents and for the TGE child, to address common presentations of family distress as it relates to a child's gender identity and expression, and to discuss pathways for families to achieve a greater level of attunement with their child's true gender self.

Structuring Sessions

When families are in distress, oftentimes they are expressing views, thoughts, and feelings that are hurtful to the child. For example, parents may be presenting in therapy saying things like, "He shouldn't be acting like a girl. It is just wrong! I refuse to see him as a girl," or "She thinks she's a little boy, which is the most ridiculous thing I have ever heard. It's breaking my heart. It's killing me." Gender affirmative treatment aims to normalize the child's gender and assist parents in helping their child develop self-esteem (Lev, 2004). One role of the clinician is to help parents understand ways in which their communications may be hurtful to their child and encourage them not to share such thoughts and feelings directly with their child. Sometimes separate sessions with parents followed by sessions with the child alone are necessary if the parents' emotions are intense and potentially harmful to the child (Coolhart, 2012; Coolhart, Baker, Farmer, Malaney, & Shipman, 2013; Coolhart & Shipman, 2017).

Sessions with the child aim to support the child's true gender self and expression of that self and build rapport for later joint sessions with parents. The clinician should be transparent with parents that the approach taken in the sessions alone with the child is informed by a gender affirmative perspective and that the clinician will be honoring the child's wishes in sessions regarding gender. For example, the clinician will be facilitating the child expressing gender in whatever ways feel most congruent for the child and the clinician will be using whatever name and pronouns the child requests. Parents in distress about their child's gender presentation may struggle with their perception that their child's gender expression is being "encouraged" by the clinician. If that becomes an issue, clinicians can explain to parents that a nonaffirmative approach may cause harm to the child and if parents are still not comfortable enough, clinicians can first work with parents alone, without meeting with the child, until enough trust is established in the therapeutic process for parents to arrive at a comfort level that would enable them to include the child in sessions that will be adopting the gender affirmative approach.

In this approach, it is important to meet parents where they are while supporting the child's gender identity and expression. The last thing we want to do as clinicians is to alienate parents, causing them to discontinue the therapy. For example, when parents are not able to tolerate the therapist using the child's chosen name and pronouns, a first step may be to avoid using a name (i.e., using "your child") and using gender neutral pronouns (i.e., "they/them"). This approach holds the parents, struggle while avoiding misgendering the child.

Ultimately, the therapeutic goal is to have joint sessions including both the parents and the child to discuss ways in which they will incorporate the child's gender identity and/or expressions into their family. We can think of these as "difficult dialogues" (Stone Fish & Harvey, 2005), as important interchanges affording family members an opportunity to process misconceptions and damaging interactions so that everyone in the family can develop a new appreciation for each other. Although these difficult dialogues facilitate treatment goals, the child's safety and well-being, along with the establishment of a gender affirming environment, should be the priority before these difficult dialogues occur. With some families, the milieu is safe enough for the child to begin family sessions immediately, whereas other families may need more time with separate parent and child sessions. When parents have had enough space to process their own positions and vent the hurtful emotions and expressions away from their child, family sessions including the child can begin. The following section discusses strategies for facilitating this work with parents.

Improving Gender Literacy: Providing Parents With Accurate Gender Education

In sessions alone with parents, clinicians can help parents sort out topics to be discussed directly with the child from those better suited for processing separate from the child. Many times, this process will include providing accurate education regarding the differences between sex, gender identity, gender expression, sexual orientation, and related concepts. Gender affirmative clinicians recommend that providing information and education about gender diversity should be a part of supportive psychotherapy; in that sense, gender affirmative therapy can also be approached as a psychoeducational opportunity (Lev, 2004; Malpas, 2011). In working with families in distress regarding their TGE child, many times the therapist functions as a teacher and a coach, providing accurate information and helping parents develop increasingly supportive responses to their child. Although this resembles a directive approach, care should be taken so that parents feel neither proselytized nor chastised. The key is to fully listen to parents' current beliefs and feelings, hold and validate their struggle, and utilize therapeutic timing to gently challenge parents to expand how they think and feel about gender diversity. Clinicians will be ineffective in helping TGE children unless they are able to establish a loving and trusting rapport with parents, valuing their challenges and strengths as parents.

Starting with the basics, sessions can be used as a space to explore, deconstruct, and expand family's beliefs about gender and sexuality. Parents can be asked to reflect on where they learned their beliefs (e.g., family of origin, society). The objective is to allow parents space to express their views within a relationship in which they can feel heard and validated. Even though their views may differ from the clinician's, the clinician should strive to understand and acknowledge parents' views and the contexts that facilitated their development. The intersections and influences of other cultural identities, such as religion, race, class, and so on, and the impact these cultural locations have on their feelings about gender can also be explored. As parents explore the origins of their beliefs, clinicians can gently challenge parents to recognize ways in which their views may be hurtful to their child, inviting them to entertain other possible views of gender and sexuality.

At this point in therapy, some parents are desperate to understand what caused the gender diversity in their child. Some parents may think it was caused by a traumatic experience in the child's life. Other parents may think that their child has been exposed to negative role models from people of their same gender, causing the child to reject that gender; that fighting in their marriage must have caused a child to align and identify with their opposite-gender parent; or that they must have done something wrong in their parenting to have caused this to happen. Clinicians should provide ample space for parents to fully express their theories and concerns about why their child is presenting as gender expansive and resist the urge to shut down their process prematurely. Parents in this stage are typically responding to the societal message that something "causes" gender diversity. Although the parents' theories can sometimes seem far-fetched to clinicians, parents should be regarded with compassion, recognizing that their need to find the cause of their child's gender diversity typically comes from a place of concern and love for their child. If parents are concerned that their child is expressing gender diversity as a response to trauma, clinicians should explore whether trauma actually occurred and what effects it may be having on the child, including possible connections to gender diversity. Such an empathic approach helps clinicians develop strong rapport with parents. While allowing space for parents to search for a cause, a gender affirmative clinician also expresses the position that gender diversity does not have a known "cause" but is something that develops naturally for people. It is helpful to communicate that gender nonconformity is rarely caused by stressors (Malpas, 2011), is most often not caused by trauma, and exists in healthy families of all kinds (Brill & Pepper, 2008). Although the field of the etiology of gender identity is young in its development, clinicians should stay up-to-date on the emerging research. For some parents, it can be comforting to hear about what is being studied, what the current theories are about how gender identity develops, and what trends are being discovered about the emergence of gender variation.

Parents' need to understand the cause of their child's gender diversity may be arising from a sense that they are "to blame." Family members or friends may have been giving them the message that they have encouraged the behavior in some way. Traditional writings from the fields of developmental and clinical psychology support such notions, only adding to parents' confusion or guilt. For example, parents may regret letting their child who was assigned male at birth play with dolls or allowing their female-assigned child to be a tomboy. In some families, one parent may blame the other parent for their child's gender diversity. Clinicians can assure parents that the gender diversity is no one's "fault," that it is something that is a part of who the child is, and that nothing they did or did not do could have caused or prevented the gender diversity.

Clinicians can also talk with parents about ways to respond when others imply they are to blame for the child's gender identity and expression. For some parents, an educational response may be the best fit, such as, "Research indicates that gender diversity is a natural occurrence with no known cause." Other parents may prefer to respond more personally—"I am only allowing space for my child to discover who they are, and I love that person!" Further, clinicians can create role-plays of situations the parents could foresee arising, allowing them to practice responses in difficult circumstances. If parents are most concerned about the questions they are getting from their own parents, the clinician can take on the role of the grandparents and ask the questions they might likely ask. As parents respond to these "interrogations," the clinician can coach them around language use, information that may be the most helpful to communicate, and clarity about information that may be nobody's business. It can often be helpful to empower the family to make their own decisions about boundaries, including whose questions they will answer and how much energy they will spend educating others, as many parents will mistakenly believe that it is their responsibility to educate anyone who asks about their child.

Parents often wonder what their child's asserted gender self means for the future: Will someone harm my child? Will my child make a gender transition? Will my child end up depressed or suicidal? Will my child be able to find a partner? If their child is requesting a gender transition, either with or without medical interventions, they may worry what will happen if their child changes their mind later or has regrets. Such angst can be particularly poignant when the child's gender story does not match the popular media representation of "the" transgender experience, that is, a clear cross-gender identification showing up by around age 4 or 5 accompanied by extreme distress when forced to live in a wrong gender box, a box matching the sex assigned on the birth certificate. Clinicians can help parents understand that a variety of gender paths exist for both gender identities and gender expressions and that often no clear future outcome is in evidence at an early age. Although gender diversity most commonly emerges in early childhood or at the onset of puberty (Brill & Pepper, 2008), it can develop at any time during childhood (or adulthood, for that matter), and different people have different experiences (see Chapter 3, this volume).

Parental understanding of the evolutionary aspects of gender serves as an important protective factor. According to Ehrensaft (2011), "Parents will have to unlearn the idea that it is our role to keep our children on the straight and narrow path prescribed by society" (p. 41). This reeducation about gender in all its iterations, countering the dominant societal narrative, can be helpful, and clinicians should communicate to parents that their child's gender presentation is not negative or pathological; rather, their child is normal regardless of how they wish to express gender.

Processing Parents' Loss and Fear

Parents in distress about their child's gender are often overwhelmed with emotions that are difficult to manage, particularly loss and fear. Two common types of losses that parents of TGE children experience are the loss of hopes and dreams for their child and the perceived loss of one child while another child emerges (Brill & Pepper, 2008). The first type of loss is often experienced as the loss of gender-related rites of passage, and the expression of grief in relation to loss. For example, some parents grieve the loss of their dream of seeing their daughter in a wedding dress on her wedding day. The second type of loss is an ambiguous loss, defined as a loss that is indistinct and confusing (Boss, 1999). Parents of TGE children may experience a "dual ambiguous loss," which is characterized by (a) the child's being physically present and psychologically absent and (b) the child's being psychologically present and physically absent (Wahlig, 2015). In the first type of ambiguous loss, the parents physically still have a child, but the child's psychological existence as a certain gender may be perceived as gone. In the second type, much of the child's personality and psychological sense of self are present, but the child's physical presence as a certain gender is gone. As with any experience of loss, these feelings take time to move through, and parents can be supported in their articulation of these feelings. Clinicians can also normalize these feelings, letting parents know that many other parents of TGE children have similar feelings. Parents may benefit from meeting other families in support groups and/or attending gender conferences, as the topic of grieving frequently arises in these settings. Helping the parents to grieve separate from the child can minimize the responsibility the child may feel for their parents' grief and also give the child space to have a separate set of feelings, especially elation and relief accompanying the freedom to live in their authentic gender.

Fear is also often central in the emotional experience of parents of TGE children and can take different forms, such as fear for the safety and well-being of the child or fear of condemnation (Brill & Pepper, 2008). Parents may also fear that their child will not be able to find love or be a parent. When parents are organized by fear, they are living in the future of "what ifs" rather than the present potentials and may be prevented from clearly seeing what is in the best interest of their child. Thus, therapy should provide space for exploring and processing parents' fears. When parents' anxiety is decreased, they can have more control over their fears and can recognize that their needs are separate from their child's (Malpas, 2011). Clinicians can help parents articulate the fears, the source of those fears, and the level of control they have over their fears being actualized. For example, parents may not have much control over the reactions of extended family members, but they do have control over their disclosure of their child's gender nonconformity, the boundaries they set in their familial relationships, their responses to conflicts, and their support of their child through the conflict. Similarly, parents may not have much control over the responses of their child's schoolmates, but they can help equip their child with love and confidence and practice strategies for dealing with mistreatment. Further, parents can advocate for their child's protection in the school setting.

Coaching Parents to Listen to Their Child

When parents are struggling to support their child's gender diversity, clinicians can reflect their feelings (e.g., "This experience is very challenging for you") while communicating to them that the statements they are making about their child's gender qualify as rejecting behavior that can have a negative impact on the child's long-term emotional and physical well-being. Parents are often worried about the discrimination their child will face, a valid concern; in these instances, clinicians can make them aware of current research which suggests parental support to be a major protective factor for children and youth in the face of any transphobic reactions. Young adults who experience high parental rejection of their lesbian, gay, bisexual, or transgender identity are more likely to attempt suicide, to report high levels of depression, to use illegal drugs, and to engage in unprotected sex (Ryan, Huebner, Diaz, & Sanchez, 2009). On the other hand, parental acceptance is predictive of higher self-esteem, social support, and better general health status (Ryan, Russell, Huebner, Diaz, & Sanchez, 2010), as well as higher grade point averages and greater levels of school belonging (Watson, Barnett, & Russell, 2016). Research on TGE people specifically corroborates these findings (Grant et al., 2011; James et al., 2016; Travers et al., 2012), confirming that the level of support parents provide to their TGE children has a long-term impact.

The first step for parents in supporting their child's gender development is to gain an understanding of their child's experience. Clinicians can coach parents to simply listen to what their child is experiencing and how their child feels. According to Ehrensaft (2011), "listening to children and paying attention to what they are telling you about their authentic gender self is the cornerstone of helping them grow healthy and strong" (p. 103). Although this sounds simple and straightforward, it is often difficult for parents to do. Their own emotional processes can get in the way of truly listening to their child. Most of the time, parents' love for their child is at the core of their distress. They do not want their child to experience the difficult path that accompanies gender diversity and possible eventual gender transition. Clinicians can access this love as the source of distress and use it as a building block for future increased attunement around gender, assuring parents that what their child needs from them the most is for them to really listen. According to Lev (2004), parents "need to learn to love their children as they are and not send messages of disappointment" (p. 335). Although parents have little control over their child's gender identity, they do have control over how they respond to their child. Their responses can have a significant effect on their child's self-acceptance, well-being, social–emotional adjustment, and safety (Malpas, 2011).

In parent–child sessions, clinicians can encourage the child to discuss their feelings and self-perceptions about their gender; when they first felt they were different, if they did, or were aware of their affirmed gender; and how it feels when forced to express gender in a way that is uncomfortable for them. During these sessions, parents may still deny or repudiate their child's experiences. The clinician's role, then, is to gently coach them to listen in a nonreactive way. For example, a parent might say, "It's just that there was no evidence of this early on. He always fit right in with the boys." In these moments, clinicians can invite parents to take seriously what their child is communicating by asking, "What if what your child is saying is true? That even though you didn't see it, your child was in pain at that time?"

Working With Siblings

Parents of TGE children often express concern about the effects of their child's gender presentations on their other children. They may worry that the child's gender diversity will cause siblings distress and confusion. Little research has been done on this topic, although anecdotally, siblings sometimes exhibit less distress regarding their sibling's gender identity or expressions than parents do, perhaps because siblings are less invested in a sibling's outcome than parents are. Siblings are also growing up in a different generation than their parents, one with more information about and exposure to diverse expressions of gender and sexuality, which may also contribute to the ease with which many of them are able to understand and support their TGE sibling.

Yet in other families, siblings may experience significant distress about having a TGE sibling, sometimes struggling more than parents (Brill & Pepper, 2008). Although parents may have fears about telling siblings about their other sibling's gender expansiveness or transgender identity, it is important that siblings be aware of and become involved in the process of their sibling presenting as their gender outside the home because the siblings may very likely receive questions and hear comments about it from their peers. In fact, it is common for peers to first ask questions of the sibling before asking the gender diverse child. Families will be best equipped if they are able to discuss gender diversity with all immediate family members, decide on the level of privacy the family wants to have (i.e., what gets to be known by whom and what stays within the immediate family), and talk about how to handle any questions or mistreatment siblings may encounter.

When siblings struggle, they, like the parents, may be experiencing feelings of loss and grief—for the sister who is no longer a sister, for example. They may have concerns about their friends' or schoolmates' reactions to their sibling's gender expression. They may be teased, bullied, or asked why their brother is wearing a dress or their sister got a buzz cut. They may feel that all the attention in the family, even if it is negative, is being given to the TGE sibling. Clinicians can create space for siblings to express these feelings, sensitizing the parents to their other children's struggles.

Siblings may have internalized transphobic messages about gender diversity. Clinicians may need to use some of the previously discussed strategies for parents with siblings as well, such as educating them about various gender paths and normalizing gender diversity. When siblings are particularly distressed, they can become the worst enemy of the TGE child, outing them at school or generally harassing or mistreating them. If this occurs, clinicians can work with parents to support the siblings who are struggling while also preventing them from abusing their TGE sibling. Clinicians can work with siblings in transitioning from enemies to allies.

Although much of the work with siblings may be done in family sessions, it may be helpful for them to also have individual sessions, depending on their level of distress. Siblings can discuss their specific concerns and fears, and clinicians can help them develop strategies for dealing with specific situations that may arise. For example, sessions can include role playing ways to tell a friend about their TGE sib or respond to a transphobic peer at school. Some siblings may do best with a response set of support and advocacy for their gender expansive sibling, in the context of a protective and proactive stance, which might include educating peers about gender expansiveness or normalizing their sibling's gender expression. Other siblings may do best with a more noninterventionist approach, such as responding to peers' queries with, "I don't really get it, it's just their thing." Clinicians can help siblings figure out an approach that feels most fitting for them.

Community Connections

Gender affirmative clinicians generally recommend that parents and children be connected with other people in the community who share their experiences (Brill & Pepper, 2008; Coolhart, 2012; Lev, 2004). It can be most helpful for families to have the opportunity to meet other children and parents face-to-face in groups where experiences can be discussed, processed, and normalized. Malpas (2011) discussed how parents who are able to engage in multifamily groups are able to not only connect with others around shared experiences but also to maintain or restore the bond with their child by having space to process their experiences in an honest, nonjudgmental space. Although therapy is a helpful setting to discuss experiences, the benefit of meeting others who are going through, or have successfully navigated, similar challenging situations can be additionally validating. Of course, group settings are not a fit for all children and parents; some may not feel comfortable sharing personal information with multiple people, and some may feel alienated by groups when their experiences differ from dominant narratives. Therefore, parents and children should ultimately decide what feels most helpful for them.

It is unfortunate that many families do not live in areas with access to supportive youth and parent groups. In these cases, parents and children can be referred to reading materials, online resources, and Internet-based support groups where they can experience some of the same benefits of mutuality and normalization. The following books, for example, can be informative, comforting, and guiding resources for parents of gender fluid children: Brill and Pepper's (2008) *The Transgender Child: A Handbook for Families and Professionals*; Tando's (2016) *The Conscious Parent's Guide to Gender Identity: A Mindful Approach to Embracing Your Child's Authentic Self*; and Ehrensaft's (2011) *Gender Born, Gender Made: Raising Healthy Gender-Nonconforming Children* and *The Gender Creative Child* (2016). Many useful resources are available online, such as Gender Spectrum (http://www.genderspectrum.org) and Trans Youth Family Allies (http://www.imatyfa.org), which provide resources for gender diverse youth and their parents and allies. Gender Spectrum Lounge (http://www.genderspectrum.org/we-can-help/the-lounge/) provides a place for gender diverse youth and parents to connect around issues related to gender identity and expressions. Many families may feel as if they are the only one dealing with gender diversity, so learning about the experiences of others can greatly reduce feelings of isolation (Lev, 2004). Additionally, families can be made aware of opportunities where they may spend time with other gender fluid children and their families (e.g., Camp Aranu'tiq or the annual Gender Spectrum/Odyssey/Infinity family conferences), although some of these may involve travel.

Pathways to Increased Attunement

As parents work through their distress, several paths may lead them to an increased level of attunement with their child's gender diversity; clinicians can help parents navigate these paths. Increased attunement can come through the realization that gender diversity is not "just a phase" but a stable part of their child's experience. Parents in distress sometimes have pathology-oriented ideas about why people develop gender diversity, which can be explored and challenged, as previously discussed. Parents may have developed these ideas on the basis of previous experiences with mental health professionals or literature, which have historically taken a more pathological view. Clinicians can talk with parents about current trends in the field, which take a more gender affirmative approach. The child, on the other hand, may have a much more naturalistic view of their gender experience, such as believing that nothing caused their gender, rather that it has always just been there. Discussing multiple perspectives can help parents expand their views and feelings about gender diversity, helping them to see that it is not a problem to be fixed but is something that will be with their child potentially for a lifetime—thus, it is something they can strive to embrace.

Parents also increase attunement by recognizing the presence of gender diversity in their child's history, if it was indeed present. Clinicians can facilitate this process by asking parents what they recall about their child's early gender expressions or assertions. By reflecting on early experiences, parents may bring into focus ways their child expressed gender diversity early in life, sometimes at as early as 2 or 3 years old. Clinicians can also ask the child to share early memories, experiences, and emotions around gender expression and socialization. Children can often recall specific times when they felt different or uncomfortable being forced into an assigned gender role. For example, a child who was assigned female at birth might remember being forced to wear a dress for their kindergarten graduation and being embarrassed and ashamed at the forced feminine expression. Similarly, a child who was assigned male may recall being punished for playing dress-up with his sisters and confused about why the sisters did not receive any punishment. Clinicians can help parents listen to and have compassion for the distress and/or dysphoria their child may have been experiencing over time as a result of being blocked from expressing externally how they have been feeling internally with regard to gender.

Finally, witnessing their child's happiness upon being afforded the opportunity to express gender in a way that feels congruent and authentic offers a third pathway for increased parental attunement. Often, as children actualize their internal gender experience more outwardly, they feel better and signs of distress decrease. Clinicians can assist parents in seeing these positive changes by inviting them to discuss their observations of their child's level of happiness before and after the gender diversity was acknowledged and addressed. Clinicians can also invite the child to talk about how it feels to be able to express their gender openly. If parents are not allowing the expression of gender diversity at home or if they limit its expression only to the home, the youth can reflect on how it feels to experience the gender safe space in therapy with no monitoring or limitations. It can also be helpful for the child to identify triggers of their gender dysphoria, if the child is experiencing dysphoria, and ways the dysphoria emotionally impacts the child. Bearing witness to their child's experience can help parents see that pushing the child toward a gender role socially congruent with the child's assigned sex but incongruent with the child's affirmed gender can be harmful to their child and that freedom of gender expression has the opposite effect—it is emotionally beneficial for the child.

As Attunement Increases

As parents' levels of distress decrease and attunement increases, they may be able to slowly tolerate broader discussions of gender identity and expressions. By this time, the clinician will have a clearer sense of the nature of the child's gender experience. For example, the clinician will likely know whether the child simply wants to be able to express "masculine" or "feminine" behaviors or whether it is the child's gender identity that needs to be addressed, or both. At this time, the clinician can begin to advocate for the child with the parents, helping them find ways to support the child's gender.

For example, if the child desires gender transition, the clinician can discuss the idea of transition and what that might look like for the family. Discussions may include parents' feelings of readiness for such a step, the potential for extended family support, the child's safety in the family's community if transition occurs, and support (or lack thereof) in the school environment. Additionally, it should be considered whether the child's personality, sensitivities, and temperament, or attributes of introversion versus extroversion would support or create challenges to a transition at this particular time. With preadolescent children, clinicians can also begin to talk about different options for gender affirmation, including social transition, disclosure to people outside the family, and, as the child approaches puberty, puberty blockers (see Chapter 12, this volume). It is important to note that gender affirmation is not a one-size-fits-all process; each person has their own unique path. Children who are experiencing significant distress and dysphoria in the gender they are living in may move through transition rapidly, whereas children who experience less distress or more gender ambiguity may take steps in transition at a slower rate or may only take one step. It is essential to listen to the child, while balancing parents' readiness and concerns, and make decisions that are in the best interest of the child and family.

Clinicians can explore with parents how they can be supportive of their child's gender self. Some children may want their parents to use a new chosen name and appropriate pronouns. Clinicians can discuss parents' comfort with this shift as well as consider situations in which the name and pronouns should be used (i.e., only in the home, everywhere). If the child is concerned more with gender expression than gender identity, the clinician can encourage the parents to take steps to support those gender expressions (i.e., allowing preferred clothing, presentation, activities) at first in the home, and then if the child desires, outside the home. The qualification here is that by delivering a message to children that at present the expressions are acceptable at home but not elsewhere, children who are eager to express themselves everywhere may internalize the message that the expressions are still something to be hidden or to be shameful about. If it is necessary to limit such a child's expressions to the home environment, it should be communicated to the child that this limitation is not because something is wrong with the child but because the world still has some learning to do about gender expansiveness (Ehrensaft, 2011, 2016). With that said, it is important to discuss with the parents the child's safety in expressing their gender, particularly outside the home. Appropriate boundary and limit setting should be discussed in therapy (Lev, 2004). Malpas (2011) promulgated a "both/and stance" in which families accept and affirm the child's gender fluidity, while still recognizing the limitations of a gender binary society, thus making decisions that both support and protect the child. Conversations should include potential challenges in settings such as school, extended family, places of worship, and other communities in which the family is embedded. As the challenges are identified, potential solutions and options can be identified before moving forward with an action. Clinicians are essentially coaching parents to move from distress to support, protection, and advocacy for their child.

Shifting into the role of advocacy can be challenging for some parents, and clinicians can support them in this role, either by physically attending meetings at school, for example, or by talking through the role of advocate with parents. When parents are in distress and expressing fear, this fear can be put into action through advocacy, for example, working to create safer places for their child. School is the most common place for needed advocacy, which can be an ongoing process requiring multiple interventions. For example, school administrators may say they will support a child's gender expression, but a child assigned male at birth may be forced to change when they wear a skirt or "girls'" shoes to school, resulting in the child feeling shamed for their gender expression. In these situations, parents can draw upon their parental instincts to protect their child and continue to "go to bat" for them, creating environments in which their child feels valued and free to express a true gender self. Going back to the messages to the child about the unfair world, rather than the transphobic messages which suggest the child is damaged because of their diverse gender and/or expression, it is important for the child to know that although people may not understand yet, "we're all working to change that" (Ehrensaft, 2011, 2016).

Case Study

Melissa and Tony sought therapy when their 9-year-old son, Andre, began to ask his parents consistently about painting his nails and wearing girls' clothes to school. Andre always liked to play "dress-up" at home, which Melissa thought was cute. She would let him use her clothes and makeup. Tony found the dressing up less amusing, and told Andre on several occasions that boys shouldn't do that. He thought that Andre would grow out of these desires, but now that Andre is wanting to dress up outside the home, both Melissa and Tony are worried. Melissa blames herself for encouraging the behavior, and both parents are concerned about other people finding out about Andre's behavior. They are also worried because Andre has already been picked on at school for not being masculine enough and they do not want him to be further bullied. They have heard about transgender people in the media and are terrified that Andre might turn out to be transgender.

During the intake call, it was evident that Melissa and Tony were not only distressed but also that their concerns were laden with transnegative thinking, stating, "I don't want my kid to turn out transgendered." Therefore, to create space for the parents to honestly discuss their feelings while also protecting Andre from nonaffirming messages, the clinician first met alone with Melissa and Tony. The history of Andre's gender expression was discussed, revealing that he had been drawn to things traditionally thought of as feminine, such as purses, dresses, and the color pink, from around age 3. Both parents discouraged any of this feminine expression outside the home, although Melissa in particular allowed him to play with his femininity at home. As a mother of two boys, she enjoyed being able to do "girly" activities with her child. This sometimes caused conflict between Melissa and Tony, and although Tony said he did not blame Melissa for Andre's expression, he felt her support of it "didn't help." The clinician began to use therapy as an opportunity for psychoeducation, pointing out that parental behaviors do not cause gender expansiveness; that the expansiveness seemed to be present in Andre from a very early age; and that the therapist's beliefs (and the beliefs of leaders in the field) are that gender diversity is a natural occurrence, emanating from the child rather than being shaped by the parents. Additionally, the clinician validated the parents' worried feelings by acknowledging that society is organized around a gender binary, so it is quite understandable that they are experiencing distress. Explaining the gender affirmative approach, the clinician requested to meet with Andre to gain more insight into Andre's gender expression.

In session, Andre described being angry when his parents would not let him wear the clothes he wanted to wear but said he usually just gave up asking because he knew they wouldn't change their minds. He expressed particular distress about his father, who "never" let him do what he wanted. As the clinician explored how Andre understood his gender, Andre reported feeling like he was a girl sometimes, and when asked if he had another name he liked to use, he said, "Sometimes I call myself 'Sparkly Diamond Rainbow.'" The clinician asked what name and pronouns he wanted used in therapy and he said *Andre* and *he/him/his* pronouns were fine. When asked what he would ultimately want if he could express gender however he desired, Andre said he wanted to be able to wear whatever he wished to, which sometimes were girls' clothes.

Further conversations with Melissa and Tony focused on the meanings they attached to Andre's feminine behavior, and they discussed and processed their feelings of guilt, fear, and embarrassment. The clinician also talked about the various paths that gender diversity could take and that Andre seemed to be telling us more about his gender expressions than his core gender identity; so, for the moment they could think about Andre as a gender expansive little boy. The clinician encouraged Melissa and Tony to listen to Andre's experience, trying to hold back on any negative reactions. They were assured that their support and protection were of the utmost importance for Andre's well-being. When their distress seemed more contained and they appeared willing to really listen to Andre, subsequent sessions included Andre together with Melissa and Tony. The clinician encouraged Andre to share pieces of the discussions they had in their individual sessions and coached Melissa and Tony to really hear his experience and the feelings accompanying that experience.

As Melissa and Tony's attunement increased, they brought up concerns about their other son, Jordan, concerned about how he would respond if Andre's feminine expression further expanded into the school setting. The clinician role played discussions they could have with Jordan, how they might let him know what was going on in the most gender affirming way that Melissa and Tony could tolerate. They ended up talking with Jordan about Andre, and although he was not surprised (as he had seen Andre playing dress-up for years), he was worried about what his friends would say and how he would be treated at school. The clinician held a family session, with all members present, and Jordan's concerns were addressed. The family negotiated an approach of baby steps, where Andre could introduce pieces of feminine expression into the school setting slowly, one at a time. The family agreed on the first step being a pair of pink sneakers. The family brainstormed possible comments from peers, for both Andre and Jordan, and role played different ways of responding to comments. Jordan took the stance that it was okay for him to think his brother was a little strange but that no one else could say anything derogatory about Andre. Therefore, protective and affirming responses were practiced that fit into Jordan's philosophy.

Conclusion

From the time their child is born, most parents view the gender matching their child's assigned sex at birth as a truth and unchangeable. Although TGE identities are becoming more visible in society, society still has a long way to go before TGE people are treated with equality, compassion, and kindness in general. Therefore, out of fear for their child's well-being, it is normal that parents experience distress when their child does not fit into the societal notion of binary gender fixed at birth. By supporting parents and families through this challenging time, clinicians have the opportunity to assist families in moving toward greater attunement to their child's gender. By allowing space for parents to experience their challenging emotions while also maintaining a gender affirmative stance, clinicians can coach parents to listen to their child and value their experience. As parents move from distress to attunement, they become better equipped to understand, support, and advocate for their child, ultimately promoting their child's long-term happiness and well-being.

References

Boss, P. G. (1999). *Ambiguous loss: Learning to live with unresolved grief.* Cambridge, MA: Harvard University Press.

Brill, S., & Pepper, R. (2008). *The transgender child: A handbook for families and professionals.* San Francisco, CA: Cleis Press.

Coolhart, D. (2012). Supporting transgender youth and their families in therapy: Facing challenges and harnessing strengths. In J. Bigner & J. Wetchler (Eds.), *Handbook of LGBT-affirmative couple and family therapy* (pp. 287–303). New York, NY: Routledge.

Coolhart, D., Baker, A., Farmer, S., Malaney, M., & Shipman, D. (2013). Therapy with transsexual youth and their families: A clinical tool for assessing youth's readiness for gender transition. *Journal of Marital and Family Therapy, 39,* 223–243. http://dx.doi.org/10.1111/j.1752-0606.2011.00283.x

Coolhart, D., & Shipman, D. L. (2017). Working towards family attunement: Family therapy with transgender and gender-nonconforming children and adolescents. *Psychiatric Clinics of North America, 40,* 113–125. http://dx.doi.org/10.1016/j.psc.2016.10.002

Ehrensaft, D. (2011). *Gender born, gender made: Raising healthy gender-nonconforming children.* New York, NY: The Experiment.

Ehrensaft, D. (2016). *The gender creative child: Pathways for nurturing and supporting children who live outside gender boxes.* New York, NY: The Experiment.

Grant, J. M., Motett, L. A., Tanis, J., Harrison, J., Herman, J. L., & Keisling, M. (2011). *Injustice at every turn: A report of the national transgender discrimination survey.* Washington, DC: National Center for Transgender Equality and National Gay and Lesbian Task Force. Retrieved from http://www.thetaskforce.org/static_html/downloads/reports/reports/ntds_full.pdf

Hidalgo, M. A., Ehrensaft, D., Tishelman, A. C., Clark, L. F., Garofalo, R., Rosenthal, S. M., . . . Olson, J. (2013). The gender affirmative model: What we know and what we aim to learn. *Human Development, 56,* 285–290. http://dx.doi.org/10.1159/000355235

James, S. E., Herman, J. L., Rankin, S., Keisling, M., Mottet, L., & Anafi, M. (2016). *The report of the 2015 U.S. Transgender Survey.* Washington, DC: National Center for Transgender Equality.

Lev, A. I. (2004). *Transgender emergence: Therapeutic guidelines for working with gender variant people and their families.* Binghamton, NY: Haworth Press.

Malpas, J. (2011). Between pink and blue: A multi-dimensional family approach to gender nonconforming children and their families. *Family Process, 50,* 453–470. http://dx.doi.org/10.1111/j.1545-5300.2011.01371.x

Ryan, C., Huebner, D., Diaz, R. M., & Sanchez, J. (2009). Family rejection as a predictor of negative health outcomes in white and Latino lesbian, gay, and bisexual young adults. *Pediatrics, 123,* 346–352. http://dx.doi.org/10.1542/peds.2007-3524

Ryan, C., Russell, S. T., Huebner, D., Diaz, R., & Sanchez, J. (2010). Family acceptance in adolescence and the health of LGBT young adults. *Journal of Child and Adolescent Psychiatric Nursing, 23,* 205–213. http://dx.doi.org/10.1111/j.1744-6171.2010.00246.x

Stone Fish, L., & Harvey, R. G. (2005). *Nurturing queer youth: Family therapy transformed.* New York, NY: Norton.

Tando, D. (2016). *The conscious parent's guide to gender identity: A mindful approach to embracing your child's authentic self.* Avon, MA: Adams Media.

Travers, R., Bauer, G., Pyne, J., Bradley, K., Gale, L., & Papadimitriou, M. (2012). *Impacts of strong parental support for trans youth: A report prepared for Children's Aid Society of Toronto and Delisle Youth Services.* Ontario, Canada: Trans PLUS. Retrieved from http://transpulseproject.ca/wp-content/uploads/2012/10/Impacts-of-Strong-Parental-Support-for-Trans-Youth-vFINAL.pdf

Wahlig, J. L. (2015). Losing the child they thought they had: Therapeutic suggestions for an ambiguous loss perspective with parents of a transgender child. *Journal of GLBT Family Studies, 11,* 305–326. http://dx.doi.org/10.1080/1550428X.2014.945676

Watson, R. J., Barnett, M. A., & Russell, S. T. (2016). Parental support matters for the educational success of sexual minorities. *Journal of GLBT Family Studies, 12,* 188–202.

Jean Malpas, Elizabeth Glaeser, and Shawn V. Giammattei

9 Building Resilience in Transgender and Gender Expansive Children, Families, and Communities

A Multidimensional Family Approach

When working with prepubertal transgender and gender expansive (TGE) children, the point of entry into care is most often led by their caregiver(s). It may also be the social service agency that orients or mandates the caregiver(s) to gender affirmative services. As service providers, we are in a unique position to work with the young person, the caregivers, and often the whole community on a journey toward support and acceptance. A similar goal can be adopted regarding building resilience, which is the ability for TGE youth, their families, and communities not only to overcome or survive adversity but to grow and flourish because of the experience (Garmezy, 1987; Rutter, 1987; Walsh, 2003).

A multidimensional approach that includes individual child well-being, family/relational support, and access to community is likely to increase resilience not only in the young person but also in their family and community. Research has demonstrated that more accepting families and communities are often associated with TGE youth who have better mental health outcomes (Olson, Durwood, DeMeules, & McLaughlin, 2016; Ryan, Russell, Huebner, Diaz, & Sanchez, 2010). For instance, TGE youth who are supported in their identities, whether by their family and/or community, have higher self-esteem, less depression or anxiety, and less occurrences of suicide attempts (Grossman & D'Augelli, 2006; Travers et al., 2012). Family support

http://dx.doi.org/10.1037/0000095-009
The Gender Affirmative Model: An Interdisciplinary Approach to Supporting Transgender and Gender Expansive Children, C. Keo-Meier and D. Ehrensaft (Editors)
Copyright © 2018 by the American Psychological Association. All rights reserved.

is a protective factor for resilience and may serve as a buffer from mental health challenges so frequently associated with the challenges of growing up in a cisnormative and transphobic world (Simons, Schrager, Clark, Belzer, & Olson, 2013).

This chapter outlines interventions to cultivate resilience in TGE children, families, and communities through the multidimensional family approach (MDFA; Malpas, 2011). We first explore the premises and history of the MDFA, then establish its levels of interventions and clinical choice points and connect the clinical model to the literature of resilience and family acceptance with TGE youth and, more specifically, methods for cultivating individual, family, and community resilience. Last, through case examples, we describe the implementation of the MDFA, demonstrating ways in which it can be applied to build resilience in families and communities with varying degrees of acceptance of gender diversity.

Multidimensional Family Approach

PREMISES AND ORIGINS

The MDFA was developed at the Ackerman Institute's Gender & Family Project and emerged from the need for gender affirmative services for families of TGE youth in New York City (Malpas, 2011, 2016). Although multiple mental health programs focused on individual support for transgender adolescents and young adults, they rarely included services for children, nor did they use a systemic approach to their existing ecological and familial contexts and relationships. The MDFA can be considered a multisystemic clinical application of the gender affirmative model's (GAM's) theoretical framework (Hidalgo et al., 2013) to TGE youth, their families, and social contexts. It is based on the common premise that gender variations are not considered disorders but rather that mental health vulnerabilities in TGE youth are most often secondary to their experiences of transphobia, cisgender normativity, and ostracism.

The MDFA, in consort with the major premises of the GAM, comprehends gender as fluid, nonbinary, culturally defined and comprising a complex combination of biological, developmental, social, and cultural influences. Core clinical objectives of the MDFA include a primary focus on creating an affirming environment where the child can freely articulate their experience of themselves and where their genuine gender identities and gender expressions can be identified and affirmed internally and in their life contexts. The MDFA takes into account both the experiences and reactions of the child's ecological environments (e.g., family, school) that inform the child's sense of self and the child's ability to actualize general mental, physical, social and in particular gender health. Finally, it offers support to both the child and the caregivers and significant players involved in his, her, or their life.

As a group of authors located in different cities and clinical contexts, we all use the MDFA in our work with families. Over the past several years, the authors of this chapter who are providers at the Ackerman Institute (Jean Malpas and Elizabeth Glaeser) learned specifically how to build services around families' needs. Beginning with a small group of families, we conducted a needs assessment and understood that families wanted multidimensional services that would include and coordinate individual, family, and larger context interventions and serve as a liaison with legal and medical services. In addition, as our program is social justice oriented, we were committed to expanding access and engaging families of TGE children and youth who were not seeking services due to sociostructural barriers or struggle with acceptance of gender diversity. To that end, we created a multisystemic program that includes (a) three parent support groups (one for parents of children, one for parents of teens, one in Spanish); (b) four support groups for youth (one play group, one tween group, one teen group, one sibling group); (c) psychological evaluations for children and youth, involving caregivers in the evaluation; (d) school, professional, and community trainings; and (e) parental coaching and family therapy.

In San Francisco, Shawn V. Giammattei, in collaboration with Mind the Gap, the mental health wing of the University of California San Francisco's (UCSF's) Child and Adolescent Gender Center (CAGC), uses a gender affirming approach that fosters resilience with the youth and families in his clinical practice. Similar to that of the Ackerman Institute, the approach at CAGC is multidisciplinary and multisystemic and offers assessments, individual and family work, teen and parent support groups, legal, medical, and educational support that includes trainings of professionals and schools. With the exception of the CAGC clinics housed in three sites of UCSF Benioff Children's Hospital, and unlike the Ackerman Institute, CAGC services are not provided in one location but are dispersed throughout the San Francisco Bay Area and function as a network of providers for the various needs of TGE youth and their families.

BUILDING INDIVIDUAL, FAMILY, AND COMMUNITY RESILIENCE

TGE youth and adults report significant levels of minority stress due to stigma, prejudice, and discrimination across the life span (Bockting, Miner, Swinburne Romine, Hamilton, & Coleman, 2013; Grant et al., 2011). Even in the most affirming families, minority stress will have an impact on TGE youth, and their families are likely to experience adversity that will create significant stressors (Greytak, Kosciw, & Diaz, 2009). At the same time, it is possible for these children and their families not only to handle these challenges but also to grow as a result of the process. The ability to bounce back from and grow through the adversity in one's life has been linked with overall success and happiness (Allan & Ungar, 2014; Trotter, 2000). Because TGE youth and their families are likely to face significant adversity in many areas of their lives, the ability to foster this resilience or ability to bounce back is an important component to successful outcomes. Given that family resilience has been shown to positively impact the individual members, and their growth, in turn, positively impacts the family (Domínguez, Bobele, Coppock, & Peña, 2015; Singh, Meng, & Hansen, 2014), the importance of building family resilience for TGE youth cannot be underestimated.

RESILIENCE-PROMOTING FACTORS AND INTERVENTIONS

Several interventions have been found to foster resilience for children, their families, and the communities within which they live. The seven resilience factors that individual, family, and community interventions can be designed to address are (a) access to material resources; (b) supportive relationships with significant others; (c) a sense of identity that fuels a sense of satisfaction or pride and purpose; (d) experiences of power and control; (e) cultural adherence, which fosters a connection to community; (f) social justice, or a sense the things are fair and equitable; and (g) a sense of social cohesion, which is often found through a connection to higher purpose or spirituality (Allan & Ungar, 2014). Depending on the context of our work, access to material resources for TGE youth and their families may be outside the scope of our practice. Regardless, it will be difficult for families to engage if their basic needs are not met. Individual-level resilience-building interventions for TGE youth and their family members should focus on increasing self-efficacy and coping skills for dealing with stress and increasing health-promoting behavior, social skills training, and the building of social support networks; improving academic skills; and engaging in extracurricular and community activities (Zolkoski & Bullock, 2012). Particularly important to TGE youth resilience is the ability to define and describe their own identities (Singh et al., 2014). Family-based resilience-building interventions should be focused on creating positive parent–child attachment and parental warmth, family cohesion and care, a close relationship with a caring adult, as well as encouragement and assistance (Allan & Ungar, 2014). Given that children spend a majority of their time at school, most community interventions are centered there, but these could translate just as well to places of worship, athletic groups, and so on. The community-focused resilience building interventions for TGE youth and their families focus on increasing supportive peer relationships, promoting positive teacher influences, and enhancing opportunities for success (Walsh, 2013).

The MDFA creates a process that can foster resilience by addressing many of the individual, family, and community resilience-building interventions. In this approach, TGE youth and their families can be helped to overcome the adversity through exposure to the practices of the GAM, such as the normalizing of gender diversity and externalizing of negative cultural reactions. In other words, the pathology is situated in the environment rather than in the child and family, freeing the family to develop their own self-confidence and strength in the face of such adversity. The ability of these families to not only nurture their TGE child but also grow through the process of acceptance and celebration of gender diversity can be healing for TGE youth, their families, and the communities in which they live.

Multidimensional Family Approach: Structure of Interventions and Choice Points

To support the child's gender health and build child, family, and community resilience, the MDFA operates with a set a sequentially ordered modalities and levels of interventions. Although the sequence of clinical intervention is flexible and always based on the needs and demands of each child, family, and community, it often unfolds in the following order.

INITIAL INTERVIEW WITH THE CAREGIVER(S) AND CHILD SEPARATELY

The initial meeting with caregivers alone presents several advantages. First, it enables the clinician to establish an alliance with the family decision makers. Second, it provides privacy to explore parents' and/or family members' genuine experiences and reactions to their child's gender diversity. Clinicians can gather an in-depth history of the child's psychological, social, and gender development and can assess the family's request for support and resources. Focusing specifically on gender development and history, the interview aims to identify the presence of discomfort with assigned sex as well as to differentiate aspects relevant to the young person's gender expression vs. child's gender identity vs. emerging sexual orientation. Third and most important, it is also a crucial time when family and individual resilience protective and risk factors can be identified, mapped out and considered for future potential supportive recommendations.

Using a dialectic perspective on resilience where both individual family members and family system resilience can modulate and potentiate each other, it is important to collect information on each family member's internal, interpersonal, and contextual resources and vulnerabilities. In coparenting families, each parent brings to the table a different set of life history and contexts, along with their respective temperament, personalities, interpersonal styles, belief systems, cultures, and social locations. Using the genogram as an organizing tool can quickly provide a map of other key family members involved in the life of the child and allows the clinician to inquire about whether these players present a source of challenges or affirmation or, most often, both.

Another section of the initial interview with caregivers focuses on the life context of the child, their school experience, and the areas of social support that might be needed. It is important to inquire with caregivers directly about their perception of their child's safety, acceptance, and integration in school, after-school programs, or other educational activities. Given TGE youth's low rates of reporting school bullying incidents (Greytak et al., 2009), a third-party direct perspective, such as a teacher's or educator's observations, is often recommended as well.

It is not assumed that TGE children need individual assessment or therapy. In some cases in which the caregivers' account shows that the child presents no sign of distress or desire to be in therapy, and evidence indicates well-established family acceptance, it is not necessary to meet the child. Supportive recommendations can be given to the caregivers directly. In most cases, however, the parents' narrative indicates that the child might be in some degree of distress—if not about their own gender diversity, then possibly about their environment's response to it. In these situations, the next step is to meet the child to get their own perspective on the situation and to evaluate best affirmative recommendations. Further gender affirming evaluation is also needed when caregivers and/or children want to clarify questions pertaining to gender identity and gender expression (Ehrensaft, 2012; Hidalgo et al., 2013; Vance, Ehrensaft, & Rosenthal, 2014).

The initial meeting with the child uses a developmentally appropriate format. If the child is particularly young, it is often necessary to spend time together with caregivers until the child feels comfortable being alone with the provider. The level of transparency about the nature of the meeting varies from one family to another. In general, it is recommended that it be made clear that the focus of the meeting(s) will be to help the child be supported for who they are—including gender identity and/or gender expression. The subsequent meeting(s) with the child focus on engaging the child in an authentic conversation about self-perception; gender identity and development; and any distress created by the reactions of their family, school, or friends. Methods used toward these goals vary depending on the age of the child. A combination of interactive, play, and observational and structured interviewing methods will be optimal (Glaeser, 2016; Kaufman, 2016a). It is unfortunate that empirically validated measures for preteens measuring gender identity and dysphoria are lacking and often too binary (see Chapter 7, this volume). Information gathered with the child helps clarify whether the child's assertions are primarily about gender expression and/or identity (see Chapter 3). On the basis of that information, caregivers are given feedback on appropriate next steps and/or recommendations (Malpas, 2014; Malpas, Davis, Colon-Otero, & Raad, 2016; Malpas & Janssen, 2015).

CHOOSING AN APPROPRIATE LEVEL AND MODALITY OF CARE

The information gathered initially helps the clinician make a collaborative and transparent decision with caregivers and children about the optimal nature of the gender affirming support. The MDFA offers a range of flexible and nonmutually exclusive services that are chosen based on several criteria: the level of distress of the child and of the family, the need for individual assessment and psychotherapy, the nature of support that will best fit the caregivers, the necessity of professional interventions in the child's social and educational environment to create more gender inclusivity, and the need to facilitate access to medical and/or legal care. The clinical choice point at the end of the set of first interviews often coalesces around several questions: whether the child needs further assessment; whether formal assessment is requested by other medical care providers; whether the child and family need therapy and/or community participation, and the type and level of gender affirming support that the child's school and communities would most benefit from. Given the young age of the children, caregivers are the cornerstones of all support modalities and are integral to their child's resilience. Their genuine engagement, collaboration, and participation will have great influence on whether the young person will have access to needed medical, legal or educational support.

When it comes to psychological services, such as psychological evaluation, individual therapy, parental coaching, or family therapy, collaborative decisions between clinicians, caregivers, children—and sometimes mandating agencies—can be made, holding multiple criteria in mind. In-depth psychological evaluations are often particularly useful in situations in which the child, the family, or the therapist are uncertain as to whether the child is gender expansive and/or nonbinary or binary transgender identified, and a finer differentiation needs to be made in terms of gender expression and/or gender identity. Some pediatric gender clinics require a more formal psychological workup before prescribing puberty suppression or hormone therapy in adolescence. In all cases, the evaluation remains systemic and integrates all caregivers' perspectives (Kaufman, 2016b). A more in-depth gender evaluation might also provide comfort to families who are more ambivalent or anxious about next steps. Following an evaluation, a comprehensive report and feedback session functions as a brief psychoeducational intervention and often engages more reluctant families into higher level of care and community participation. Some families who enter the gender evaluation with disbelief and hope that their child's assertion will be denied find in the report's in-depth history and narrative reasons to give their child's assertion and urgency more credibility. Similarly, although some children and adolescents are reluctant to discuss gender in depth, many of them experience the process of gender affirmative evaluations as the opportunity for a more supportive and honest engagement among all family members.

Individual and/or family therapy is not always needed, and a referral to a support group for children and for parents is often the appropriate level of care. However, individual, family therapy, and caregiver coaching are sometimes necessary when the child's distress has impacted the child's emotional, relational, social, or educational development or when the family's response to gender diversity has eroded or complicated family relationships and greatly increased the risk factors that impair resilience. Working with the family is helpful when the tension triggered by the child's gender diversity and the caregivers' reactions has disrupted family relationships, communication and attachment; such work can also provide support to the family as they navigate their internal and external developmental tasks. When caregivers are particularly resistant to gender diversity, we have found that meeting with them alone and taking the time to understand their dilemmas has been effective. Rather than driving a gender inclusive agenda that might alienate the caregiver and ultimately jeopardize the child's access to a gender affirmative team, the provider can focus on meeting caregivers where they are and developing a compassionate understanding of the individual, cultural, or relational factors that prevent the parent from adjusting to the child's emerging gender identity and/or expression (Sheinberg & Brewster, 2014).

Additionally, it is vital that caregivers are given the opportunity to discuss additional stressors, such as racism and other forms of marginalization based on the family's social location, within the context of services for TGE youth. A color-blind mentality, or failing to name differences in experience of various social identities, can alienate caregivers who then would likely not return for services (Sue & Sue, 2016).

Whether accompanied by individual or family therapy, the multifamily groups offer a unique and essential sense of belonging to a community of peers where children get to meet other gender diverse children and grow older together and where caregivers also find a community of peers. The groups offer a resilience-building intervention by fostering social support, a sense of identity, cultural adherence, and an opening for learning new coping skills. Multifamily groups meet for 2 hours once per month and are structured according to identity and developmental criteria. A playgroup for children (age 5–9) and a support group for tweens (10–13) meets at the same time as a caregiver support group. Siblings are invited to join the youth group or meet on their own. Families can come together, or caregivers of children of those ages can come without their child. Every 3 months, the caregivers group opens up to welcome extended family members. A similar set of support groups exists for adolescents and their families, as well as for Spanish-speaking families. Children groups' activity and goals are organized by developmental criteria: The elementary school-age group focuses on arts, crafts, and interactive expressive activities, and the tween group is more process oriented and provides a safe space for youth to begin addressing questions pertaining to identity, socialization, family, and school disclosure, as well as developing peer connections and support. Although youth coming from accepting families are more likely to be affirmed and to have socially transitioned or be receiving puberty-suppressing medication or hormone therapy, they also can benefit from a community of peers of the same age. Meeting other TGE children allows for the creation of meaningful friendships, a space where children's identity is affirmed, and a community where resources and experiences can be exchanged and supported.

Caregivers' support groups focus on making room for a range of experiences from shock, fear, ambivalence, and grief to hope, joy, empowerment, and mutual support. The group emphasizes caregivers' own social location and intersectionality of race, class, gender, sexual orientation, and religion (Malpas et al., 2016). It encourages caregivers' genuine expression of their journey while processing parenting experiences, dilemmas, and solutions. The themes that have emerged in the caregivers' support groups show that cisgender parents have a variety of reactions to their TGE youth. These experiences are contextualized by their own life history, the "gendered" expectations they had for their child, the larger cultural systems, and the communities with whom they affiliate. Families rarely have homogenous experiences, and different caregivers or members of the same family might "hold different voices," some expressing unconditional love more easily and others articulating fear, grief, or denial.

Initially, many parents experience a sense of shock and disbelief. They feel disoriented and uncertain as to how to handle the gender expression and/or identity of their child. The emerging narrative presented by the child comes to challenge the conscious or unconscious cisnormative expectations they had for their child's emotional, social, and gender development. This shift in perspective can trigger a sense of grief in relation to the cisgender, gender conforming child they always assumed they would have. When parents have moved past shock, fears tend to invade the scene, triggering anxiety as they face the developmental unknown of their child. Whether accepting or not, most caregivers are quick to read everything they can online. Typically, the first pieces of information they take in are the horrifying statistics regarding suicide rates, bullying, and violence committed against transgender youth, particularly youth on the feminine spectrum and youth of color. No parent would ever want that for their child, and fear can easily become a paralyzing factor, pushing the parent to become more rigid, less open to dialogue and collaborative problem solving with their child. Within that dynamic, rejection can sometimes be a misplaced initial attempt at protection.

The caregivers' groups support members in their own coming-out process. They must grapple with their own transition from a position of privilege to one of minority status: They are now the parent of a transgender or gender expansive child. Parents may feel their own fears of shame, stigma, failure, or disconnect as their identity is different from that of their child, and now that of their own family and community. Parents must figure out how to "come out" to their extended family and community and how to re-affiliate themselves with their child, while simultaneously figuring out their own identities in the process (Giammattei, 2015). Questions of gender identity in children can cause complications in parental and marital relationships. Relational ruptures in the coparenting or family systems are not atypical. Navigating the various difficulties, uncertainties and conflicts are part of the pathway toward acceptance of their child's gender identity.

Last, the MDFA takes into account the multiple systems in which the child and family are involved. For instance, providers and support groups inquire about the multidisciplinary needs of the child and family and facilitate referrals to medical and/or legal services when needed or appropriate. In addition, the MDFA operates with the contextual and psychosocial premises according to which the range of interventions each family will need to span a spectrum from most individualized and psychological to those mainly affecting the larger systems impacting the life of the family. The direct community around the caregivers and child, and in particular, their school, are of utmost importance in fostering resilience. Affirming the child's gender and improving their mental health necessitates taking into account any instance of oppression, danger, and marginalization they might be experiencing in a systematic or daily way. These interventions are especially important for TGE youth because they are disproportionately victims of bullying and harassment in school (Greytak et al., 2009; Ryan, Huebner, Diaz, & Sanchez, 2009). In the MDFA intake process, the provider asks caregivers and the child about academic performance and school climate. Direct inquiry with school teachers are made with permission from the family. In our experience, most children experience a degree of discomfort or harassment based on their gender expression, identity, and level of disclosure and/or social transition in school. Even in schools in which the child is accepted and affirmed, most educators and administrators often feel underequipped to optimally support the child and their family or integrate gender diversity as a core component of the school's educational program and social climate. The collaboration between the clinician and the school trainers offers the family the chance to have a coordinated impact on their larger systems and builds individual, family, and community resilience.

However, it is important to not underestimate the young person's distress and need for individual support (Hendricks & Testa, 2012; Testa, Habarth, Peta, Balsam, & Bockting, 2015), independently from the level of family support or community access that they are receiving. Fostering individual resilience, although strongly connected to family and community support, sometimes requires a therapeutic space in which the young person can express the hardship of living in a cisnormative and transphobic world. Although supportive parents are fundamental to a child's well-being, they might struggle to understand and validate the experiences of challenging gender stereotypes and expectations. Referrals to individual therapists with extensive experience with gender diversity may be recommended. Whether services are integrated inside one institutional team or through the coordination of multiple independent providers, optimal care of TGE youth needs to take into account the emotional, developmental, and relational factors impacting the child's gender health and overall well-being. Emphasizing only individual and developmental parameters out of social context can risk missing much of what is to be known about a child, factors best learned through family participation and awareness of potential social stressors. On the other hand, family support alone does not always provide enough containment and empowerment for the young child who needs a space to elaborate and articulate complex feelings and experiences, often about family relationships and stressors, and to build gender resilience.

Caregivers' Process of Acceptance

Despite our belief that all parents love and want the best for their children, research results and clinical evidence show that many parents of TGE youth have parenting behaviors that can be described as rejecting and ambivalent (Malpas, 2011; Ryan et al., 2009). For many years, we have wondered about the process that makes a loving and well-intended parent become an undermining factor for their child's development and resilience. To answer that question, we have found it helpful for clinical intervention to keep in mind the parenting mandates that become conflicted in situations of unexpected identity differences in the family.

PARENTING FUNCTIONS

In a Western context, parental tasks include the following:

- *Nurturance:* Parents are both wired genetically and trained to form an attachment relationship that will become the container for very important interpersonal experiences, such as emotional availability and attunement, bonding and mutual love.
- *Acceptance:* On the foundation of a hopefully solid and nurturing bond, caregivers are providing contexts and resources for the child to develop. Month after month, they discover the personality, temperament, and singularities of their child. An important function is the acceptance of these idiosyncratic features by the caregivers that will allow the child to feel seen and loved for who they are.
- *Transmission:* From a historical and multigenerational standpoint, the caregiver's role is also to pass on defining and differentiating characteristics of the family. The beliefs, behaviors, language, and interpersonal habits are informed by cultural, social, and familial histories.

- *Socialization:* The caregiver's role includes teaching their children the cultural and social norms of the group they intend their child to affiliate with. Caregivers methodically and repeatedly role model and train children in specific behaviors that the child is expected to uphold to fit in with the social group.

GENDER AND PARENTING

In families where parents and children share cisgender identities and a predilection toward conventional binary conforming expressions, gender operates as a platform for positive interpersonal experiences where nurturance, acceptance, transmission, and socialization can all happen at once and without conflict. For instance, a masculine cisgender male caregiver can enjoy teaching sports to his masculine cisgender male child.

Reviewing each of these parental functions reveals that any one of them can become conflicted when caregivers' and children's experiences of gender do not fit within the same models. TGE youths' gender identities may not systematically align with their assigned sex at birth and their gender expressions often defy the typical norms of gendered roles in the family, community, and culture with which the caregivers affiliate:

> Whether accepting or struggling, parents face the difficult task of having to position themselves, at home and in the world, at the intersection of two parenting mandates that usually do not conflict as acutely: nurture their child's personhood while promoting [the child's] adjustment to consensual social realities. (Malpas, 2011, p. 454)

When developing interventions with parents who are experiencing such conflicts in their parental tasks, it is important to help parents understand that rejecting behaviors, such as "I will not let my child wear a dress in public because he might be bullied," can unwittingly come from a loving and protective place. In building resilience, parents need to be given the space and the tools to explore conflicts they experience in the execution of their parental tasks and ensuing fears and desires to protect their children from harm.

Case Study

Through our experiences, we have identified three groups of caregivers and families, ranging from exhibiting most- to least-accepting behaviors in response to their children's gender identity and expressions (Malpas & Janssen, 2015). These groups are, respectively: accepting, ambivalent, and rejecting. Fostering resilience in each group requires different approaches and modalities. For the purposes of illustration, we have chosen a case example from the third group, as these are often the most challenging in our resilience-building work.

Winston is a 10-year-old biracial child who was assigned male at birth; with feminine expressions, she asserts a gender identity of "girl." She presented with her mother and father at the Gender & Family Project. Bill, an African American cisgender businessman in his 50s and Monique, a White cisgender music teacher in her 40s, had been divorced for 5 years. Following an initial intake with each parent separately, a meeting with them together, and preliminary meetings with Winston, it became abundantly clear that Winston had been experiencing a clear and high level of distress about her assigned gender since at least first grade. She said she was 80% sure she was a girl, but she didn't know whether the remaining 20% of doubt was because of her parents' refusal to believe her or because she simply wasn't sure yet. Both Bill and Monique were progressive and connected to the gay community in New York City. However, despite Winston's ongoing claims that she was not a gay boy but a straight girl, they were adamant in refusing a social transition until after puberty, "if she had not changed her mind by then." Winston had always excelled at sports and had a promising future in basketball, with potential scholarships at the best high schools. By the time they came in for services, Winston presented with depression and suicidal ideation, which had increased in recent months. Monique started to wonder whether they were taking the right path. But Bill was certain that puberty suppression, a potential next step given Winston's gender assertions, would only influence his "son" in the worst way: "If he isn't really transgender, these medications will convince him he is," he exclaimed many times.

The recommendation for affirmative care had to be carefully crafted in this situation. Monique was moving from rejecting to ambivalent, but Bill was not ready for the approach taken with the MDFA model. Neither one of them was open to participating in a caregiver or family group. Bill kept asking for arguments to be convinced that Winston's gender assertions and expressions weren't a call for attention or a product of the negative influence of living in "crazy NYC." The team decided that a family-centered evaluation would provide everyone the chance to "tell their side of the story" and that a serious psychological workup might influence Bill's perception, assuming he recognized it as legitimate. The recommendation of moving forward with the evaluation was a way of showing Winston that everyone took her distress and desire to transition seriously. As puberty was nearing fast, it could also be used to support medical care if needed. The lengthy process of evaluation confirmed Winston's transgender identity and revealed that the relationship between Winston and her dad had worsened in the past year. Fights escalated often, and her dad became verbally abusive.

Family therapy was strongly recommended, which the family accepted. The family therapy modality was used flexibly—sometimes mom and daughter were seen, sometimes dad and daughter, sometimes parents alone, and only when necessary, the divorced coparents together. Over time, the treatment helped Monique identify the sources of her ambivalence. She feared for Winston's future but also felt guilty and ashamed. Disconnected from her own parents, Monique felt that having a transgender child would prove to her friends and extended family that she had failed as a parent and that she was more wounded than she thought. Differentiating her own narrative from her child's experience helped her to want to join the parent support group. Bill, on the other hand, was struggling to perceive the risks of his approach, agreeing to disagree with the information provided by the therapist. As a person of color, he feared for his child's safety and worried that he was the only person who truly understood the harsh reality of being a Black transgender woman. He was prepared to protect Winston's safety at all costs. Yet he also did not want to lose his relationship with his child. The family therapist, who also identified as African American, was able to involve Bill's new wife and join him in understanding the challenges of raising Winston as a transgender girl who he thought needed to be a "strong Black man." Although Bill never accepted joining a parent support group, he accepted education and sought information from doctors about puberty suppression. In addition, he reached out to friends in his community and found support as a gender affirming dad. After 2 years of a slow and careful process, Winston socially transitioned and was started on puberty blockers. She joined the tween group at the clinic and started meeting other transgender youth "in real life, not just online," as she said excitedly. In this case, the clinical approach toward gender resilience had combined slow and flexible engagement with parents, affirming feedback with the child, and subtle but clear messaging with the father about the potential risk of a rejecting stance toward his child. The treatment was layered with an in-depth exploration of each caregiver's experience and belief system, enabling the provider to have a more intimate understanding of their struggle and a more compassionate delivery of psycho- and socioeducation.

Conclusion

The MDFA is a gender affirming, resilience-building, multimodal intervention for working with TGE youth, their families, and communities. This model is a multimodal clinical application of the GAM. The approach is comprehensive, meeting families where they are and offering the interventions needed to affirm and advocate for their child. The clinical approach emphasizes taking into account the multiple perspectives and varying degrees of comfort with gender diversity that exist in the family. A crucial aspect of the stance is its flexibility with sequence and modalities of interventions. Different youth and families require different points of entry and catalysts for change depending on their social location, access to resources, gender identity development, belief systems, and larger cultural contexts.

The MDFA addresses key factors of individual, relational, and family resilience. In addition to pointing families and communities in the direction of resources and support, it engages all the relevant individuals in the life of the TGE youth to develop a more coherent, empowering, and culturally relevant narrative of the family's relationship with gender diversity. The model lessens restraining forces and conflicts for caregivers, enabling them to find their way back to their functions of positive socialization, nurturance and acceptance. By involving all family members and relevant members of the community, the MDFA gives youth and families a sense of control, agency, and connection to a greater sense of purpose. Optimally, gender diversity is then no longer divisive but instead becomes the source of bonding and pride.

References

Allan, R., & Ungar, M. (2014). Resilience-building interventions with children, adolescents, and their families. In S. Prince-Embury, D. H. Saklofske, S. Prince-Embury, & D. H. Saklofske (Eds.), *Resilience interventions for youth in diverse populations* (pp. 447–462). New York, NY: Springer. http://dx.doi.org/10.1007/978-1-4939-0542-3_20

Bockting, W. O., Miner, M. H., Swinburne Romine, R. E., Hamilton, A., & Coleman, E. (2013). Stigma, mental health, and resilience in an online sample of the U.S. transgender population. *American Journal of Public Health, 103*, 943–951. http://dx.doi.org/10.2105/AJPH.2013.301241

Domínguez, D. G., Bobele, M., Coppock, J., & Peña, E. (2015). LGBTQ relationally based positive psychology: An inclusive and systemic framework. *Psychological Services, 12*, 177–185. http://dx.doi.org/10.1037/a0038824

Ehrensaft, D. (2012). From gender identity disorder to gender identity creativity: True gender self child therapy. *Journal of Homosexuality, 59*, 337–356. http://dx.doi.org/10.1080/00918369.2012.653303

Garmezy, N. (1987). Stress, competence, and development: Continuities in the study of schizophrenic adults, children vulnerable to psychopathology, and the search for stress-resistant children. *American Journal of Orthopsychiatry, 57*, 159–174. http://dx.doi.org/10.1111/j.1939-0025.1987.tb03526.x

Giammattei, S. V. (2015). Beyond the binary: Trans-negotiations in couple and family therapy. *Family Process, 54*, 418–434. http://dx.doi.org/10.1111/famp.12167

Glaeser, E. (2016, June). "What does it mean to socially transition: A pilot measure." In Kaufman, R. (Chair), *Social transition & systemic clinical care of prepubertal transgender and gender nonconfirming children in the United States*. Symposium at the World Professional Association of Transgender Health Conference, Amsterdam, Netherlands.

Grant, J. M., Motett, L. A., Tanis, J., Harrison, J., Herman, J. L., & Keisling, M. (2011). *Injustice at every turn: A report of the national transgender discrimination survey*. Washington, DC: National Center for Transgender Equality and National Gay and Lesbian Task Force. Retrieved from http://www.thetaskforce.org/static_html/downloads/reports/reports/ntds_full.pdf

Greytak, E. A., Kosciw, J. G., & Diaz, E. M. (2009). *Harsh realities: The experiences of transgender youth in our nation's schools*. New York, NY: GLSEN. Retrieved from http://www.teni.ie/attachments/c95b5e6b-f0e6-43aa-9038-1e357e3163ea.PDF

Grossman, A. H., & D'Augelli, A. R. (2006). Transgender youth: Invisible and vulnerable. *Journal of Homosexuality, 51*, 111–128. http://dx.doi.org/10.1300/J082v51n01_06

Hendricks, M. L., & Testa, R. J. (2012). A conceptual framework for clinical work with transgender and gender nonconforming clients: An adaptation of the minority stress model. *Professional Psychology: Research and Practice, 43*, 460–467. http://dx.doi.org/10.1037/a0029597

Hidalgo, M. A., Ehrensaft, D., Tishelman, A. C., Clark, L. F., Garofalo, R., Rosenthal, S. M., . . . Olson, J. (2013). The gender affirmative model: What we know and what we aim to learn. *Human Development, 56*, 285–290. http://dx.doi.org/10.1159/000355235

Kaufman, R. (2016a, June). Social transition: Pre-pubertal TGNC children. In R. Kaufman (Chair), *Social transition & systemic clinical care of pre-pubertal transgender and gender non-confirming children in the United States*. Symposium at the World Professional Association of Transgender Health Conference, Amsterdam, the Netherlands.

Kaufman, R. (2016b, June). Trauma and gender. In A. Tishelman (Chair), *Complex clinical cases of transgender and gender nonconforming youth in the U.S.* Symposium at the World Professional Association of Transgender Health Conference, Amsterdam, the Netherlands.

Malpas, J. (2011). Between pink and blue: A multi-dimensional family approach to gender nonconforming children and their families. *Family Process, 50*, 453–470. http://dx.doi.org/10.1111/j.1545-5300.2011.01371.x

Malpas, J. (2014). *Fifty shades of purples: Supporting gender variant children and their families on the gender spectrum*. Paper presented at the World Professional Association for Transgender Health, Bangkok, Thailand.

Malpas, J. (2016). The transgender journey: What role should therapists play? *The Psychotherapy Networker*. Retrieved from https://www.psychotherapynetworker.org/blog/details/772/the-transgender-journey

Malpas, J., Davis, B., Colon-Otero, S., & Raad, M. (2016, June). *The ethics of intersectionality and allyship in clinical work: Power analysis of racial and gender locations in mental health and community work with transgender clients*. Paper presented at the World Professional Association for Transgender Health, Amsterdam, the Netherlands.

Malpas, J., & Janssen, A. (2015, November). *Between pink & blue: Combining affirmative and evidence-based approaches to transgender & gender nonconforming youth & their families*. Paper presented at the Ackerman Institute for the Family, New York, New York.

Olson, K. R., Durwood, L., DeMeules, M., & McLaughlin, K. A. (2016). Mental health of transgender children who are supported in their identities. *Pediatrics, 137*, e20153223. http://dx.doi.org/10.1542/peds.2015-3223

Rutter, M. (1987). Psychosocial resilience and protective mechanisms. *American Journal of Orthopsychiatry, 57*, 316–331. http://dx.doi.org/10.1111/j.1939-0025.1987.tb03541.x

Ryan, C., Huebner, D., Diaz, R. M., & Sanchez, J. (2009). Family rejection as a predictor of negative health outcomes in White and Latino lesbian, gay, and bisexual young adults. *Pediatrics, 123*, 346–352. http://dx.doi.org/10.1542/peds.2007-3524

Ryan, C., Russell, S. T., Huebner, D., Diaz, R., & Sanchez, J. (2010). Family acceptance in adolescence and the health of LGBT young adults. *Journal of Child and Adolescent Psychiatric Nursing, 23*, 205–213. http://dx.doi.org/10.1111/j.1744-6171.2010.00246.x

Sheinberg, M., & Brewster, M. K. (2014). Thinking and working relationally: Interviewing and constructing hypotheses to create compassionate understanding. *Family Process, 53*, 618–639.

Simons, L., Schrager, S. M., Clark, L. F., Belzer, M., & Olson, J. (2013). Parental support and mental health among transgender adolescents. *Journal of Adolescent Health, 53*, 791–793. http://dx.doi.org/10.1016/j.jadohealth.2013.07.019

Singh, A. A., Meng, S. E., & Hansen, A. W. (2014). "I am my own gender": Resilience strategies of trans youth. *Journal of Counseling & Development, 92*, 208–218. http://dx.doi.org/10.1002/j.1556-6676.2014.00150.x

Sue, D. W., & Sue, D. (2016). *Counseling the culturally diverse: Theory and practice*. Hoboken, NJ: Wiley.

Testa, R. J., Habarth, J., Peta, J., Balsam, K., & Bockting, W. (2015). Development of the gender minority stress and resilience measure. *Psychology of Sexual Orientation and Gender Diversity, 2*, 65–77. http://dx.doi.org/10.1037/sgd0000081

Travers, R., Bauer, G., Pyne, J., Bradley, K., Gale, L., & Papadimitriou, M. (2012). *Impacts of strong parental support for trans youth: A report prepared for Children's Aid Society of Toronto and Delisle Youth Services*. Retrieved from http://transpulseproject.ca/wp-content/uploads/2012/10/Impacts-of-Strong-Parental-Support-for-Trans-Youth-vFINAL.pdf

Trotter, J. (2000). Lesbian and gay issues in social work with young people: Resilience and success through confronting, conforming and escaping. *British Journal of Social Work, 30*, 115–123. http://dx.doi.org/10.1093/bjsw/30.1.115

Vance, S. R., Jr., Ehrensaft, D., & Rosenthal, S. M. (2014). Psychological and medical care of gender nonconforming youth. *Pediatrics, 134*, 1184–1192. http://dx.doi.org/10.1542/peds.2014-0772

Walsh, F. (2003). Family resilience: A framework for clinical practice. *Family Process, 42*, 1–18. http://dx.doi.org/10.1111/j.1545-5300.2003.00001.x

Walsh, F. (2013). Community-based practice applications of a family resilience framework. In D. S. Becvar & D. S. Becvar (Eds.), *Handbook of family resilience* (pp. 65–82). New York, NY: Springer. http://dx.doi.org/10.1007/978-1-4614-3917-2_5

Zolkoski, S. M., & Bullock, L. M. (2012). Resilience in children and youth: A review. *Children and Youth Services Review, 34*, 2295–2303. http://dx.doi.org/10.1016/j.childyouth.2012.08.009

Robert J. McLaughlin and Robbie N. Sharp

Working With Parents and Caregivers When Conflicts Arise

10

For the clinician, the crux of addressing the needs of the transgender and gender expansive (TGE) child in a consistent and loving way is to facilitate parental cohesion, despite differences in parents' worldviews and disagreements that may be exacerbated by the child's unexpected gender identity or expression. Whether they present as an intact parental unit or as separated coparents, all major caregivers are central to defining the social and emotional context for the child's development, including identity resolution and consolidation. When caregivers are in strong opposition regarding responses to the child's gender identity or expression, this discord threatens the child's well-being, particularly if family factions form within and across generations. The goals of clinical intervention are to bring caregivers together to develop a clearer understanding of their TGE child's needs, along with their own concerns and needs, and to help them create an environment that supports their child's exploration of identity. When conflicts persist, the tasks of the clinician may expand to encompass work with caregivers, the child, the siblings, and the extended family system to reduce threats to the child's healthy attachments, social emotional stability, and gender health.

Although differences in parental approaches to management of a child's gender identity or expressions commonly appear in clinical practice, scant literature exists to guide the family or the clinician in these situations (Dreger,

http://dx.doi.org/10.1037/0000095-010
The Gender Affirmative Model: An Interdisciplinary Approach to Supporting Transgender and Gender Expansive Children, C. Keo-Meier and D. Ehrensaft (Editors)
Copyright © 2018 by the American Psychological Association. All rights reserved.

2009). In our experience, even parents who agree to see a therapist and attend together may have disparate ideas about what is going on with their child and the best ways to support their child's healthy gender development. A parent can find support for rewarding conformance to traditional gender expectations and for punishing gender diversity (e.g., Zucker & Bradley, 2005), as well as for affirming the child's gender expression and fostering the child's "true gender self" when it becomes clear (Brill & Pepper, 2008; Ehrensaft, 2011). When such disparate notions are expressed in therapy, parents can often collaborate on ways to proceed—in the short term and the long term—and voice important questions leading to cooperative strategies that promote their child's healthy development.

In this chapter, language that refers to "parents" means "prominent adults in the child's life" and does not assume dyads, spousal relationships, different-gender couples, or intact families. Our experience includes biological parents who are raising the child together or while separated or divorced, single parents with and without coparents, single and coupled adoptive parents, foster parents, and kinship parenting collectives including grandparents and others. The term *parents* reflects appreciation of all such caregiver influences in a child's household—and across households—regardless of family constellation, in recognition that conflicts can erupt in any caregiving system that addresses gender identity and expression.

We propose that clinicians use thorough and ongoing assessment to aid understanding of parental discord about the child's gender identity or expressions; to suggest interventions to reduce that discord in service of the child's development; and to inform treatment, as needed, for the child, the caregiver system, and the extended family. Presenting parental conflict has roots in individual histories, biases, and assumptions, and resides within the context of the relationship history and balance of parenting styles. Uncovering these issues requires attention to each parent's personal history and perspective, as well as an understanding of the dynamics and influence of extended families with attendant loyalties that may be hidden or unconscious. Differences among the parents or caregivers can be intense and even volatile. Effective interventions, therefore, require the clinician to relate to each caregiver, in consideration of family values, culture, community, and other influences, while focusing on the well-being of the child.

Initial Family Presentation

Families of TGE children present in myriad ways with varied levels of conflict and skills for dealing with conflict. The initial presentation usually informs the therapist as to how extensive the assessment process must be and suggests interventions.

LOW CONFLICT

In some families, minor conflicts can be resolved with information and guided reflections that highlight parental agreement on core values. In these families, each parent may demonstrate the intent to support the child despite skepticism or concern regarding gender identity/expressions or may simply want an affirming place to talk. The child in these cases is often doing well at home, school, and in the community. Such parents may need only a safe place to learn about resources and verify that they are meeting their child's needs in healthy ways (Riley, Sitharthan, Clemson, & Diamond, 2013). Often, one parent has taken the lead to understand gender issues and find resources, yet sufficient parental compatibility exists to propel them as a unit to establish an affirming family environment for the child. Additional guidance, and even advocacy, may be needed to help them develop strategies to engage outside systems, such as extended family, neighbors, parents of the child's friends, schools, faith communities, and formal support organizations. Their child will typically not need treatment; episodic parent consultations may suffice that are mostly psychoeducational, such as providing guidelines to promote healthy development in lesbian, gay, bisexual, and transgender (LGBT) youth (Substance Abuse and Mental Health Services Administration [SAMHSA], 2014) or that merely provide a safe place for facilitated discussion, airing of differences, or addressing fears and questions as they arise.

Case Study One

Rosie and George are university professors, both upwardly mobile heterosexual cisgender individuals from middle-class Euro American backgrounds. Their only child, Chris, was assigned male at birth, and was a spirited child, preferring dance and music to sports and outdoor activities. Chris had both boys and girls for friends, and tended to engage with serious, verbal children with like interests. Chris did well in school, excelled in piano lessons, and participated in a modern dance team sponsored by the school. With the onset of puberty at 11, Chris became withdrawn and showed reluctance to continue with piano or dance. After a particularly trying day, Chris broke down at the dinner table and cried inconsolably, ultimately blurting, "I am a freak because I am really a girl," and expressing stress in coping with a "boy body." The parents assured Chris they would do everything they could to be supportive. Internet searches led them to information about "sex reassignment surgeries" and historic biographies of transgender individuals. When they sought counseling, their questions were whether a child could understand gender identity enough to be transgender, how they should parent differently, and what should they do next. The therapist connected them to information resources more relevant to children and encouraged them to discuss their fears; their initial inquiries set the stage for productive ongoing dialogue.

MODERATE CONFLICT

In other families, one parent's reluctance to accept or affirm the child's gender identity and expression may strain the parental unit or relationship with the child, necessitating more therapeutic work, potentially to include the child and the parents. In these families, despite obvious conflict, strengths are evident in the relationships, in communication, and in sensitivity to many of the child's needs. Although the families present in conflict, their disagreements tend not to be so rancorous as to damage the family unit. The child may be aware of tension about gender identity and expression based on disparate parental responses to the child, but may also experience parental support. Depending on the assessment discoveries, the therapist may evoke productive discussions about gender identity and expression, concerns, questions, and fears; share information about community resources for their child and for them; and impart skills to negotiate future conflicts (Riley et al., 2013).

Case Study Two

Maria, a lesbian cisgender woman, conformed to gender expectations while growing up in a large Mexican American extended family. As a teenager, she resisted her romantic attraction to women and became pregnant, having a child who was assigned male at birth. As a single mother, she moved across town and got an office job in a department store. She remained somewhat close to her family but was discrete about her sexual orientation, and vowed that her children would not suffer the cultural constraints she experienced. When her toddler evidenced a compelling preference for pink and "girly" things, was seen to play only with girls at Head Start, and began to assert being a girl, Maria saw a therapist to determine how best to support the child's emerging gender. Maria accepted the child's choice to be called "Norah" and worked with the preschool to accept Norah as a girl; she was relieved that kindergarten and first grade proceeded without incident.

During the first-grade year, Maria introduced Norah to her new girlfriend, Toni, who adored Norah and helped her develop a love of cooking. Although she was from the same Mexican American cultural community as Maria, Toni's family had encouraged her self-expression and supported her to acquire the culinary training to become a chef. Toni had come out in her early teens and was mostly well accepted by her family as a somewhat masculine lesbian, but she firmly resisted when her cousins joked about her being a man. When Maria and Toni decided to combine households after dating a year, Maria told Toni that Norah "was born a boy" and later told the therapist she was surprised when Toni "freaked out."

Maria brought Toni to a session with the therapist, where they were able to lay out their perceptions about transgender identity and clarify misunderstandings. Toni's concerns about Norah included confusion about whether she might "grow out of it" and come to identify as a gay man, instead. They discussed the variety of ways transgender identity and sexual orientation are expressed as well as their mutual concerns about discrimination Norah might face as a transgender woman of color, as her "true self" became known. This led them to address other assumptions and expectations about moving in together: trust, household responsibility, finances, and parenting.

HIGH CONFLICT

The most complex families present with severe schisms, even separation and divorce, usually based on factors apart from the child's gender expressions or identity, although purportedly irresolvable differences in the parents' responses to the child's gender may play a role in the estrangement. High conflict arises when one parent refuses to accept the child's verbal and behavioral assertions and expressions of gender, engages in disrespectful language or treatment of the child, or threatens to divorce or sue for sole custody in response to the child's gender identity and/or expressions. Engaging these parents in productive discourse is extremely challenging, and sometimes impossible, whether the conflict is due to the child's gender or to other disputes; separate but coordinated consultations with each parent may be the best initial course of assessment and treatment to reconcile disparate approaches. Often, the child or siblings have been co-opted into the conflict and need to be included in therapeutic interventions—sometimes with one or both parents, sometimes alone—to address estrangement when it has occurred and to minimize misinformation and confusion. The clinician must attempt to manage not only the gender concerns but also high-conflict dynamics and dispute resolution. It may be necessary to adopt a team approach, where resources permit. We have had success when one clinician assumes therapy to address the children's feelings, beliefs, and loyalties, and another addresses the parents' management of conflict. With appropriate consents and disclosures, additional therapists who see the parent(s) separately may be included in team consultations, which may include an *ad litem* attorney to protect the children's interests, as well as additional attorneys involved in the parental dispute.

Case Study Three

Jeremy's parents, Sherry and Ed, are cisgender Euro American individuals who have each had occasional heterosexual relationships since they divorced when Jeremy was 4 and his brother was 2. Both maintain steady employment, Sherry as office support for a small company and Ed in a series of computer service jobs. Jeremy, assigned female at birth, declared at age 8 that he was a boy. He was not sure how "God made a mistake" but asserted that everyone who called him a girl had got it wrong. He was a good student entering third grade at a Catholic school. Sherry chose her battles about clothes and hair length, but the Lower School uniform for girls was a jumper and blouse and Jeremy was not allowed to wear polo shirts and shorts. Ed had limited contact with the children, but when Jeremy told him at his next visit that he wanted to wear the boys' uniform, Ed became furious. He blamed Sherry for coddling him and called Jeremy ugly names, telling him no child of his was going to be "a fag." He refused to allow Jeremy to visit him unless he wore "girl" clothes and responded to *she/her/hers* pronouns. When Jeremy refused, Ed stopped inviting him to visit and castigated Jeremy's 6-year-old brother, who tried to get his father to understand.

A school counselor referred Sherry to an affirming therapist who was not able to engage Ed in treatment but who helped Sherry identify support in her extended family and referred her to a support group with affirming parents. Jeremy adopted a gender neutral hairstyle and clothing for visits with his paternal grandparents, who supervised Ed's brief contacts with Jeremy and encouraged their shared interests in country music, sports, and video games. After several months, Ed joined Sherry at two counseling sessions, where it became evident he had watched a TV documentary on transgender children. Ed listened as the therapist voiced potential emotional risks as Jeremy approached female pubertal development. Ed opposed any consideration of treatment to suppress Jeremy's puberty but agreed to a "watch and wait" approach and let Sherry transfer Jeremy to a public school where he was not required to wear a jumper or dress. Jeremy, now 10, was thrilled when Ed accompanied him to a men's restroom at a sports arena and agreed to call him "Jay." Sherry sees the therapist every few months and reports that Ed remains "chilly" with her but listens when she or Jeremy share with him about Jeremy's gender experience.

By the time any family presents for treatment, multiple social interactions have influenced the child's self-acceptance and sense of welcome in the world. Clinicians can help parents recognize and establish positive connections, as well as mitigate negative influences. Clinicians should evaluate the potential to engage supportive parental practices and omit nonsupportive ones (SAMHSA, 2014). Clinicians must also assess damage caused by denying acceptance and support to the child because of gender identity and expression (Pyne, 2014). Although the following assessment dimensions focus on primary caregivers, all are fruitful areas of inquiry and potential resolution applicable to the child's broader social system.

Assessment Dimensions

We recognize five broad areas for assessment of parental conflict: (a) attitudes and parental responses of each major caregiver to the child's gender identity and/or expression, including gender concepts, religious beliefs, and family norms; (b) the character and intensity of parental discord and how the child's gender is involved; (c) alliances among the caregivers, child, and siblings, and important relationships beyond the nuclear family; (d) the child's responses to each parent, and awareness of and response to the discord itself; and (e) determinants of strength, congruence in parental goals, and expectations for supporting the child in exploring gender identity and/or expression and for developing healthy family relationships. These dimensions are explicated next.

PARENTS' GENDER IDEOLOGIES

At face value, it is important to assess the attitudes and behaviors of the major caregivers toward the child and, specifically, to the child's gender assertions and expressions. Chief among them are the parents' capacities for attunement, for validation of the child's lived experience, and for meeting the child's needs to explore gender. Sessions with the clinician typically reveal whether the parents are attuned to the child and in general agreement about their approach to the child's gender-typed behaviors or hold disparate views that have compromised their ability to work together on child management. Each parent's gender beliefs, attitudes, and values emerge from unique multicultural influences and intersectional identities, and are played out across multiple venues. Broad influences can be attributed to the parents' demographic and cultural identities, even though beliefs, attitudes, and values about gender vary within demographic strata and cultures. Parents can be helped to examine the degree to which their views of gender adhere to fixed, binary concepts and the manner in which their views have been shaped by their own gender identity, gender expression in their families, race, ethnicity, religious community, and socioeconomic circumstances, historically and in the present. Membership in faith communities and interpretation of religious proscriptions weigh heavily in some parents' gender beliefs and biases and may surface in treatment as the basis to oppose gender diversity. Even parents from the same faith community usually had different religious experiences and incorporated nuanced messages with varied levels of intensity. In many Western religions, beliefs and expectations about gender emerge more through innuendo or absence of discussion than through study of doctrine, while other religions and cultures are highly proscriptive about deviations from accepted gender identities and expressions. Parents may struggle to reconcile their love for the child and their love for the place of worship, which now coexist in tension. Parents may need opportunities to clarify their values about caregiving and about nurturing their child's emerging self apart from religious doctrine. Individuals differ widely in the manner in which they resolve such crises of faith, and outcomes range from rejection of either child or religion to tortured ambivalence to well-integrated resolutions. Each parent needs a safe, nonthreatening place to work through their concerns. Here, as in other intensely personal struggles, clinicians may help parents find the patience and wisdom to face these challenges while attending to their child's needs.

Clinicians may encourage parents to seek affirming congregations within their faith base that accept gender diversity or celebrate individual expression. Affirming clergy, directed readings, or discussion with other parents who have faced this dilemma may be useful. Resources exist. For example, the Family Acceptance Project, under Caitlin Ryan's direction, has produced literature specifically to address religious beliefs and parenting LGBT children in Mormon families (http://familyproject.sfsu.edu/family-education-booklet-lds).

Regardless of cultural and religious contexts, each parent is also subject to idiosyncratic personal narratives regarding gender and sexuality, which many have never explored or questioned. These influences can be difficult to discern and may emerge in therapy as they find meaning of experiences, relationships, and associations beyond the nuclear family, from the present and past. For example, one mother attributed her distress that her son was transgender to her personal history of abandonment by her father, who had left his family to "be a transvestite in New Orleans and die of AIDS." The therapist helped her consider that her transgender child could have a different outcome.

In treatment, parents can examine their personal experiences of adequacy in their gender identity and expression tied to narratives that emerged in their formative relationships. How have they experienced reward or condemnation throughout their lives for perceived deviations from gender expectations? How was gender valued and rewarded? How did primary role models reflect feminine or masculine cultural norms? What instances of sexual or other abuse were attributed to gender identity or gender expression? What media depictions shaped their perceptions and continue to influence their beliefs and attitudes, explicitly or subtly? To what degree is each aware that these influences affect their opinions of, unconscious assumptions about, and reactions to their child's gender? The clinician hopes to establish the degree to which each parent is able to relinquish a stronghold on their own expectations and goals for the child in service of larger goals for the child's intact sense of self and value, of integrity and self-acceptance.

CHARACTER OF CONFLICT

Having identified likely areas of disagreement regarding gender concepts and tolerance of gender expansiveness, it is important to explore the intensity of the discord. Clinicians can help parents contextualize their conflict with regard to its specificity to gender identity/expressions, its appearance across myriad aspects of their child's current and future happiness and functionality, or its sources apart from the child's gender. Overt conflicts may reflect true differences in gender beliefs or may be manifestations of pervasive relationship conflicts between the parents, rivalries over the child's affections, or styles of management of the child's behavior.

FAMILY ALLIANCES

Beyond the particular gender attitudes and behaviors of each parent, to what degree do alliances about gender exist among each caregiver and the child or siblings, and how do these influence the relationship between the child and the other parent? Triangulation will exacerbate challenges in the parental relationship. How have members of the nuclear family been co-opted into these alliances with and against the other parent or other members of the family? What is the role of grandparents, each parent's siblings, and other extended family in supporting the gender biases of one parent over another, and how have these played out regarding parenting decisions? What other influences impinge upon the child and the family system? Has either parent co-opted others in the multisystemic community in order to alienate the child from the other parent if the child does not conform to gender stereotypes? In facilitating parents' recognition of the ways in which these potential support systems have been engaged or corrupted, the clinician may also help them find compatible strategies to support the family as a whole and resist alliances that contribute to further estrangement.

Parents' different expectations may manifest in competing behavioral management strategies around gender identity and/or expression. How openly do they acknowledge discrepancies in treating gender issues or, for that matter, other parenting issues? How transparently do they face these differences, and what is each parent's level of insight into the differences? Effective practices to resolve differences in other areas may be applied to resolve disputes about gender. On the other hand, if previously successful parental strategies do not work in this particular arena, why not? Have traditional means to soothe tensions broken down around gender and, if so, at what point did that occur? What efforts have been made to reconcile differences and how did those unfold?

CHILD'S RESPONSES TO EACH PARENT AND TO PARENTAL CONFLICT

Parental insight may or may not extend to recognizing ways in which the child has responded to either parent around gender issues and, important, to the parental conflict itself. Parents will typically report if the child has sought refuge in the more supportive parent or become estranged from the other but may not be aware of the effects of the conflict itself on the child. Each may lack insight regarding the ways they have estranged or exploited the child based on their personal beliefs or attitudes or how the conflict itself has been exploited, sometimes by a parent and sometimes by the child.

In explicating the effects of parental conflict about gender, it can be helpful to explore the child's behavioral and emotional functioning in each caregiver's presence rather than rely on parental report. How does the child alter their gender assertions and expression in each parent's presence, in deference to or in defiance of that parent's perceived preferences or demands? How disparate are the child's presentations with one parent versus the other? What is each parent's awareness of the different ways the child presents, relates to, or responds to that parent and the other parent? If the child's gender-specific behaviors vary in intensity across settings or social contexts, such as in the grandparents' presence, at temple, school, or with peers, what might that mean about the nature of the child's authentic self in those settings? To what degree are the child's statements or actions related to real or perceived parental discord about gender? Is the child's behavior acting out conflict avoidance or, alternatively, attempting to provoke or exacerbate tensions between the parents, and what does this suggest about avenues of potential intervention? To what degree is the child aware that their gender expression contributes to the conflict between the parents, and what is each parent's response to that awareness? How does each parent's reaction to the child's gender affect the child's self-esteem? Have parent responses facilitated or compromised the child's gender identity formation?

PARENTAL CONGRUENCE IN GOALS AND EXPECTATIONS

While assessing areas of disagreement, it is essential to elicit and reinforce parental areas of agreement. It is particularly critical to evoke alignment of parental long-term goals and expectations for the child's happiness, functionality, and well-being. How similarly do the parents regard the child's needs to be heard versus to be compliant, and to be accepted and feel safe, and do they agree on how well these needs are being met? How well can they address whether their own and one another's needs to deal with the situation of their child's gender are being met?

Interventions

Interventions to reduce discord in parents' responses to, and influences on, a child's gender expression can occur at multiple levels and utilize a range of modalities that include psychoeducation, family systems therapy, cognitive–behavioral interventions, and skill-building, as well as child and adult individual and conjoint therapy. Treatment options vary, depending on who attends sessions and what issues require focused attention. Clinicians may choose various modalities, but the focal areas explicated next are generalizable to interventions with one or more parents, and with or without the TGE child, siblings, or extended family.

INTERVENTIONS WITH PARENTS

Generally, when parents are in conflict, one parent is the driving force to seek help. This parent may depict the other parent in many ways, from supportive, to neutral or disengaged, to hostile about the child's gender expression or identity. If both parents cannot be engaged directly, the presenting parent can be helped to identify common ground with the coparent or find ways to affirm the child's gender while working to bring the other parent along. If parents are separated or divorced, the stakes can be high because potential court battles revolving around disagreements about their child's gender are both emotionally and financially costly.

One parent's purported reluctance to engage in treatment may indicate underlying parental conflicts beyond gender issues and it must be recognized that the presenting parent may misperceive or misreport the other's motives, attitudes, and behaviors. True resistance can reflect emotional estrangement between the parents, or between a parent and the child; however, the child's experience of either parent might be quite different from what the parent describes. Likewise, the child may experience either parent differently than the clinician anticipates. The child may feel compelled to choose sides and may adopt inaccurate perceptions of parent attitudes and behaviors that serve some purpose in the parental conflict, such as siding with the parent with the greater power or financial wherewithal to meet the child's wants.

Understanding these family dynamics is critical to deciding how to proceed. Strategies may be employed to pique interest in attending conjoint parent consultations or individual sessions with the clinician. Determining where and with whom to begin intervention is difficult, but in the best of circumstances both parents are sufficiently invested in relieving their family stress to participate in the process and attempt new ways to interact.

Key's (2014) framework outlines considerations for consistent parenting in gender-related areas. These include consulting a therapist to negotiate conflict over handling gender issues; recognizing that differences of opinion are likely based on shared goals of what is best for the child; looking at caregivers' understanding of the perceived issues, concerns, and barriers; evaluating the child's level of distress; mutual gathering and sharing of information and knowledge about gender identity; and setting aside relationship difficulties as much as possible, particularly in divorce and separation situations.

When consulting a therapist, parents may feel pressed to stress their differences before they can consider similarities, because discord typically brings them to the consultation. It is critical to help parents clarify shared values and expectations for their child's long-term well-being. Typically, parents want their child to be happy, healthy, and functional. Expansions on these themes involve being safe, capable of intimate personal relationships and friendships, and employable. The clinician can help parents address a gender diverse future for their child (Riley et al., 2013). Although it is important to point out that the child may attain positive outcomes regardless of gender expression or gender identity, parents need to understand that their child's health and safety depend on caring and affirming parental responses. They need opportunities to air their fears and concerns, including differences from one another, and they need to be aware that not meeting the child's need to be affirmed, loved, and accepted poses a risk, no matter what their gender.

The importance of finding common ground in the parents' long-term hopes for their child cannot be overstated. Almost invariably, commonalities in the parents' hopes can be found to anchor treatment goals and create touchstones to which the clinician can return when salient differences surface. Fruitful strategies include asking each parent's wishes for the child even before birth, how those wishes were affected when each parent learned the child's sex, and whether those wishes have changed. It can be important to contextualize rapid changes in social strictures in recent generations that are changing still, such as that gender restrictions imposed on the grandparents' generation were diminished for the parents and will lessen further for their children (Pyne, 2014). Despite an individual's opinion toward cultural shifts in gender expectations, parents likely agree that some benefits have accompanied these shifts. For example, not long ago, women in the workplace were an anomaly, yet many households today depend on income from all adults in the home and recognize women's participation in the workforce as progress.

Parents may be guided to see that their child is happier or less withdrawn when their asserted gender is affirmed. This simple acknowledgment, with strategic reinforcement from time to time, lays the groundwork for acceptance and may be critical in bringing parents toward shared perspectives that incorporate greater gender flexibility for their child. When differences in opinions emerge about managing the child's gender identity or expression, it can help to explore when the parents first noticed that each responded differently and what meaning they assigned to that. For example, did conflicts emerge in the child's infancy with regard to parent choices in sex-typed clothing, in early childhood when the child displayed unexpected behaviors, or in later childhood when the child verbally asserted clothing, hairstyle, and play preferences? To what degree were these gender expressions perceived as a parent's decision versus the child's assertion? In retrospect, what meaning does each parent attribute to the emergence of these themes?

At some point, the parents noticed discrepancies between their child's asserted interests and behaviors and cultural stereotypes for the child's assumed gender. Did they discuss these observations when they arose? What were their reactions in those first stages of awareness? Some parents can discuss highly charged topics like gender and sex and reach resolution; others agree peaceably to a shared stance despite differences of opinion; and still others engender tension by working at odds with one another in reacting to their child. How did these parents' management of gender issues resemble their resolutions of other disagreements in parenting approaches and expectations for their child? In what areas were they able to reach agreement, and why did they fall short in reaching resolution regarding dimensions of gender? Can they take gender out of the equation and resolve their differences? How important does each judge gender identity to be in a child's development? Parents often have differences in their tolerance of their child's individuation. How have they worked to maintain relationships with one another and with the child throughout their child's unfolding development?

Persistent differences in the parents' approaches may necessitate discussing whether each parent believes it is possible to reach agreement or to establish tolerance regarding differences in expectations and limits for their child's gender expression. If the parents perceive their differences as irresolvable, are they hopeful about learning to live with the discord, and how do they expect the discord itself will affect the child in the present and moving forward? How will the discord likely affect the child's relationship with each parent? What reverberations will occur in the nuclear and extended family? How will the discord affect the parents' relationship? The child's progressive milestones may be accompanied by an increase in the significance of gender expression and identity, such as entering school, developing independent friendships, having sleepovers, approaching puberty, and desiring to date. How will the gender issues that present themselves in these contexts affect the parents' ability to manage differences moving forward?

Where disagreement cannot be resolved, disputes over management of a child's TGE status can be severe enough to result in, or become a part of, custody disputes and visitation battles, leaving the child feeling responsible for the family breakup or animosity (Ehrensaft, 2011). In such situations, the parent who supports the child's gender identity/expression is encouraged to document adherence to mental health and medical advice from professionals with expertise in these matters and ensure that the documentation includes evidence of efforts to involve the other parent (Broadus & Minter, 2014). Parents may need referrals to attorneys with experience in gender diversity or to organizations that provide legal advice to the LGBTQ community, such as the Transgender Law Center, the National Center for Lesbian Rights, GLAD Legal Advocates and Defenders, or the American Civil Liberties Union. When a parent's responses to the child's gender assertions are abusive, steps must be taken to institute protections for the child that shelter their developing sense of self-worth and sometimes even physical safety.

INTERVENTIONS INVOLVING SIBLINGS

Multiple aspects of the family system might provide support and influence toward greater parental congruence and, on the other hand, fuel parental conflict about gender. If the child has siblings, their responses to the child's gender and to each parent's approach can reverberate throughout the system. It is common for siblings to be approached with questions about their gender diverse sibling. In many families, siblings readily adapt and demonstrate acceptance of various expressions of gender, taking protective postures toward the TGE child. Siblings may also alienate and reject the child, or become hostile toward the child in public to avoid social ramifications, most notably teasing from their peers. In response, parents may attempt to suppress a child's gender expression to spare siblings from feared social ostracism, privileging the siblings' well-being over the TGE child's freedom to express their gender authentically. Whether protective or rejecting, siblings need to be included in family sessions.

Sibling sessions without the gender diverse child present may enable them to vent negative feelings and fears and learn coping skills, while at other times, conjoint sessions that include everyone may be critical to reduce family conflict.

INTERVENTIONS INVOLVING EXTENDED FAMILY

Extended family members play central roles in shaping parental attitudes about gender and determine the level of support for the TGE child. Parents may adopt positions regarding gender expression based on anticipation of their own parents' and siblings' responses or in the face of actual responses. Because grandparents, aunts, uncles, and stepparents can inflame or alleviate family tensions, family therapy sessions that include such key individuals may be indicated. Family members who influence the less affirming parent may play a productive role if they are motivated to shift the focus from gender tension toward family unity. Likewise, joint sessions with a supportive parent may enlist skeptical relatives to ensure the child's safety at family gatherings. Grandparents might be the source of restrictive traditional gender stereotypes, yet just as often are sources of unconditional love and acceptance for grandchildren. Cousins may support TGE children more readily than siblings, lacking a sibling's fear of rejection by association with the identified child.

We have worked with parents who encountered both accepting, supportive responses and rejecting, divisive responses from extended family. Parents who agree to affirm their TGE child can respond by attempting to share information and provide opportunities to interact with their family, while insisting on enforcing boundaries to protect the child. Our work has generally aimed to help the parents and child address extended family issues as they arise. When members of the extended family have been unavailable or declined to attend family sessions, we have sometimes had success engaging them in local educational conferences.

Special challenges when dealing with extended family exist when parents disagree about affirming the child's gender expression or identity. One parent may wish to protect the child from extended family members who object to the child's gender, while the other may overtly engage those relationships specifically to reinforce disapproval of the child's gender identity or expression. Critical treatment tasks include helping the child and the affirming parent find positive ways to respond in these situations, to utilize respectful but firm statements of their choices, and to reach resolution about managing toxic emotional environments. This might mean limiting or supervising extended family or intergenerational gatherings where the child would be exposed to disaffirming or disrespectful attitudes and behaviors and avoiding venues in which the child would interact with particular rejecting family members.

INTERVENTIONS WITH THE CHILD

Particularly when parental agreement is a distant ambition, direct therapeutic work with the TGE child may be needed to help the child cope with and adapt to incompatible parental expectations. Optimally, if influences are not so strong as to disaffirm the child's identity or worth, the child can be supported to maintain relationships with each parent and with other family members. It might be possible to exploit common interests and goals in ways that build upon strengths in those relationships and minimize gender conflicts.

When there is disagreement regarding the child's gender, one parent may insist that the child be exposed to venues where gender diversity is not supported. In such circumstances, the clinician may help an older child weigh the value of choosing to adapt gender expression to the social context, both in and outside the family, versus choosing not to adapt and rather to cope with the consequences of rejection and exclusion. The clinician can guide the supportive parent to endorse the child's decision, and to help the child maintain personal integrity by affirming the validity of such decisions for the purposes of avoiding irresolvable discord and retaining family alliances. For example, a father objected to his child's gender expression (i.e., clothing and hairstyle) and insisted that the child conform to the father's sense of gender appropriateness or be excluded from family celebrations. In response, at those events, the child chose to don a "costume" associated with the assigned sex and later cast off the costume and resumed expressing their authentic self. By regarding the "costume" as simply an adaptive social performance for the benefit of others who were not yet enlightened about gender expansiveness, the child could maintain an integrated sense of self while staying connected to the family. The clinician and supportive parent jointly strategized to shore up the child's resolve that this was at least for now a solution to minimize family rifts. These challenging situations reflect reality when a parent does not accept the child's true gender self and when continuation of the relationship is conditional on the child's temporary compliance with the parent's gender biases.

HELPING PARENTS ATTEND TO COMMUNITY AND LARGER SYSTEMS

Broader community systems influence each parent's attitudes and behaviors, and parents might draw upon them to support their gender biases. Clergy and congregants may support or refute a position that inflames parental conflict. Nearly all parents wish their child to be protected from bullying and harassment, but parents with limited appreciation of the child's experience of rejection by neighbors or peer groups might insist that the child engage in aversive and damaging social activities. One parent may be an advocate for a child who is gender expansive and work to remove barriers; another may support gender-restrictive policies and even reinforce social admonishments for perceived gender transgressions and regard the negative treatment as a natural consequence of the child's defiance of prevailing norms. The clinician must address the parents' conflicts about safe environments and how they will intervene to protect their child.

LONG-TERM MANAGEMENT

Many coparents ultimately reach agreement in addressing the child's emerging gender identity and diversity of gender expression. If each parent stays engaged with the child and can value the child in ways that transcend gender stereotypes, supportive attitudes may enable healthy development of gender identity. Optimally, the clinician is a part of the support team and can connect parents to community resources, collaborate with educational, legal, and medical professionals, and facilitate family decisions about gender care.

Parental conflict regarding gender may erupt whenever parent opinions differ in what to allow, where, and when. The clinician can help parents anticipate and address differences as developmental challenges emerge. Even a resistant parent may tolerate variable gender expression in early childhood, but the child's gender expansiveness may become more emotionally charged for that parent as the child matures. Schools, places of worship, and neighborhoods may become reactive and intensify parental intolerance.

Some touch points for increased risk of conflict between parents are predictable. When the child begins preschool or kindergarten, comparisons with gender-typed behaviors of peers are frequent and persistent, and parents might be expected to bring their child into compliance with community norms. Another touch point is when the child asserts preferences for clothing, toys, and hairstyles, and objects to parental choices that reflect gender restrictions. The onset of puberty is a major trigger because the child's body dysphoria and emerging sexuality command attention. Desires to seek a social, legal, or medical gender transition for a transgender child are further major areas for parent conflict. If parents cannot agree how to proceed, conflict is likely.

At any age, when a child becomes reactive to gender pronouns, names, or nicknames with strong gender implications or to relational words depicting gender (e.g., *daughter, sister, son, brother*), the child's objections can provoke ruptures in the parents' ability to find common ground to tolerate the child's gender identity. Parents who have not developed a united approach to accept and affirm their child's gender identity can clash about how to respond.

Conclusion

Issues of gender and sex can be highly charged for parents and are laid open when a child is gender expansive or transgender. Ensuing parenting challenges can strain knowledge, beliefs, and attitudes beyond what many loving caregivers can imagine, and parental discord and conflict frequently arise. The parental tasks of being loving and accepting of a child's exploration of gender identity must be balanced with the child's needs to be safe, secure, and resilient. When there is parental discord as to how to create this balance, accomplishment of these parental tasks can be greatly facilitated by the intervention of knowledgeable and skilled therapists. We have grown to know many courageous, loving, strong parents of delightful, smart, inventive children; we have all learned together to celebrate the creative wonders of gender diversity and its capacity to override familial and extrafamilial conflict.

Resources

American Civil Liberties Union: https://www.aclu.org
Family Acceptance Project: http://familyproject.sfsu.edu
National Center for Lesbian Rights: http://www.nclrights.org
GLAD Legal Advocates and Defenders: https://www.glad.org

References

Brill, S., & Pepper, R. (2008). *The transgender child: A handbook for families and professionals*. San Francisco, CA: Cleis Press.

Broadus, K. W., & Minter, S. P. (2014). Legal issues. In L. Erickson-Schroth (Ed.), *Trans bodies, trans selves: A resource for the transgender community* (pp. 174–211). New York, NY: Oxford University Press.

Dreger, A. (2009). Gender identity disorder in childhood: Inconclusive advice to parents. *The Hastings Center Report, 39*, 26–29. http://dx.doi.org/10.1353/hcr.0.0102

Ehrensaft, D. (2011). *Gender born, gender made: Raising healthy gender-nonconforming children*. New York, NY: The Experiment, LLC.

Key, A. (2014). Children. In L. Erickson-Schroth (Ed.), *Trans bodies, trans selves: A resource for the transgender community* (pp. 409–445). New York, NY: Oxford University Press.

Pyne, J. (2014). Gender independent kids: A paradigm shift in approaches to gender non-conforming children. *The Canadian Journal of Human Sexuality, 23*, 1–8. http://dx.doi.org/10.3138/cjhs.23.1.CO1

Riley, E., Sitharthan, G., Clemson, L., & Diamond, M. (2013). Recognising the needs of gender-variant children and their parents. *Sex Education, 13*, 644–659. http://dx.doi.org/10.1080/14681811.2013.796287

Substance Abuse and Mental Health Services Administration. (2014). *A practitioner's resource guide: Helping families to support their LGBT children* (HHS Publication No. PEP14-LGBTKIDS). Rockville, MD: Author. Retrieved from https://store.samhsa.gov/shin/content/PEP14-LGBTKIDS/PEP14-LGBTKIDS.pdf

Zucker, K., & Bradley, S. (2005). Gender identity and psychosexual disorders. In J. M. Wiener & J. K. Dulcan (Eds.), *The American Psychiatric Publishing textbook of child and adolescent psychiatry* (3rd ed., pp. 813–836). Washington, DC: American Psychiatric Association. Retrieved from http://focus.psychiatryonline.org/doi/abs/10.1176/foc.3.4.598

Randi Kaufman and Amy Tishelman

Creating a Network of Professionals

11

Gender is fundamental to interpersonal interaction. Much has been written about gender stereotyping and the impact of gender on functioning and development across interpersonal, academic, social and occupational realms. Given that gender is intrinsic to self-concept, self-understanding, and the perceptions and expectations of others, gender development that varies from conventional trajectories can be a profound experience for a child. Creating a network of educational, medical, mental health, legal, and sometimes spiritual professionals who are trained in understanding transgender and gender expansive (TGE) children, and the issues that often arise, is an integral part of facilitating a positive developmental trajectory for a child. Such a network is a central factor in the child's psychosocial adaptation and adjustment. Through access to this interdisciplinary collaborative network, the family can thoughtfully create and shape opportunities and environments that best suit the needs of their child and their own personal situation.

Ecological Model

Children are, by definition, part of an ecological system, meaning that their development takes place through "progressively more complex reciprocal interaction" between themselves and "the persons, objects and symbols"

http://dx.doi.org/10.1037/0000095-011
The Gender Affirmative Model: An Interdisciplinary Approach to Supporting Transgender and Gender Expansive Children, C. Keo-Meier and D. Ehrensaft (Editors)
Copyright © 2018 by the American Psychological Association. All rights reserved.

in their environment (Bronfenbrenner, 1994, pp. 1643–1647). This ecological system typically broadens with development. Infants must rely on others for survival, including all important decisions regarding their care and health. Although this reliance increasingly relaxes as the child approaches mid- to late adolescence, the child's ecological world has a profound impact on their life experience and developmental trajectory. A number of studies suggest that ecological factors can be protective, harmful, or both (e.g., Belsky, 1993; Tishelman, Haney, Greenwald O'Brien, & Blaustein, 2010). An intersectional ecology model applied to lesbian, gay, bisexual, transgender, and questioning (LGBTQ) populations has been proposed (Mink, Lindley, & Weinstein, 2014), observing that the high risks and adversities associated with sexual and gender minority status are often related to social context.

General developmental literature also informs understanding of risks and protective factors with TGE youth, in the service of fostering positive development from early childhood. This literature consistently emphasizes that development is cumulative, with each phase being a foundation for future development (Sroufe, 2013), and past development as a shaper of future development (Masten & Cicchetti, 2010). Change is possible for an individual at any point, but the person is also constrained by past experience (e.g., Sroufe, 2013). *Developmental cascades*, or the cumulative effect of multiple interactions in the ecological environment on a child's development, are believed to alter the course of development, with consequences that are not transient (Masten & Cicchetti, 2010, p. 491). Therefore, with regard to TGE children, it is critical to understand the many factors that impinge on development and the child's sense of comfort, confidence, and self-esteem, and to foster the situations that facilitate positive relationships, happiness, and success at meeting one's own personal goals.

Importance of Coordination Among Professionals

A retrospective study of TGE adults found that their most commonly identified childhood needs were educated authority figures, acceptance and support to discuss their gender diversity, freedom of identity expression, validation, and recognition (Riley, Clemson, Sitharthan, & Diamond, 2013). The needs most commonly endorsed for parents were access to information, education, peer support, and educated professionals. Professionals frequently involved with a TGE child and family include school officials, educational advocates, medical and mental health providers, legal advisors, and pastoral and/or spiritual advisors. Creating such a network is important to ensuring a smooth, successful transition for TGE children across various domains. Optimally, at least one or more of these professionals has expertise in working with TGE youth. In settings in which such access is impossible, modern technology enables professionals to communicate and access consultation and resources remotely.

Coordinated care involves identifying problem areas, knowing what types of professionals to bring on board, intervening appropriately and with sensitivity, and helping families access other resources. Although things can go awry for many different reasons, having professionals work together in a coordinated way buffers a negative outcome. For example, when a TGE child wants to make a social transition, the participation of an experienced mental health provider or advocate to help the family navigate challenges at school, religious institutions, and other important contexts may be essential. This coordinated care approach can be individually tailored, taking into account the child's and family's unique circumstances to optimize support, facilitating a sense of safety and acceptance for a child.

Educational Professionals

The Gay, Lesbian, & Straight Education Network published a National School Climate Survey in 2013, which included sobering statistics (Kosciw, Greytak, Palmer, & Boesen, 2014). The survey reported high levels of harassment and assault, discriminatory school policies and practices, and a lack of safety for LGBT students. With regard to transgender students specifically, 42.2% had been prevented from using their chosen name, 59.2% had been required to use a bathroom or locker room of their legal sex rather than their gender identity, and 31.6% had been prevented from wearing clothes considered by the school to be inappropriate based on their assigned sex. The report noted that students experiencing higher levels of victimization were more than 3 times as likely to have missed school in the past month compared with other students. Victimized students had lower grades, lower levels of self-esteem, and higher levels of depression, and they were twice as likely to report that they did not plan to pursue any postsecondary education.

When children come out to their family as TGE, one of the first questions to arise is whether, and how, to tell the school. When a child comes out to a teacher or guidance counselor before telling their family, the school may be the first setting for initial stages of social transition. In either case, teachers and school personnel are often some of the first professionals to be brought into the network that forms around the child, and need to know how to accommodate the child in school. School personnel generally want to do what is best to foster a child's well-being but cannot do so if they are uninformed. In addition, school professionals who are not gender affirming might engender negative and harmful experiences for the child, either wittingly or unwittingly. Regrettably, it is often left up to the family to take responsibility for educating school personnel or finding other professionals to come into the school to provide training. Increasingly, schools are taking the initiative to bring gender trainings to their academic community. In either case, children will most likely thrive if the families are proactive in advocating for their TGE child with the school (Brill & Pepper, 2008), which becomes one more task for the family that already has many. Unfortunately, children already at risk because of family conflict or rejection will be at even higher risk because they will lack parents willing to take on that task of family advocacy with the school. Typically, children spend the majority of their day in educational settings; therefore, TGE-friendly schools are essential in fostering learning in a safe and nontraumatizing environment.

Speaking with school leadership is an important first step in advocating for a TGE child. A point person, often the principal, will be an integral figure in developing a plan for the child, as well as in setting a positive tone regarding acceptance of gender diversity. When change is initiated from the top down, it often fosters an environment in which other personnel adapt better to implemented changes (Cole, Eisner, Gregory, & Ristuccia, 2013). School psychologists and guidance counselors can also be helpful in decision-making regarding which staff needs to know about a specific child's situation (National Association of School Psychologists, 2014). A child's gender identity is part of their medical history, and school personnel do not necessarily have access to this information. Balancing issues of confidentiality with support for a child's gender-related preferences requires careful discussion and collaboration. If the school's core policies do not include specific language around gender nondiscrimination, it will be important to work with the principal to clarify that diverse gender identity and expressions are to be accepted along with other personal identifiers such as race, nationality, religion, sexual orientation, and so on.

Teachers often have the most contact with students on a daily basis, and therefore need to be informed about the child's chosen name and appropriate pronoun, and the importance of using them consistently. Being referred to correctly is one of the most basic ways for a gender diverse child to feel recognized and validated. Not only does proper use of name and pronouns affirm the child's identity, it helps to create a cultural norm that models acceptance and respect. This may be particularly important when the child's name has not been legally changed, and therefore does not appear on the attendance roster and other school documentation. In such cases, school personnel may incorrectly assume that using a nonlegal name in the classroom is inappropriate, and/or not know how to explain a name change to other students or parents who make inquiries. School administrators will need to ensure that staff are aware of policies allowing children to use nonlegal names in the everyday school environment, even if legal names are retained for official documentation, such as report cards. A system for keeping the chosen name and pronoun in place is very important for situations such as substitute and adjunctive teachers, so professionals who are less familiar with the child have a clear guideline for their contact with the child. Having professionals who are educated about gender transition be part of the child's interdisciplinary network will allow for guidance around these issues.

Case Study

A TGE school-aged youth was placed in a therapeutic boarding school because of developmental and behavioral issues at home. An educational advocate worked closely with the child's family, outpatient psychologist, and the child's former school to coordinate care around finding a residential setting that was gender affirming and had appropriate educational and behavioral health services based on the child's unique set of needs. The boarding school also agreed to work on a continuing basis with the child's outpatient therapist who had been involved with the child and family for several years before the placement. This care coordination helped to avoid further complications and potential adversities related to gender, and facilitated successful implementation of services in this setting so that this child could thrive.

Medical Professionals

All children require wellness and illness care, provided through both primary care settings and specialized services. TGE youth encounter the same array of medical issues as any other child, and therefore can be expected to interface with the medical community on a routine basis.

Although TGE youth have always existed, issues related to their well-being and development went unnoticed until recently, when both media attention and gender-specific services started burgeoning. Most licensed physicians were trained well before issues related to TGE youth came to the forefront, and even now structured training programs on TGE children and youth are few and far between. Therefore, only the rare primary care physician (PCP) with particular interest in this population will likely have knowledge or expertise, and specialized practitioners will likely have even less training. For TGE children, routine medical care can therefore entail a number of risks and hardships, both medically and emotionally. Lack of training and exposure to TGE youth leaves these children vulnerable to encountering medical professionals who are misinformed or have personal biases, which can then be transmitted directly to a child and/or their family. An example of this occurs when the pediatrician reassures the parents, "Don't worry, it's only a phase," in response to a TGE child. Given that pediatricians are often viewed as authorities on all issues relevant to children, families may be prone to embrace their advice, including in situations when it is counter to their actual experience and factually incorrect. In some situations, the physician's uninformed or biased communications to the child and parents can set up a tension between family members, some of whom will either be persuaded or reinforced in their own views by physician-initiated misinformation, pitted against other family members who reject that advice. The PCP's stance on the child's gender expansiveness can even create conflicts between various physicians involved in a child's care. For instance, a pediatrician who refers a TGE child to an endocrinologist because of concerns that the child is diabetic may ignore that endocrinologist's recommendation to have the family consult with a gender specialist.

Other important risks can arise from child–physician interaction. Being examined by a physician who may be unaware of, minimize, or even reject gender identity concerns can be distressing or even traumatizing. For children who are uncomfortable with their bodies, without acute sensitivity on the physician's part, the medical examination can exacerbate feelings of embarrassment around their genitals. For example, a medical provider who comments on how wonderful it is to see the child maturing, may inadvertently cause a child distress, as puberty may be less than wonderful for this particular child. Such negative encounters can create a context of conditioned mistrust and discomfort associated with medical care. This can lead to active avoidance of necessary and routine medical care, risking an exponential increase in a TGE child's medical vulnerability. Given that past development is a shaper of future development, negative medical experiences in childhood can lead to continued avoidance over time of potentially shaming medical situations. Examples include trans feminine adults who refuse to have prostate exams, and trans masculine adults who refuse regular pelvic exams, putting both groups at risk for missing early detection of treatable cancers. Further, uncomprehending medical professionals can interpret gender expansive expressions or identities as a mental health condition to be "cured" through mental health intervention. This can engender further confusion and alienation for a child who may be struggling to affirm something that they cannot modify.

In contrast to uninformed providers, knowledgeable, sensitive, and supportive medical professionals can increase a child's hope, sense of esteem, and trust in adults and authority figures, a psychological gift for a young child who may feel bereft or confused. Invested medical personnel can outreach to mental health providers or schools to coordinate best care, and can refer children and families to gender specialists, support groups and organizations, such as PFLAG (Parents, Families and Friends of Lesbians and Gays) and, to help families garner support. Thus, a medical provider can provide comfort, support, and resources for families trying to cope in positive ways with challenging circumstances. In addition, because medical professionals are mandated to report concerns of child maltreatment, they can be protective forces for highly vulnerable children who are being emotionally or even physically abused by caregiving figures who are hostile to, and/or naive about, the children's gender identities or presentations.

Typically, TGE youth do not require medical intervention related to gender identity until they enter the very first stages of puberty. Gonadotropin-releasing hormone agonists are prescribed by medical providers to pause the onset of puberty. These medications, commonly referred to as *puberty blockers*, may then be initiated to buy time for the child and family to further evaluate whether, and when, to initiate a cross-sex puberty (for further details, see Chapter 12, this volume). Access to puberty blockers can be extraordinarily therapeutic to children and their families. For youth who may be dreading the physiological changes associated with a gender that they reject, their impending puberty can be alarming, threatening to upend their lives. Puberty blockers can alleviate some of the anxiety and dysphoria that often accompanies the progression of a biologically programmed gender that is a mismatch with identity. Having an informed, sensitive medical provider to communicate this information in a timely manner can make all the difference in a gender diverse child's level of well-being.

Mental Health Professionals

As with medical providers, mental health professionals can be involved with TGE youth and families in a number of roles. These roles can encompass acting as consultants, psychotherapists, educators, advocates, evaluators, providers on an interdisciplinary team, and collateral informants offering guidance to families, educators, other therapists, media, legal professionals, policymakers, and others. Similar to the Endocrine Society Clinical Practice Guidelines, the American Psychological Association Task Force on Gender Identity and Gender Variance (2009) supports the "efficacy, benefit, and medical necessity of gender-transition treatments for appropriately evaluated individuals" (p. 67). Parallel to concerns regarding medical professionals, underinformed mental health providers risk creating harm, mistrust of mental health interventions, stigma, and destructive developmental progressions that cannot be undone. Ethically, however, a conundrum occurs when youth and families need mental health services to help navigate the social and family challenges related to being transgender, but practitioners with the requisite expertise are unavailable. Therefore, it is imperative for mental health professionals to find ways to access the necessary resources to be able to properly serve gender diverse children, who inevitably will be coming their way, if not now, in the future. This can be accomplished through involvement with professional organizations such as the American Psychological Association and the World Professional Association for Transgender Health. In addition, mental health providers are encouraged to be proactive, take the initiative to form peer support groups, attend gender conferences, keep up to date with research as it becomes available, and consult with more experienced providers, to achieve a current level of knowledge. Given the breadth of resources on the Internet, including professional e-mailing lists, it is also possible to reach out to experts nationally and internationally for input about practice issues, professional trainings, and other resources.

PEDIATRIC SETTINGS

Pediatric psychologists and other mental health professionals often see youth in pediatric settings, as members of interdisciplinary teams housed in endocrinology, pediatrics, or adolescent medicine. Families frequently call to consult with gender teams when youth are prepubescent, requesting education and sometimes evaluation and guidance from an expert regarding issues such as social transition; disclosure; and navigation of the considerable cultural, social, and family dynamics and challenges that can emerge as a child explores gender identity and expression. Families with older children approaching puberty may seek information regarding puberty blockers.

Practice across gender centers differs with regard to a variety of issues, including the model used, the composition of the team, the range of services provided, and the age or developmental stage used as a benchmark for intervention. Some of these choices may be decided in part by the availability of providers with expertise. Other times, policies at the institution may override the gender clinic's recommendations, which may not be understood by a larger administration that lacks gender expertise. Many gender clinics housed in hospitals follow a model that includes prerequisites before medical intervention, such as a certain amount of time in gender-based psychotherapy and/or a comprehensive psychological and gender assessment. This evaluation is typically conducted by a mental health professional who is able to work closely with a family and interface with the rest of the team. Tishelman et al.

(2015) described one center's approach to evaluation of children in this context, but many approaches exist (see Chapter 7, this volume), and we anticipate they will be modified over time as research continues to inform best practices. In general, such an evaluation can be described as a way to best understand a child and family's needs, provide education, help them to review options based on their unique profiles, facilitate access to services, and reach out to others in a child's environment to help the child and family optimize environmental supports.

Child and other psychologists are trained in the skills utilized in these evaluations, as well as in therapy and consultation roles. They typically receive broad mental health, clinical, and developmental training in a tradition of working in multi- and interdisciplinary settings, with expertise in complex assessment and in the integration of multiple sources and methods of information. In addition, psychologists are trained to administer and interpret psychometric and projective measures with children, which can add an important dimension to an evaluation. This type of evaluation is particularly helpful when working with TGE youth and families, as a more superficial assessment may not be able to fully comprehend a child's experience within the context of multiple forces of influence, including family dynamics, religion, and social interactions with peers. As is known from other areas of psychology, young children can be especially susceptible to adopting the beliefs and assumptions of caregivers and others in authority. Care needs to be taken to understand a child's gender issues in the context of their multiple ecological influences.

PUBLIC OR PRIVATE PRACTICE SETTINGS

Mental health professionals often work with TGE youth and families outside of medical gender clinics because gender clinics, although growing in number, continue to be sparse throughout the United States. Any clinician who works with youth and families is likely to encounter concerns related to gender at some point. Because of this, it is critical for graduate programs to require training to ensure a basic level of skill for all new mental health clinicians. The complexities of work with TGE youth can sometimes be manifold. Some research suggests that certain issues, such as autism spectrum disorder, are more likely in youth with gender identity concerns (Shumer, Reisner, Edwards-Leeper, & Tishelman, 2016; Strang et al., 2014). These added layers of complexity present unique treatment needs and require specialized knowledge. It is well established that TGE children and youth have high rates of depression, anxiety, suicidality, and self-harm, particularly in the context of a rejecting or nonsupportive family. Mental health clinicians can provide necessary support and psychological interventions in such situations. They also may impart education and feedback to medical providers about a child's gender issues and needs prior to the initiation of medical intervention. Mental health clinicians, along with medical providers, school personnel, and other authorities entrusted with a child's welfare, may be compelled to file a report with child protective services if a child is being maltreated, and in rare cases, may need to inform courts regarding a child's best interests. In many ways, a mental health clinician can be a pivotal presence, informing the others in a child's ecological universe, and tracking a child's well-being throughout.

CASE EXAMPLE

A 12-year-old asserted and affirmed boy (assigned female at birth), who socially transitioned to living as a boy at age 7, has started to develop breast buds. He is very distressed about this and wears several layers of clothing to hide his chest, despite becoming overheated as a result. He is increasingly anxious that although he is nondisclosing of his transgender status, he will be "outed" as a result of the pubertal changes to his body. He has also become anxious as he anticipates the onset of menstruation. He is so preoccupied with this fear of the start of menses that he has begun to leave class frequently without permission to go to the bathroom to check his underwear. In addition, his anxieties have interfered with academic focus and concentration, and he was referred by his teacher, who was unaware of his gender concerns, for an evaluation for a possible attention or learning disorder. His parents took this opportunity to consult with a child psychologist with gender expertise, who was able to provide psychoeducation about medical intervention around pubertal changes. After evaluating the child, the therapist recommended moving forward with puberty blockers and facilitated a referral to a medical provider with the appropriate expertise. The physician evaluated this child medically and initiated puberty blocking medication, which gave the child great relief. His therapist obtained consent from his parents to speak with the school and educated the guidance counselor regarding this child's gender journey, suggesting that with academic support and empathy, this child might be able to return to his previous level of school functioning and adjustment.

Spiritual Counselors

Although some families do not choose to participate in religious or spiritual practices or institutions, or may not have access, for families who do, spiritual counselors can be integral components of a family's system of support. Although religious and spiritual practices can vary enormously, having a person of faith as a trusted resource can be beneficial and healing for families, and can provide another safe space for a TGE child and their family. Over time, as society becomes more knowledgeable about TGE individuals, accommodations are increasingly being made in religious and spiritual settings, even in instances that seem improbable. For example, despite the strict sex segregation of Orthodox Jews, accommodations of TGE students in Orthodox day schools and synagogues are being increasingly demanded, some of which are beginning to make changes. Similar to families, religious institutions can undergo a process of change and transformation, sometimes as a result of a TGE individual in their midst who brings the issue to ground level rather than being an ideological percept.

When religious or spiritual settings are not willing to accommodate TGE children, families may experience upset, feelings of rejection, and the need to evaluate undesirable or unsustainable options. Some families may willingly choose to change their place of worship, such as opting for a similar place of worship that will be accommodating, finding a less conservative branch (e.g., Reform Judaism vs. Orthodox), choosing welcoming/open churches or temples, or even changing their religious affiliation (e.g., to the Unitarian Universalist Church) to find a spiritual home that is supportive. However, such options may include the experience of loss of their spiritual home and community, and the new place may not fully meet the family's desires. Some families may feel they need to choose between their child and their religion, and may opt for undesirable choices, such as putting the child in an untenable situation of not actualizing their gender identity to attend the house of worship or leaving their TGE child home while the rest of the family participates, despite the experience of being invalidated, unsupported, and discriminated against. In such cases, it may be beneficial for a gender specialist to consult with the family's religious leader, to provide education on gender development and the direct correlation between gender-affirming responses and a child's well-being. This type of intervention may legitimize the situation and lead to acceptance of the TGE child and their family.

Legal Professionals and Issues

TGE youth and families can be involved with a variety of legal professionals regarding a host of issues, including (a) name changes, gender marker changes, and other legal documentation; (b) child protection; (c) child custody; (d) civil rights, such as public bathroom use and access to sports teams and other gender-specific school activities; and (e) health care. In addition, it should be noted that adolescents can also be directly involved in the legal system for reasons related to sexual exploitation and delinquency, both of which are risks for youth who are rejected at home or at school. TGE youth are more likely than same-age peers to run away from home, and/or to be subject to abuse at home, as well as exploitation on the street. Some older youth may explore legal means to establish emancipation, motivated by a need to forge a gender path independently, without the restrictions or aspersions of their family. For some children who are not accepted by their families, knowledgeable outside supports can help to stem long-term damage through advocacy, including through state child protection programs. Therefore, to ensure a child's well-being, school personnel, medical providers, mental health practitioners, and others involved with a TGE child may need to bring in the assistance of legal professionals if a child is living in an unsustainable and damaging environment.

CHILD PROTECTION AND SUPERVISION

Family courts may become involved when a report is made to child protective services or a family member seeks assistance to help manage their child, such as filing a child in need of supervision (CHINS) petition. Care and protection hearings can also occur for the court to move toward removal of a child from home in situations of maltreatment. In such situations, when one of the issues is a child's gender, it is imperative for mental health and medical professionals, educational professionals, or others experienced with gender identity and expression to educate the legal providers about the basic issues associated with gender diversity, to support the child through this stressful process and advocate for their best interests. It is important to understand the common occurrence of maltreated children maintaining secrecy related to abuse for many reasons, including fear of the consequences of disclosure, attachment to family members despite abuse, desire to remain in their communities and maintain friendships and valued activities, and lack of knowledge regarding who to trust. Close and trusting relationships with adults outside of the family can be crucial for TGE youth who are enduring any form of maltreatment. Such individuals may begin to suspect a child's victimization on the basis of behavior or the child's emotional state, or a child may eventually be comfortable enough to speak with them directly about their situation. In such instances, having a trusted adult already knowledgeable about the child's gender identity can be a critical part of the effort to protect a child while averting harm, and it can allow for important advocacy.

CHILD CUSTODY ISSUES

Family stress and division around issues of gender are not uncommon. In addition, family stressors may predate gender issues, and a TGE child can be a lightning rod for family dysfunction (see Chapters 8 and 9, this volume). Divorce, custody, and visitation are areas where legal professionals are poised to provide extremely important assistance, particularly when they are working within an interdisciplinary collaborative model. When a child's custody is at question following a marital separation or divorce, custody evaluators will often turn toward others who are involved with the child for input regarding the child's welfare. The critical role legal professionals can play is even more important in situations when parents are not in agreement with how they view or understand their child's gender identity and expression and needs. Situations such as one parent blaming the other for "causing" the child's gender issues, believing the child will outgrow their transgender identity, or believing that supporting the transgender identity is sinful in the context of their religious beliefs can compound already complex family issues. The child or supportive parent may realistically fear that a parent who is unsupportive may disallow gender transition or want to reverse it, refuse to allow appropriate medical and/or mental health support around the asserted gender, prohibit the child from dressing the way that affirms their gender identity, or not use the child's chosen name or pronouns when visiting with that parent. In worst-case scenarios, an unsupportive parent may attempt to take legal action against the supportive parent. Because research shows that parental support and acceptance is a protective factor for TGE children's well-being, having an experienced professional bring this information into a custody proceeding can be critical for the child.

DOCUMENTATION

Documentation is another area in which families may want or need the assistance of a lawyer. Changing a legal name or gender marker is frequently done as part of a social gender transition, and although it is a fairly straightforward process that many families undertake on their own, legal consultation may be desirable, or it may be required by certain courts. Legal counsel may be helpful in making decisions about when to initiate a legal name change, as well as regarding issues around protecting the child's privacy and safety. Some courts require the notice to be posted in a local newspaper and/or reflect the name change in public documents, which may appear on the Internet. Having a legal representative can be helpful in having a judge waive posting requirements to protect the child's privacy or safety, and it may even allow for the records to be sealed. Legal providers can also be hugely informative for other adults involved with a child's collaborative care, such as reassuring a school that they are able to use the child's chosen name in class and on attendance rosters, even when a legal name change has not taken place.

CIVIL RIGHTS ISSUES

Civil rights issues, including being able to use public bathrooms and locker rooms, and having access to sex-segregated activities in accordance with a child's gender identity, are another area where the assistance of legal professionals may be necessary and extremely helpful. Title IX, the portion of the U.S. Education Amendments of 1972 that states people will not be excluded from participation or denied benefits for being subject to discrimination under any education program or activity that receives federal financial assistance, received greater enforcement nationwide under the Obama administration. However, shortly after taking office, Donald Trump rescinded protective school guidance for transgender students. The case of Gavin Grimm, a transgender boy in Virginia who was refused access to the boys' restroom and the consequent rejection of the United States Supreme Court to hear his case in March 2017 turned back progress and is a stark reminder of how critical it is for transgender children to have a supportive network of adults who can continue to fight for their health and well-being. Although many people do not think twice about going to the bathroom in public settings, cases such as Grimm's underline the vital importance of civil rights issues in constructing and keeping a supportive, validating system around a TGE child and the critical role of the mental health professional coordinating with the legal community to secure these rights.

MEDICAL INSURANCE

Families may also wish to consult with a legal professional around medical insurance. Insurance varies widely among insurance carriers, and in different states. This will vary according to whether the insurance coverage is public or private, what regulations must be observed because of the size of the business offering the insurance, what options and riders a particular employer or educational institution decides to include in the plan they offer, and what local or state mandates dictate. At this time, insurance for transgender-related medical care is far from standardized, and insurance coverage ranges from no coverage to a few rare situations of full coverage. The Patient Protection and Affordable Care Act (ACA), signed into law by President Barack Obama in 2010, banned the denial of health care based on gender identity. However, the change of administration to Donald Trump in 2017 brought an immediate challenge to repeal the ACA, which continued to be in flux with an uncertain outcome as of this writing. It is important to keep up-to-date regarding state regulations, insurance plan policies, and changes at the federal level. Having an interdisciplinary team work collaboratively with the family and insurance company can mean the difference between receiving and not receiving coverage for certain interventions. Those who are not experienced gender specialists, such as insurance clerks, are often uneducated about the needs of transgender youth and may view medical or surgical intervention as elective rather than necessary. Insurance denials can frequently be reversed with an appeals process when gender-experienced providers can speak to the medical necessity of such intervention.

CASE STUDY

In a gender clinic, the interdisciplinary team working with families divides up issues related to insurance coverage in a routine manner. Their director of nursing negotiates with the insurance companies but calls on the clinic's legal director in instances of questions of patient rights violations. The social worker interfaces with the family throughout the very frustrating process to get approval, seeing them through one, or often several, appeals. Through their combined experience this team has learned best practices in interfacing with both insurance programs and families so that they are very effective in obtaining coverage while simultaneously helping the family tolerate the stress of the process.

Case Study of Coordinated Care

BACKGROUND INFORMATION

Ian is a 9-year-old White and Latinx TGE child who attends public school in a large city. The father, a Caucasian Jew, is a homemaker, and the mother, a Puerto Rican Catholic, supports the family through her job as a highly specialized nurse in a major hospital. Ian was assigned male at birth and is being raised Jewish. Ian came out to their parents as gender fluid after attending a family wedding where relatives repeatedly asked why Ian had long hair. Ian told their parents that they did not feel either male or female, and asked parents to use *they/them/their* pronouns. Ian's parents had some knowledge of transgender youth but were unaware that children could come out so young and were unfamiliar with nonbinary identities. Ian stated that they wished to continue using their given name and wanted to start wearing their hair back with ribbons and hair clips but had no desire to change their androgynous style of clothing.

PROFESSIONAL INPUT AND COORDINATION

Mental Health

Ian's father began searching the Internet for support services and made an appointment with a local mental health agency that specializes in working with TGE children and youth. He began educating himself through reading books, watching documentaries, and doing research on the Internet. Ian's mother was reluctant to take action, stating that this was likely a phase, but agreed to meet with the mental health provider. At the provider's suggestion, Ian's father began attending a local support group for parents of TGE children, but Ian's mother refused, stating she was too busy with work and too tired when not working. With repeated encouragement from the gender specialist over a few more meetings, Ian's mother agreed to attend the parent support group, and agreed that Ian could begin attending a play group for TGE children. She also watched some documentaries on TGE children that the therapist recommended (*Growing Up Trans* on *FRONTLINE* [Navasky & O'Connor, 2015], *TRANS* [Schoen & Arnold, 2012]), and agreed to continue attending sessions with Ian's father so they could receive support as a couple, along with further psychoeducation. After Ian joined the sessions with the gender specialist, they revealed that they had been getting teased in school for the past 2 years, often being called a girl. Upset to hear this, Ian's father asked the gender specialist to help get support for Ian at school.

School

The mental health provider arranged for outside consultation from an agency that conducts school trainings for TGE children, and a series of meetings began with school staff to identify the needs of the administration, the students, and their parents. Formal training was then given to the teachers and administration on several separate occasions, followed by discussion and training with the PTA. School staff began to use *they/them/their* pronouns with Ian and integrated discussion of TGE identities into classroom curricula at all grade levels. When given a choice between boys' bathroom and the nurse's, Ian started to use the nurse's bathroom, and although allowed to opt out, chose to continue to attend gym, using the nurse's restroom to change.

Religious/Spiritual

Ian's father then asked the agency that conducts trainings to meet with the rabbi of their temple, and a gender training was arranged in their Jewish center for both staff and congregants. Ian's mother shared with her husband in therapy that she no longer wanted to practice Catholicism because of her upset that Ian's identity was not affirmed by her priest. She refused further support around this but eventually did talk about it in the parental support group.

Medical

The mental health provider arranged for a referral to a pediatrician who was familiar with caring for TGE children. The doctor was able to inform Ian's parents about where Ian was in puberty, as well as to review information on puberty blocking medications. As Ian did not show signs of beginning puberty yet, a plan was made for the family to return every 6 months to monitor Ian's pubertal development. Continued input from Ian and their mental health provider would be sought regarding whether puberty blockers would be indicated.

Outcomes

Ian's parents noticed that Ian, who had become increasingly quiet over the past year, was now much more talkative, cheerful, and spontaneous in their interactions. They developed more friendships, and cut back on playing video games alone. Their grades in school, which had been in the B–C range, became solid A's. Ian's mother told the gender therapist that despite continued worry that Ian's identity was a symptom of another problem, she nevertheless could see a tremendous positive change in Ian's mood and daily life. She entered her own therapy for additional support and continued to attend the parent support group with father. The school year ended with Ian asking to deliver a personal speech at the school assembly, explaining their gender story to the school and thanking everyone for their support.

Conclusion

Gender has a profound impact on the development of a child. TGE children are at great risk for negative social, psychological, and academic outcomes if they are not correctly identified, supported, and provided with necessary services to enable healthy, appropriate development. Creating a network of school, medical, legal, and spiritual professionals enables a healthy comprehensive, coordinated holding environment in which the ecological world of the developing child can take place with healthy reciprocal interactions that enable resilience and positive development to build upon themselves. Such collaborative care in an affirming environment will set the stage for TGE children to move forward in their development in healthy ways, towards becoming happy, resilient, children, and eventually adults. As Laverne Cox, transgender actress, said, "When you put love out in the world it travels, and it can touch people and reach people in ways that we never even expected" (Fallon, 2016).

References

American Psychological Association, Task Force on Gender Identity and Gender Variance. (2009). *Report of the APA Task Force on Gender Identity and Gender Variance.* Retrieved from http://www.apa.org/pubs/info/reports/gender-identity.aspx

Belsky, J. (1993). Etiology of child maltreatment: A developmental–ecological analysis. *Psychological Bulletin, 114,* 413–434. http://dx.doi.org/10.1037/0033-2909.114.3.413

Brill, S., & Pepper, R. (2008). *The transgender child.* San Francisco, CA: Cleis Press.

Bronfenbrenner, U. (1994). Ecological models of human development. In T. N. Postlethwaite & T. Husen (Eds.), *International encyclopedia of education* (2nd ed., Vol. 3, pp. 37–43). Oxford, England: Elsevier.

Cole, S., Eisner, M. A., Gregory, M., & Ristuccia, J. (2013). *Helping traumatized children learn: 2. Creating and advocating for trauma-sensitive schools.* Boston, MA: Massachusetts Advocates for Children.

Fallon, K. (2016, June 15). Laverne Cox talks love, healing, and pride. *The Daily Beast.* Retrieved from http://www.thedailybeast.com/laverne-cox-talks-love-healing-and-pride

Kosciw, J. G., Greytak, E. A., Palmer, N. A., & Boesen, M. J. (2014). *The 2013 National School Climate Survey: The experiences of lesbian, gay, bisexual and transgender youth in our nation's schools.* New York, NY: Gay, Lesbian, & Straight Education Network.

Retrieved from http://www.glsen.org/sites/default/files/2013%20National%20School%20Climate%20Survey%20Full%20Report_0.pdf

Masten, A. S., & Cicchetti, D. (2010). Developmental cascades. *Development and Psychopathology, 22,* 491–495. http://dx.doi.org/10.1017/S0954579410000222

Mink, M. D., Lindley, L. L., & Weinstein, A. A. (2014). Stress, stigma, and sexual minority status: The intersectional ecology model of LGBTQ health. *Journal of Gay & Lesbian Social Services, 26,* 502–521. http://dx.doi.org/10.1080/10538720.2014.953660

National Association of School Psychologists. (2014). *Position statement: Safe schools for transgender and gender diverse students.* Retrieved from http://www.nasponline.org/assets/documents/Research%20and%20Policy/Position%20Statements/Transgender_PositionStatement.pdf

Navasky, M., & O'Connor, K. (Writers, Producers, & Directors). (2015). Growing up trans [Television series episode]. In D. Fanning (Executive producer), *FRONTLINE.* Boston, MA: Outpost.

Patient Protection and Affordable Care Act, 42 U.S.C. § 18001 et seq. (2010).

Riley, E. A., Clemson, L., Sitharthan, G., & Diamond, M. (2013). Surviving a gender-variant childhood: The views of transgender adults on the needs of gender-variant children and their parents. *Journal of Sex & Marital Therapy, 39,* 241–263. http://dx.doi.org/10.1080/0092623X.2011.628439

Schoen, M. (Producer), & Arnold, C. (Director). (2012). *Gender dysphoria: The lived experience TRANS* [Motion picture]. United States: TRANS.

Shumer, D. E., Reisner, S., Edwards-Leeper, L., & Tishelman, A. C. (2016). Evaluation of Asperger Syndrome in youth presenting to a gender dysphoria clinic. *LGBT Health, 3,* 387–390. http://dx.doi.org/10.1089/lgbt.2015.0070

Sroufe, L. A. (2013). The promise of developmental psychopathology: Past and present. *Development and Psychopathology, 25,* 1215–1224. http://dx.doi.org/10.1017/S0954579413000576

Strang, J. F., Kenworthy, L., Dominska, A., Sokoloff, J., Kenealy, L. E., Berl, M., . . . Wallace, G. L. (2014). Increased gender variance in autism spectrum disorders and attention deficit hyperactivity disorder. *Archives of Sexual Behavior, 43,* 1525–1533. http://dx.doi.org/10.1007/s10508-014-0285-3

Tishelman, A. C., Haney, P., Greenwald O'Brien, J., & Blaustein, M. (2010). A framework for school-based psychological evaluations: Utilizing a 'trauma lens'. *Journal of Child and Adolescent Trauma, 3,* 279–302.

Tishelman, A. C., Kaufman, R., Edwards-Leeper, L., Mandel, F. H., Shumer, D. E., & Spack, N. P. (2015). Serving transgender youth: Challenges, dilemmas, and clinical examples. *Professional Psychology: Research and Practice, 46,* 37–45. http://dx.doi.org/10.1037/a0037490

U.S. Education Amendments, 20 U.S.C. §§ 1681–1688 (1972).

Arlene I. Lev and Carolyn Wolf-Gould

Collaborative Treatment Across Disciplines

Physician and Mental Health Counselor Coordinating Competent Care

12

> The future of health care delivery will require interprofessional teams of health care professionals working together to provide patient-centered care.
>
> —American Academy of Family Physicians and American Academy of Physician Assistants, 2011

The surge in families of transgender and gender expansive (TGE) children and youth seeking services in the United States is unprecedented, but most families will not have access to interdisciplinary pediatric treatment centers, which are scattered in a few urban areas (Edwards-Leeper & Spack, 2012; Sherer, Rosenthal, Ehrensaft, & Baum, 2012) and will seek care from providers in their local communities. The vulnerability of families with gender expansive children (Ehrensaft, 2012) and the evolving but limited research to guide gender transitions necessitate collaborative work across disciplines to facilitate comprehensive treatment plans. To meet the complex needs of this population in a variety of urban and rural settings, primary medical and mental health providers must develop new skills and create informed interdisciplinary systems.

In this chapter, we outline a collaborative and gender affirmative model (GAM) of care for use in small cities or rural communities where services are less accessible. Our approach requires regular communication between

http://dx.doi.org/10.1037/0000095-012
The Gender Affirmative Model: An Interdisciplinary Approach to Supporting Transgender and Gender Expansive Children, C. Keo-Meier and D. Ehrensaft (Editors)
Copyright © 2018 by the American Psychological Association. All rights reserved.

providers and is based on honoring the child's emerging gender identity and development, addressing the parents' concerns for their child's well-being, and recognizing the complexity of social and medical transitions and the need for integrated treatment plans that evolve over time.

We developed our collaborative care model over a period of years by working closely together with a large number of TGE children and youth and their families. Arlene I. Lev is a family therapist and social worker with 30 years of experience as a gender specialist. She and her staff provide individual, couple, family, and group therapy for children, adolescents, and adults in Albany, New York. Carolyn Wolf-Gould is a family physician in Oneonta, New York, a small town 90 minutes from Albany. She provides transgender health services for all ages as part of her family practice.

The Value of Collaborative Care

In the past 2 decades, treatment protocols have shifted from viewing gender diversity as a pathologizing psychiatric condition to a natural and healthy variation of human diversity but one that may require medical treatment and present with complex psychosocial sequelae (Coleman et al., 2012; Lev, 2004). The *Standards of Care* (*SOC*) developed by the World Professional Association for Transgender Health (WPATH; 2011) no longer recommend intensive, long-term psychotherapy for all transgender adults before medical treatment and suggest a briefer gender assessment or even a one-session assessment within an informed consent model (as cited in Coleman et al., 2012). Although briefer evaluations are appropriate for some adults with consolidated gender identities, in contrast, youth and their families will benefit from comprehensive and ongoing collaborative care, both because of the youths' relative immaturity and because the youth are still reliant on the care and nurture provided by their families.

TGE people are often best served by integrated medical and mental health services (Feldman & Goldberg, 2006; Schechter, 2009). Solely focusing on medical needs often minimizes the painful social challenges of TGE people and their families (Lev, 2004). The growth of affirmative modules of treatment (Hidalgo et al., 2013; Hill, Menvielle, Sica, & Johnson, 2010; Lev & Gottlieb, in press; Malpas, 2011; Vanderburgh, 2009) for children and youth necessitates a wider scope of practice that integrates medical and psychological treatment of the child with the complex needs of parents and caregivers. Standard wisdom suggests that the highest level of care is possible only in integrated models housed within the same physical location (Feierabend & Bartee, 2004). Specialized treatment centers for TGE children and youth are emerging in the United States, built on the success of the multidisciplinary and collaborative model developed at The Amsterdam Center of Expertise on Gender Dysphoria, Vrije Universiteit University Medical Center, the Netherlands. These multidisciplinary clinics offer medical, mental health, and sometimes educational and legal services for children and support for parents under one roof (Sherer et al., 2012; Tishelman et al., 2015). An ideal treatment team would include physicians, therapists, social workers, educational specialists, legal consultants, pediatric psychologists, and psychiatrists.

Although we recognize the advantages of these models, they are difficult to create. In our service area, we have minimal access to pediatric psychologists or psychiatrists with training in TGE health, and few medical providers and therapists committed to serving this population. We have to make do with available resources. But our experience has shown that with a commitment to a collaborative approach, quality care coordination is possible.

We believe best practices of the GAM are embedded in this collaborative approach and include (a) nurturing the emerging gender identity and expression of children and youth; (b) developing protective strategies to support children and youth who are living in hostile environments; (c) supporting families and social institutions to become more gender flexible, so that TGE children are integrated within their families and communities; and (d) supporting those parents and institutions that are already advocating for their children, a needed service as they are often isolated and under public scrutiny as a result of their gender advocacy and practices (Lev & Alie, 2012). Additionally, the fifth component related to medical care is (e) supporting and educating children and families about the risks and benefits of medical interventions, which could include puberty-blocking medication, hormone treatments and surgical procedures, and assisting families in choosing appropriate treatments.

The Practice of Collaborative Care

As von Trotsenburg (2014) stated, "The necessity and the advantages of a team brought together to serve transgender patients will hardly be questioned, but the task of realizing a true 'gender team' is something difficult and challenging" (p. xvii). The practice of collaborative care is an art that requires commitment to relational issues, discipline, and regular application (Gagné, 2005). Similar to many relational skills, interdisciplinary collaboration is rarely a part of formal education. Absent such training, providers must first recognize the need for a team approach, then identify providers working across disciplines, and then develop the necessary professional relationships (Doherty, McDaniel, & Baird, 1996; Seaburn, Lorenz, Gunn, Jr., Gawinski, & Mauksch, 1996). Given the fragmentation and stress of the mental health and medical systems, fostering frequent, supportive communication across disciplines can be challenging (Woltmann et al., 2012).

Although we recognize the difficulties, we maintain that attending to the tasks of collaborative work is essential to care. These tasks include (a) written referrals and sharing of documentation generated during office visits; (b) scheduled meetings, in person or online; and (c) frequent phone calls or e-mail communication regarding patient care. Our providers use detailed referral letters/notes to introduce each other to our patients and to present an initial assessment. Usually, the families seeking medical interventions present to the therapist first, receive a comprehensive mental health assessment, and are then referred to the medical doctor with a letter from the therapist. The physician then completes a medical assessment with attention to the psychosocial issues that present in the medical setting and sends that information to the therapist. The process of formulating and reviewing referral letters and medical assessments is the first step in sorting through the complex biopsychosocial issues families bring to our offices.

Genograms, a graphic representation of a person's family relationships and medical history over several generations (McGoldrick & Gerson, 1985), are used by all providers as part of the intake history and serve as an effective way to document and share nuances of the family's social structure. While sketching the genogram, we uncover family beliefs and dynamics over generations, including medical, behavioral, and mental health problems. We use the visual patterns to elicit mental health concerns: "I notice a history of suicide in your family—do you worry about that with Kathryn?" Medical information surfaces as well: "My mother and I both carry the *BRCA* cancer gene—What will that mean for our child if she wants feminizing hormones?"

Face-to-face meetings among providers offer an opportunity to process care plans. We aim for a monthly meeting, both to discuss complex clinical situations and for formal continuing education, by training one another or bringing in experts for chosen topics. This enables support and collegiality in what might otherwise be an isolated field. Between meetings, we collaborate by e-mail. For example, the physician wrote, "Sophia is still struggling with the bullies at school and Dad is setting up a meeting with the principal." The therapist, who does school advocacy, was then able to reach out to the family and offer support, and ultimately provide an educational training on transgender policies to personnel at Sophia's school.

Occasionally, we find it necessary to meet together with families, a powerful intervention during times of resistance, indecision, or crisis. The process of calling a meeting with all parties emphasizes the importance of each of the contributing voices in the system. Parents and youth experience the team listening and responding from different perspectives and understand that we believe their struggles deserve attention.

The Goals of Collaborative Care

Our goal is to identify and explore the needs of each family system so that we can facilitate the work of therapy and carry out appropriate medical interventions. We see the exploration of identity as normal transactional processes that affect the entire family, not simply an internal experience for the child (Malpas, 2011; Walsh, 2011). The parents' views of gender will influence the child's experience of gender, and the parents' own experience of their own gendered childhoods will also impact the experience of gender diverse children. Rather than label the child as the "identified patient," we view the child as an extension of, and embedded in, a larger familial system (Lev, 2004; Malpas, 2011; Stone Fish & Harvey, 2005). The position the parent takes regarding their child's emerging gender identity may be the single most salient influence on the child's mental health during childhood (Ryan, Huebner, Diaz, & Sanchez, 2009). It is this relationship that we honor and prioritize.

Anxiety within the family is usually the catalyst for seeking professional care. As such, it serves an important therapeutic function. But family anxiety can run amok and spread to the medical or mental health setting, making it difficult to effect meaningful interventions. We have found that through careful collaboration we are better able to (a) alleviate the anxiety of parents, (b) alleviate the anxiety of children and teens, and (c) alleviate the anxiety of professional caregivers so that the necessary work of adjustment and change can take place.

ALLEVIATING THE ANXIETY OF PARENTS

Parenting is a heroic act even in the best of circumstances. Parenting a gender creative child and negotiating the many medical, psychological, and social challenges associated with gender exploration or transition can be overwhelming. Parents often present with intense anxiety, and a team approach for assessment, followed by education to explain that a child's gender identity is the result of complex biopsychosocial processes, may lower their anxiety.

Parents usually question the etiology of their child's gender expression and often feel guilty, thinking that a "mistake" they made during pregnancy (e.g., alcohol or drug use) is the cause. They may wonder if there is a genetic problem or an intersex condition and request medical testing. Seeking substantive medical "proof" can be both the driving force behind and the hoped-for alleviation of a parent's anxiety. Lesbian, gay, bisexual, transgender, and queer (LGBTQ) parents may wonder whether they have passed some poorly understood genetic predisposition to their child or if their family structure was responsible. Adoptive parents may worry whether the gender expression is inherited from the child's birth parents or fear being blamed by the birth family for not being good enough parents. Some parents wonder whether their family dynamics or their own personal or interpersonal problems have created an environment that caused gender expansive behaviors to emerge. Even LGBTQ parents may be confused by the emerging gender identity options available (i.e., genderqueer, nonbinary, gender fluid), not just those embedded in a rigid gender-binary belief system. It is unfortunate that all of these worries have been fueled by mental health and medical systems that in previous eras, and up to the present, promote theories that blame parents for their children's "gender confusions." Thus, within the GAM, it is essential to work across disciplines to address both the medical and psychological concerns parents are expressing. Only then can parents "control their fears and reactivity and differentiate their child's needs from their own" (Malpas, 2011, p. 457).

Parents of TGE children come to professionals with many questions regarding diagnoses and medical treatments, school-related concerns, and trepidation for their children's safety. Some parents resist their child's expansive expression and are punitive and rejecting. Others wonder if it is "just a phase." Many parents state that gender changes appeared to come out of the blue in the teen years and link it to new friendship networks or online social media, rather than emerging identities. Parents of youth entering puberty often fear the potential health risks of puberty blockers, coexisting with concerns for missing the time-sensitive window of this developmental transition from prepuberty to puberty. Their anxiety is extreme and palpable and can be assuaged by explanations from both medical and mental health providers about normal trajectories.

Encouraging parents to keep an open mind about their child's gender identity is an important focus of treatment, and clinicians can explain that it may remain fixed but might evolve and change during childhood and adolescence and even into adulthood. Maintaining a position of trusting "self-affirmed gender identity while recognizing and accepting the fact that it may be fluid" (Edwards-Leeper & Spack, 2012, p. 323) is indeed the greatest challenge for parents. Malpas (2011) suggested that parents raising TGE children face an intersection of two conflicting parenting mandates—nurturing the child's identity while helping them adjust to social expectations, which are often judgmental of the family's position of supporting their child's gender expression.

Parents with rigid ideas on gender usually feel greater anxiety than those with less pressure to behave in traditional ways. One family consulted us because their son liked playing with Barbie dolls, indeed was stealing them from his sister's room, and was repeatedly and harshly punished for his transgression. The child's clothing, mannerisms, and identity were identified by both the medical and mental health providers as typical of a cisgender "boy"; he exhibited no distress about gender at all, no dysphoria, no body dysmorphia—he simply liked to play with Barbie dolls. The treatment plan developed was simple: Buy the child his own Barbie dolls so he will not have to steal them and counsel the parents about being less rigid in their gender expectations of children's play. Having a physician validate that there were no medical or diagnostic concerns for this child enabled the family to trust the work of the therapist—which pushed them outside of their gendered comfort zones but allowed them to feel held within the collaborative team approach.

Parenting TGE children presents an ambivalent loss (Boss, 2006) for families. Parents must change their assumptions and expectations about a child: "We thought we knew her, but we didn't"; "Even though she's still the same person, we have to see her as different in important and confusing ways." They must manage their own conflicting emotions and remain present and supportive of their child, whom they may not understand (Stone Fish & Harvey, 2005). Teens who identify as genderqueer or nonbinary often request the use of gender-neutral pronouns *they/them* and can present in a gender-blended manner (skirts and unshaved facial hair), which can be unsettling for parents (Tilsen, 2013). In these instances, both parents and children will benefit from education and support. When the collaborative team models respect toward these youth, they help "normalize" out-of-the-box gender expressions for the parents.

Providers can reassure parents that their child's behaviors are healthy and shared by many children today and that it is not their "fault." Educating parents about hormonal treatments, timing, and the wide window of puberty is important for alleviating anxiety. Assisting them to connect to other parents, through support groups, can be another essential step toward lessening isolation and fear. All parents require support in addressing anxiety-provoking situations, such as advocacy in school systems, coming out to extended family members, challenging rigid public policy, and navigating complex social situations. The collaborative team amplifies the message that these struggles are normal, healthy, and expected and hearing similar advice from different providers reinforces the value of suggestions.

More recently, gender issues have become more prominent in U.S. media and culture, and parents are voicing concern that their child's behavior is linked to copycat phenomena or influenced by online social media. The effect of a rapidly changing society on youth has not yet been well analyzed or articulated, and some providers are also expressing concerns about the new, atypical ways teens present. The team must validate and carefully assess these concerns to ensure that all providers and family members are comfortable moving forward with medical or social interventions.

ALLEVIATING THE ANXIETY OF CHILDREN AND ADOLESCENTS

Children often present to therapists and physicians with a great deal of anxiety about their situation. Gender dysphoria can be emotionally painful, disrupting normative development and social relationships, and creating disturbances in family dynamics. The distress can interfere with learning and developing educational goals, impact relational intimacy, or confound sexual maturity.

Some youth are able to identify anxiety and address it, whereas others express their anxiety through physical or behavioral symptoms. TGE children may present to the doctor solely with medical complaints, and it can be challenging to sort out which symptoms have organic causes, which are somatic, and which are a combination. For example, a child with gender dysphoria with incapacitating migraines will benefit from input from both the physician and therapist on developing coping mechanisms for stress and medical management of headaches. The therapist can then delve deeper into the underlying causes of the stress and headaches, with the goal of removing environmental impingements and treating core anxieties. A 10-year-old trans masculine child in our care who had been put on puberty blockers focused his anxiety around his Lupron injections, voicing complaints that pain from his shots prevented him from attending school or participating in gym. After helping him identify that most of his angst was related to locker room logistics and changing his puberty-blocking medication from Lupron to the Histrelin implant to avoid painful shots, the child became less anxious and began to thrive both at home and in school.

Children may have worries about their bodies that they are afraid to verbalize. We cared for a 7-year-old trans feminine child who wanted to wear a girl's swimsuit to a party, but worried about her genital bulge. She had been putting a Band-Aid on her penis to "make it stay down." During examination, she discussed her worries with her physician, and was then able to participate in conversation with her parents, doctor, and therapist about tucking and compression garments.

Children are influenced by their parents' reactions to their gender expression. One transgender girl told her therapist, "I avoid Daddy because I know he hates my dolls, and that means he hates me because I love my dolls. He wants me to be somebody I'm not." Both providers encouraged this father to explore his own issues and concerns in therapy, not as a projection of his child's issues but as part of his own personal journey living in a society where deviations from expected manhood come with a high price. They normalized this father's response to the dolls and his child as a normal stage for a struggling parent and provided a safe space for him to share the residual pain from his own childhood, where "girly" behavior would not have been tolerated. Most parents pass through their own transformative process as they learn to first accept and later embrace the experience of parenting a TGE child. The therapeutic team must create a safe space for all family members to express and process feelings that impact the health of the system. Working in a team enables a sturdy holding environment for the family, and the family knows that both their medical and therapeutic issues are being addressed.

Adolescents may be reluctant to see a therapist for something they perceive to be a medical problem. Often, their primary source of information about transition comes from YouTube or Tumblr. These venues may portray therapists as gatekeepers who block the way to "real" (i.e., medical) treatments. They may not see value in therapy and perceive it as a hoop they must jump through on the path to puberty blockers or hormones. However, when they meet with the medical provider, many youth express anxiety about school, bullying, and discrimination, and articulate fears about being outed or hurt by others. A medical provider can encourage youth and families to see this as an issue that is best addressed in therapy by affirming the importance of tending to the emotional issues that arise during hormonal interventions. When youth come to see the therapist as an advocate for a medical referral, as well as someone educated about transition, they often become more open to the collaboration.

Adolescents often see even supportive parents as "enemies." Many express fear that their parents will disown them, punish them, and refuse to get them the help they want. When the therapist points out that their parents drove hours to the therapist's office, are using their requested pronouns and names, and have said they would do anything to help them, they often nod but repeat that they are still anxious about what might happen. Some of this might be because of the influence of social media in their lives, with reported tales of rejection and hostility from other youth who may not have supportive parents. Some of it is a reflection of their deep desire to be mirrored and loved by their parents, and their fear of rejection, or that the parents will accept parts of their journey but fall short in allowing appropriate medical interventions. Some of it may be a reaction to the microaggressions that parents unintentionally communicate to their children, either by their own unresolved issues about transition or by simply being cisgender and not fully understanding their child's experience of gender dysphoria. Some of this experience is simply developmental, normative adolescent turbulence, related in part to the maturational processes of the prefrontal cortex of the brain.

Due to their different training and specialization, medical providers and therapists often see different sides to the child's anxiety and may be able to offer insight to one another when issues surface in different venues. For example, one 7-year-old told her physician, "What I'm most anxious about is *bugs*. My therapist wants to talk about gender all the time, but I don't want to talk about that. I'm scared of spiders." Determining what is true arachnophobia and what is displaced gender anxiety may be the work of therapy, but working in a collaborative team allowed the physician to share the child's frustration with the therapist, which in turn helped to refocus the therapeutic conversation—from gender to bugs.

ALLEVIATING THE ANXIETY OF PROVIDERS

Providers are challenged by the complex needs of families with gender diverse children and must rely on one another to stay grounded and focused. Some families experience multiple crises and extended periods of difficulty, and their needs can be taxing. Families rely on us to be the experts, but gender transitions in childhood are relatively recent phenomena, and the protocols for treatment rely on evidence that is still emerging. The "true gender" of a child is not determined with a simple lab test but is revealed over time, relationally, and developmentally. The pressure on providers to know what is essentially unknowable—the outcome of a particular child's gender identity—can be as anxiety producing for them as it is for parents. Providers are under intense scrutiny by colleagues and the media—who are often skeptical and hostile—as well as the families, who rely on them to "get it right." They are under enormous pressure to contain their emotions, while making decisions that will have a lasting and impactful effect on the lives of those in their care. Having colleagues to rely on, to brainstorm and commiserate with, and to sometimes play "good cop/bad cop" can not only make this work less stressful and isolating but also can allow for multiple perspectives on clinical issues and ease the burden of having "the buck stop here." We are continually enriched by the opportunity to educate and learn from one another.

Evolving Tasks for the Collaborative Team

By far the most challenging aspects of working with families of TGE children and youth are issues of social and medical transitions. Families may initially present in either the medical or the mental health setting with a child in any of the developmental/physical stages. The first task for the provider making initial contact with a family is to quickly assess, identify necessary collaborative services, and refer across disciplines. Tasks for the collaborative team depend on the age and developmental stage of the child and family and if warranting gender affirming medical care, are organized around medical interventions that fall into three categories: completely reversible (social transition, puberty-blocking medication), partially reversible (hormone therapy), and irreversible (gender transition-related surgeries; Coleman et al., 2012).

Although the medical and mental health providers have distinct tasks, there is considerable overlap, and all team members should be familiar with the biopsychosocial issues faced by a family. The comprehensive mental health assessment includes attention to intrapsychic issues, personality, cognitive ability, social relationships, personal strengths, cultural/familial and racial/ethnic identities, mental health and trauma history, level of school supports, family culture, beliefs and level of acceptance regarding gender issues, family dysfunctions that may exacerbate gender difficulties, societal oppression, and family hardship. The work of the therapist includes gender assessment and history taking, ongoing psychotherapy, family assessment and therapy, group sessions with nuclear and extended families, mental health and psychiatric assessment (including medication referral as necessary), and outreach to schools and community organizations. The comprehensive medical assessment includes a gender history, a medical history, family history, social history, psychiatric history, medication history, physical examination, and appropriate medical testing. The work of the medical provider involves attention to changing bodies; anticipatory guidance; management of coexisting medical problems; education about medical interventions, including fertility education and consultation; and outreach to schools with questions that arise from a lack of understanding of gender issues or ways to create safe spaces for TGE students.

PREPUBERTAL CHILDREN AND/OR COMPLETELY REVERSIBLE INTERVENTIONS

For prepubertal children, the therapeutic team will counsel and advise about interventions that are completely reversible, with minimal side effects. It is important to stress the fluidity of gender identity and expression, and to encourage parents to create a safe environment where children can explore their emerging sense of self. Some parents and children arrive at the office at a young age ready to take immediate steps to transition their child from one gender to the other, whereas other parents expect help in trying to "make their child stop twirling in skirts." It is important for the therapeutic team to meet families where they are, normalize behaviors, and explain the wide trajectory of possible outcomes. The pressure on TGE children to conform to simple binaries and rush medical treatment during the assessment process may increase parental anxiety. Despite their stated goals of moving cautiously, the child's insistence may weaken the parents' resolve and compel them to want to socially transition their child quickly. The gender binary often exists as a fact in the cisgender adult world and transitioning (i.e., if the child is not a boy, then they must be a girl) may prematurely appear to "fix the gender problem" that has rocked their family's life. Frequent reminders by the team to commit to the "not knowing" stance can empower parents to think outside the box: that is, the team can send strong messages of loving the child regardless of their gender identity, while also providing accurate medical information about medical treatments and therapeutic support for the complications caused by gender ambiguity. Suggestions by therapists that have the "official stamp" from a physician always carry more weight, which can be helpful in family interventions and in assisting in school-related advocacy.

A young child's gender dysphoria presents with symptoms and behaviors rather than words, and providers may need to interpret the meaning of those actions. Children may present to the physician with school failure, anxiety, mood disorders, or attention-deficit/hyperactivity disorder; for instance:

> My 4-year-old son disrupts the whole class with his tantrums every time they make him take off his ballerina costume. His teacher thinks he's bipolar. I wonder, too—though he's better at home, if I just let him wear what he wants.

By recognizing the complex ways gender dysphoria presents in young children, the team can start the process of sorting out which behaviors are related to gender issues and which are not. In this case, the medical provider referred the family to a therapist, and the collaborative team reached out to school personnel to assist with training and education. As the child's gender expression was affirmed by allowing him to wear what he desired, the tantrums diminished. The team also diagnosed autism spectrum disorder in addition to gender dysphoria in this 4-year-old child and developed an educational plan to better meet the child's needs.

Some children need to socially transition at a young age to thrive, and the families of these children may struggle with issues related to transparency. Problems related to disclosure, or "going stealth," versus "being out" may consume them. Although nondisclosing children may benefit from being affirmed in their gender, this advantage can come at the price of intense anxiety and fear for the family: "We've got a secret and what if it's found out?" On the other hand, families with a child who is "out" (fully disclosing their social transition and transgender identity) may face scrutiny and criticism by other parents and children. The provider team can assist by identifying the physical and emotional manifestations of stress and reaching outside the family system to educate, and garner support, while helping the child and family develop a psychological toolbox for confronting bullying and transphobic reactions. Counseling families to support their children's "next steps" (coming out at school, dressing in the clothes they like, telling grandparents about their new name and pronouns) is often difficult and tedious work. Coping with fear and anxiety, school policies, neighborhood judgments, and an ever-present sense of walking into the unknown makes these steps challenging. Assisting families in balancing complexities, particularly regarding transparency versus privacy, is the most difficult part of any social transition, and the therapeutic team must commit to helping each family find their own path.

Research has shown that transgender children who have lived in their affirmed identity show the same gender cognition consistency as cisgender children, that is, their clarity about their expressed gender is indistinguishable from cisgender children's (Olson, Key, & Eaton, 2015). The process of negotiating social transition at any age involves multiple systems—certainly the familial system, as well as larger cultural systems, including schools, neighborhoods, and religious institutions. This negotiation is often a difficult process for parents, with no exemption for those who support their TGE child and believe that a social transition is the right step for their child. Even a step that feels right can be frightening, even terrifying, when the parent is unsure or skeptical or when parents cannot agree on whether a social transition is in the child's best interests. The therapeutic team can help to keep families grounded as their world shifts by providing a protective cocoon for the process.

ONSET OF PUBERTY/COMPLETELY REVERSIBLE INTERVENTIONS

The first medical interventions are offered at the onset of puberty, when youth face unwelcome physical and emotional changes related to their assigned gender. Gonadatropin-releasing hormone (GnRH) agonists may be used in the early stages of puberty to halt the development of secondary sex characteristics by pressing a "pause button" on the release of the adult hormones that stimulate that development (Delemarre-van de Waal & Cohen-Kettenis, 2006; WPATH, 2011). GnRH agonists, used safely for years in the treatment of precocious puberty, are a completely reversible intervention. If the medications are stopped, the child will progress through puberty consistent with the sex assigned at birth. Introducing puberty blockers can prevent worsening distress for a dysphoric youth and allows the family time to consider the risks and benefits of proceeding with gender transition. The use of this intervention, which dates back to the 1990s as a treatment for precocious puberty, has revolutionized the treatment of TGE youth by preventing the stigmatization of being perceived as visibly transgender. GnRH analogues can be administered by injection on a monthly or quarterly schedule, or implanted subcutaneously, to provide slow release of the drug for 1 to 2 years. Puberty blockers are most effective if started early in puberty, at Tanner Stage 2, and youth who first present to therapists during this time should be referred relatively quickly for medical assessment. Although long-term data to demonstrate safety are lacking, the efficacy of these medical interventions for gender dysphoric children has been well-documented (Cohen-Kettenis & Pfäfflin, 2003; Delemarre-van de Waal & Cohen-Kettenis, 2006; Rosenthal, 2014). However, the decision to proceed may evoke ethical questions for parents and providers (WPATH, 2011). The therapeutic team must educate patients and families about the medical and psychological risks and benefits of puberty blockers. In our collaborative model, we obtain informed consent from all parental figures, when possible, taking time to be sure that everyone understands the value and limitations of this intervention. We take heed of Gooren and Delemarre-van de Waal's (1996) reminder, "It is to be remembered that giving, but also withholding, endocrine treatment is a momentous and responsible decision" (p. 69). One cannot sidestep the ethical dilemmas by merely avoiding them, especially given the potentially devastating impact of puberty in a discordant gender. It is important to note that puberty-blocking medication is costly and coverage is not guaranteed under most insurance plans in the United States (Edwards-Leeper & Spack, 2012), requiring the team to advise families about insurance options and medical alternatives.

Anatomical dysphoria, or aversion to one's own body parts, can be profoundly disturbing for youth. Physical exams may be traumatic, and medical providers should be attentive to the use of gowns and drapes and should ask permission to touch. Therapists can assist by preparing children for the visual inspection of breasts and genitalia necessary for Tanner Staging. Our physician shows the child a diagram with Tanner Staging and asks for the child's assistance in assessing pubertal development. This helps to distract from embarrassment and also reassure the youth that providers are aware of the unwanted changes the youth see in their bodies.

For some families, the decision to proceed with puberty-blocking medication may be relatively easy, and others will struggle with fear and ambivalence about starting a process they are not sure they can stop. We weigh fears for the future against the immediate risks of untreated gender dysphoria, such as depression, substance abuse, school failure, and suicidality (Bonifacio & Rosenthal, 2015; Peterson, Matthews, Copps-Smith, & Conard, 2017; Ryan et al., 2009) that often manifest during puberty. To date, we have no evidence of untoward risks as a result of puberty blocking (Carel, Eugster, Rogol, Ghizzoni, & Palmert, 2009). Most dysphoric teens get significant psychological relief from puberty blockers, which can lead to less stress in the family. The therapeutic team will continue to monitor the physical and emotional response of the child and family and make use of the extra time from puberty blockers to continue exploration of the child's gender identity and gender expression and to determine whether further medical interventions make sense for the child (de Vries et al., 2014).

Discussions around loss and/or preservation of fertility are some of the most difficult and require collaborative effort; both therapist and medical provider need to be skilled in talking about fertility preservation. At this point in history, if a youth begins blockers early in puberty, before the body develops mature eggs or sperm, and then moves directly to hormone treatment, that youth will forfeit the opportunity to build a family with gametes of their own. If a youth has already begun to produce mature eggs or sperm, they can cryopreserve gametes to use through assisted reproductive procedures later in life. Advances in cryopreservation of ovarian and testicular tissue in prepubertal children with cancer, although still experimental, give hope that TGE children may eventually have more options for preservation of fertility, without the need for in vivo maturation of gonadal tissue and the resulting pubertal changes (De Roo, Tilleman, T'Sjoen, & De Sutter, 2016; Estes, 2015; Johnson & Finlayson, 2016). Providers must describe the processes for harvesting gametes, which may induce dysphoria by requiring masturbation for sperm donation or the use of a vaginal ultrasound probe to monitor ovarian follicular development. Often, the youth are unconcerned about potential loss of fertility: "I'll just adopt," they shrug. But parents may understand that feelings about having genetically related children can change over time and that their child may regret fertility loss when older. Parents' own desires to become grandparents may blur their vision regarding the pressing and primary gender health needs of their child. It is helpful for medical and mental health providers to have an understanding of the available technologies and costs (both financial and emotional), as well as the grieving process that may occur when options to preserve fertility are abandoned. Some young children already yearn to be parents and are painfully aware that their struggle for authentic expression is tied to the loss of having genetically related offspring. The therapeutic team can offer a safe space to express and process this grief or to assist a child in living in a discordant gender until gametes are harvested for preservation of fertility.

INITIATING HORMONE THERAPY/PARTIALLY REVERSIBLE INTERVENTIONS

Feminizing and masculinizing hormone therapy is considered a partially reversible intervention, as the development of secondary sex characteristics congruent with gender identity is partially dependent on the continued use of hormones. Some of the changes that occur, such as breast development, hair growth or suppression of hair growth, voice change and clitoral enlargement, will not be reversed if the hormones are stopped. Other changes, such as cessation of menses, loss or increase in muscle strength, and redistribution of fat, will revert without continued use of the hormones. For medicolegal reasons, we prefer that all members of the family and therapeutic team be in alliance before taking this step. We value the input of all family members, and sometimes find that even disenfranchised or difficult members will come on board when included in the care of the child. However, at times this is not possible, and the risks of not treating a child may trump the needs of a parent without legal rights. In situations of divorce where it is stipulated in custody agreements that both parents must sign off on all major medical decisions, sometimes the only choice is to take the issue to court if parents are in disagreement about going forward with treatment or one parent refuses to be involved in the decision-making process. Although it is critical that the therapists on the team review the medical and psychological risks and benefits of hormone therapy with all family members, signed consent will necessarily occur in the medical provider's office.

The WPATH *SOC* are intended to be flexible to meet diverse health needs; however, they also recommend waiting until age 16 to begin feminizing or masculinizing hormone therapy (Coleman et al., 2012), which may sometimes be overly cautious. This recommendation is based on Dutch protocols and law, which require waiting until the age of legal consent (age 16) to begin hormone therapy. But some children are unable to obtain puberty-blocking medication and are suffering from severe dysphoria. For others, particularly those who started blockers at a young age, beginning hormones younger than 16 may be both psychologically and medically appropriate; the alternative is keeping them stalled in a prepubertal state for an extended period of time, putting these youth out of sync with their same-aged peers, who will all have gone through a full puberty by age 16 (Rosenthal, 2014).

The onset of puberty comes with new issues about gender and sexuality for the child and family. Our therapeutic team begins to ask age-appropriate questions about developing (and often shifting) sexual orientation and explores the child's relationship with their own body. One child, assigned male at birth, who lived as female from age 6 to 14, decided to cease transition when feminizing hormones became part of the discussion. He said, "As I enter puberty, I realize that I like girls, but I don't like girls the way a girl likes girls, but the way a boy likes girls." The team concurred that we were not sure exactly what this shift meant, but we did not doubt that the child understood something about his developing identity. Although this could be a kind of internalized homophobia (in this case, not wanting to be a lesbian), careful assessment indicated the authenticity of the emerging male gender identity. Changes in sexual orientation attractions and identities are common during social and medical gender transitions (Katz-Wise, Reisner, Hughto, & Keo-Meier, 2016; Meier, Pardo, Labuski, & Babcock, 2013), and medical and mental health clinicians can normalize this experience for parents and youth.

The onset of puberty for sexually maturing bodies is an opportunity to create safe spaces to obtain sexual histories and ask about high-risk sexual behaviors or concerns about sexual intimacy. Youth need guidance about when and how to safely disclose facts about their anatomy to potential partners and practical advice about safe sex and prevention of sexually transmitted infections. As the risk of depression, self-harm, bullying, poor self-esteem, abuse, school failure, family conflict and substance abuse are high in this population, we screen for these issues. We also ask about self-treatment with hormones obtained on the Internet or on the street, and review safe versus unsafe techniques for tucking, binding, packing, and using stand-to-pee devices. As parents may be reluctant to visit the websites or shops where such devices are sold, the physician or therapist can show youth and parents appropriate equipment in the controlled office environment and demonstrate safe use.

REFERRALS FOR SURGERY/IRREVERSIBLE INTERVENTIONS

The collaborative team must also be ready to discuss available surgical procedures with children and families, often at a very young age. People are curious, planning ahead, wondering how "all this really works." Young children may have unrealistic expectations regarding surgical procedures; for example, they may think, "After I have surgery to remove my penis, I'll be able to have a baby!" Thus, education must begin early and continue over a period of many years. Although questions about long-term options for care must be addressed, the team needs to communicate with youth in ways that are age appropriate and avoid an upsurge in anxiety by flooding them with confusing information.

The seventh version of the WPATH *SOC* recommends waiting until age 18 for these irreversible interventions, although again, at times, proceeding earlier may be indicated. Trans masculine teens that have severe breast/chest dysphoria may refuse to participate in athletics or swimming events. They may get bullied in school for their anatomical mismatch, and these may be good reasons to proceed before age 18 with surgical chest reconstruction. Most providers discourage proceeding with phalloplasty, metoidioplasty, or vaginoplasty until the individual is ready to assume the responsibility for postoperative care, including management of operative complications (common with phalloplasty) or following the demanding schedule for dilation of the neovagina. Without regular dilation, the neovagina will close, and it is imperative to wait until a teen is mature enough to take responsibility for this task. Most parents find it hard enough to get their teen to take out the garbage and prefer not to nag about vaginal dilation. Other teens demonstrate remarkable maturity and can follow through with necessary self-care. Letters from both medical and mental health providers are required for referrals for surgical services, and should include the providers' thoughts about timing and ability to follow through with postoperative care.

In unclear situations, surgical providers can be asked by the therapeutic team to assist with decision making by carefully reviewing the risks and benefits of all procedures with the youth and family.

Conclusion

The success of gender transition when treated with a multidisciplinary team approach has been well-documented (de Vries et al., 2014). Our collaborative model extends gender affirmative treatment for use in small cities or rural communities where specialized treatment centers do not exist. Our treatment philosophy aims to help lower families' anxieties about the choices they are making, assist them in understanding that identity and maturity emerge slowly over time, and enhance their ability to see their child's gender identity not as an ever-narrowing window of opportunity with a need for immediate decision making but rather as both the child's and the family's ever-expanding exploration of gender expression, identity, and family cohesion. Through this collaborative model, we have learned the value of supporting one another both personally and professionally and that this collaboration creates a secure, expansive holding environment for the family to explore gender and opportunities for growth. Caring for this population can be challenging as well as rewarding, and each of us has benefited enormously from the wise counsel of the other, as well as from the wisdom of the families in our care.

References

American Academy of Family Physicians and American Academy of Physician Assistants. (2011, February). *Family physicians and physician assistants: Team-based family medicine.* Retrieved from https://www.aafp.org/dam/AAFP/documents/practice_management/admin_staffing/AAFP-AAPAJtPaper.pdf

Bonifacio, H. J., & Rosenthal, S. M. (2015). Gender variance and dysphoria in children and adolescents. *Pediatric Clinics of North America, 62,* 1001–1016. http://dx.doi.org/10.1016/j.pcl.2015.04.013

Boss, P. (2006). *Loss, trauma, and resilience.* New York, NY: Norton.

Carel, J. C., Eugster, E., Rogol, A., Ghizzoni, L., & Palmert, M. (2009). Consensus statement on the use of gonadotropin-releasing hormone analogues in children. *Pediatrics, 123,* 752–762.

Cohen-Kettenis, P. T., & Pfäfflin, F. (2003). *Transgenderism and intersexuality in childhood and adolescence: Making choices.* Thousand Oaks, CA: Sage.

Coleman, E., Bockting, W., Botzer, M., Cohen-Kettenis, P., DeCuypere, G., Feldman, J., . . . Zucker, K. (2012). Standards of care for the health of transsexual, transgender, and gender nonconforming people (7th version). *International Journal of Transgenderism, 13,* 165–232. http://dx.doi.org/10.1080/15532739.2011.700873

De Roo, C., Tilleman, K., T'Sjoen, G., & De Sutter, P. (2016). Fertility options in transgender people. *International Review of Psychiatry, 28,* 112–119. http://dx.doi.org/10.3109/09540261.2015.1084275

de Vries, A. L. C., McGuire, J. K., Steensma, T. D., Wagenaar, E. C. F., Doreleijers, T. A. H., & Cohen-Kettenis, P. T. (2014). Young adult psychological outcome after puberty suppression and gender reassignment. *Pediatrics, 134,* 696–704. http://dx.doi.org/10.1542/peds.2013-2958

Delemarre-van de Waal, H. A., & Cohen-Kettenis, P. T. (2006). Clinical management of gender identity disorder in adolescents: A protocol on psychological and paediatric endocrinology aspects. *European Journal of Endocrinology, 155,* 131–137. http://dx.doi.org/10.1530/eje.1.02231

Doherty, W. J., McDaniel, S. H., & Baird, M. A. (1996). Five levels of primary care/behavioral healthcare collaboration. *Behavioral Healthcare Tomorrow, 5,* 25–27.

Edwards-Leeper, L., & Spack, N. P. (2012). Psychological evaluation and medical treatment of transgender youth in an interdisciplinary "Gender Management Service" (GeMS) in a major pediatric center. *Journal of Homosexuality, 59,* 321–336. http://dx.doi.org/10.1080/00918369.2012.653302

Ehrensaft, D. (2012). From gender identity disorder to gender identity creativity: True gender self child therapy. *Journal of Homosexuality, 59,* 337–356. http://dx.doi.org/10.1080/00918369.2012.653303

Estes, S. J. (2015). Fertility preservation in children and adolescents. *Endocrinology and Metabolism Clinics of North America, 44,* 799–820. http://dx.doi.org/10.1016/j.ecl.2015.07.005 (Correction published 2016, *Endocrinology and Metabolism Clinics of North America, 45,* p. xiii. http://dx.doi.org/10.1016/j.ecl.2015.12.001)

Feierabend, R. H., & Bartee, Z. L. (2004). A collaborative relationship between a community mental health center and family practice residency program. *Families, Systems, & Health, 22*(2), 231–237. http://dx.doi.org/10.1037/1091-7527.22.2.231

Feldman, J. L., & Goldberg, J. M. (2006). Transgender primary medical care. *International Journal of Transgenderism, 9,* 3–34. http://dx.doi.org/10.1300/J485v09n03_02

Gagné, M. (2005). *What is collaborative mental health care? An introduction to the collaborative mental health care framework.* Mississauga, Ontario, Canada: Canadian Collaborative Mental Health Initiative. Retrieved from http://www.shared-care.ca/files/02-Framework-EN.pdf

Gooren, L., & Delemarre-van de Waal, H. (1996). The feasibility of endocrine interventions in juvenile transsexuals. *Journal of Psychology and Human Sexuality, 8,* 69–84. http://dx.doi.org/10.1300/J056v08n04_05

Hidalgo, M. A., Ehrensaft, D., Tishelman, A. C., Clark, L. F., Garofalo, R., Rosenthal, S. M., . . . Olson, J. (2013). The gender affirmative model: What we know and what we aim to learn. *Human Development, 56,* 285–290. http://dx.doi.org/10.1159/000355235

Hill, D. B., Menvielle, E., Sica, K. M., & Johnson, A. (2010). An affirmative intervention for families with gender variant children: Parental ratings of child mental health and gender. *Journal of Sex & Marital Therapy, 36,* 6–23. http://dx.doi.org/10.1080/00926230903375560

Johnson, E. K., & Finlayson, C. (2016). Preservation of fertility potential for gender and sex diverse individuals. *Transgender Health, 1*, 41–44. http://dx.doi.org/10.1089/trgh.2015.0010

Katz-Wise, S. L., Reisner, S. L., Hughto, J. W., & Keo-Meier, C. L. (2016). Differences in sexual orientation diversity and sexual fluidity in attractions among gender minority adults in Massachusetts. *Journal of Sex Research, 53*, 74–84. http://dx.doi.org/10.1080/00224499.2014.1003028

Lev, A. I. (2004). *Transgender emergence: Counseling gender-variant people and their families*. New York, NY: Taylor & Francis.

Lev, A. I., & Alie, L. (2012). Transgender and gender nonconforming children and youth: Developing culturally competent systems of care. In S. K. Fisher, J. M. Poirier, & G. M. Blau (Eds.), *Improving emotional and behavioral outcomes for LGBT youth: A guide for professionals* (pp. 46–66). Baltimore, MD: Brookes.

Lev, A. I., & Gottlieb, A. R. (Eds.). (in press). *Families in transition: Parent perspectives on raising gender diverse children*. New York, NY: Harrington Park Press.

Malpas, J. (2011). Between pink and blue: A multi-dimensional family approach to gender nonconforming children and their families. *Family Process, 50*, 453–470. http://dx.doi.org/10.1111/j.1545-5300.2011.01371.x

Meier, S. C., Pardo, S. T., Labuski, C., & Babcock, J. (2013). Measures of clinical health among female-to-male transgender persons as a function of sexual orientation. *Archives of Sexual Behavior, 42*, 463–474. http://dx.doi.org/10.1007/s10508-012-0052-2

McGoldrick, M., & Gerson, R. (1985). *Genograms in family assessment*. New York, NY: Norton.

Olson, K. R., Key, A. C., & Eaton, N. R. (2015). Gender cognition in transgender children. *Psychological Science, 26*, 467–474. http://dx.doi.org/10.1177/0956797614568156

Peterson, C. M., Matthews, A., Copps-Smith, E., & Conard, L. A. (2017). Suicidality, self-harm, and body dissatisfaction in transgender adolescents and emerging adults with gender dysphoria. *Suicide and Life-Threatening Behavior, 47*, 475–482.

Rosenthal, S. M. (2014). Approach to the patient: transgender youth: Endocrine considerations. *The Journal of Clinical Endocrinology and Metabolism, 99*, 4379–4389. http://dx.doi.org/10.1210/jc.2014-1919

Ryan, C., Huebner, D., Diaz, R. M., & Sanchez, J. (2009). Family rejection as a predictor of negative health outcomes in white and Latino lesbian, gay, and bisexual young adults. *Pediatrics, 123*, 346–352. http://dx.doi.org/10.1542/peds.2007-3524

Seaburn, D. B., Lorenz, A. D., Gunn, W. B., Jr., Gawinski, B. A., & Mauksch, L. (1996). *Models of collaboration: A guide for mental health professionals working with health care practitioners*. New York, NY: Basic Books.

Schechter, L. S. (2009). The surgeon's relationship with the physician prescribing hormones and the mental health professional: Review for Version 7 of the World Professional Association for Transgender Health's *Standards of Care*. *International Journal of Transgenderism, 11*, 222–225. http://dx.doi.org/10.1080/15532730903439468

Sherer, I., Rosenthal, S. M., Ehrensaft, D., & Baum, J. (2012). Child and Adolescent Gender Center: A multidisciplinary collaboration to improve the lives of gender nonconforming children and teens. *Pediatrics, 33,* 273–275. http://dx.doi.org/10.1542/pir.33-6-273

Stone Fish, L., & Harvey, R. G. (2005). *Nurturing queer youth: Family therapy transformed.* New York, NY: Norton.

Tilsen, J. (2013). *Therapeutic conversations with queer youth: Transcending homonormativity and constructing preferred identities.* New York, NY: Jason Aronson.

Tishelman, A. C., Kaufman, R., Edwards-Leeper, L., Mandel, F. H., Shumer, D. E., & Spack, N. P. (2015). Serving transgender youth: Challenges, dilemmas, and clinical examples. *Professional Psychology: Research and Practice, 46,* 37–45. http://dx.doi.org/10.1037/a0037490

Vanderburgh, R. (2009). Appropriate therapeutic care for families with pre-pubescent transgender/gender-dissonant children. *Child & Adolescent Social Work Journal, 26,* 135–154. http://dx.doi.org/10.1007/s10560-008-0158-5

von Trotsenburg, M. (2014). Building a center for gender dysphoria research and transgender health care: The road from wishful thinking to reality. In B. C. P. Kreukels, T. D. Steensma, & A. L. C. de Vries (Eds.), *Gender dysphoria and disorders of sex development: Progress in care and knowledge* (pp. xvii–xix). New York, NY: Springer.

World Professional Association for Transgender Health. (2011). *Standards of care for the health of transsexual, transgender, and gender nonconforming people* (7th version). Retrieved from https://www.wpath.org/media/cms/Documents/Web%20Transfer/SOC/Standards%20of%20Care%20V7%20-%202011%20WPATH.pdf

Walsh, F. (2011). *Normal family processes: Growing diversity and complexity.* New York, NY: Guilford Press.

Woltmann, E., Grogan-Kaylor, A., Perron, B., Georges, H., Kilbourne, A. M., & Bauer, M. S. (2012). Comparative effectiveness of collaborative chronic care models for mental health conditions across primary, specialty, and behavioral health care settings: Systematic review and meta-analysis. *The American Journal of Psychiatry, 169,* 790–804. http://dx.doi.org/10.1176/appi.ajp.2012.11111616

Diane Ehrensaft and Colt Keo-Meier

Where Do We Go From Here? 13

We have had the opportunity to learn from an esteemed group of experts throughout the United States. They have enlightened us on the gender affirmative model (GAM) from every angle we have been able to capture as essential to the gender health of all the children who come to us, as clinicians and mental health providers, for help with their gender identity, their gender expressions, or both. Gender stress, gender distress, gender dysphoria, and gender resilience have been woven together to create the fabric of the myriad banners of gender exploration and gender consolidation under which we do our work as gender affirmative mental health professionals. Yet any good professional will admit to a healthy agnosticism—we know what we know, but we also know that what we know today may not prove to be true tomorrow, or was clearer to us than it ought to have been. With that said, what do we now want to say to ourselves about the GAM and its viability as a treatment modality for transgender and gender expansive (TGE) children?

What Others Are Telling Us

We completed this volume in a tumultuous time in U.S. history. We presently live under a federal administration that appears to be intent on dismantling some of the important gains made for TGE people of all ages: At present,

http://dx.doi.org/10.1037/0000095-013
The Gender Affirmative Model: An Interdisciplinary Approach to Supporting Transgender and Gender Expansive Children, C. Keo-Meier and D. Ehrensaft (Editors)
Copyright © 2018 by the American Psychological Association. All rights reserved.

Title IX, which protects against sex discrimination in public education, according to present executive order, is not to be interpreted as pertaining to TGE students, undoing the expansive interpretation of the law proffered by the Obama administration in 2016. Throughout the country, unless state laws to the contrary have been put in place or advocates wage successful legal battles against local school systems or municipalities, transgender students are being barred from using the bathrooms that match their gender identity. This present battle within many states pits school boards against transgender students, using arguments making no more sense than, and infused with, the same pernicious prejudices that once barred Blacks from using the same restroom as Whites throughout the South. In an atmosphere of conservative thinking and open criticism of those who do not conform to traditional values, the GAM of care for youth has been singled out for attack. In July 2017, Michelle Cretella, the president of the American College of Pediatricians, a group of Christian conservative medical professionals, published the following account: "I'm a Pediatrician. How Transgender Ideology Has Infiltrated My Field and Produced Large-Scale Child Abuse." To be precise:

> Today's institutions that promote transition affirmation are pushing children to impersonate the opposite sex, sending many of them down the path of puberty blockers, sterilization, the removal of healthy body parts, and untold psychological damage. These harms constitute nothing less than institutionalized child abuse. (Cretella, 2017, "Bottom Line," paras. 3–4)

We hope to have made clear in this volume that no gender affirmative practitioner would ever push a child to "impersonate" anything or wittingly or unwittingly send a child down the path of sterility, body mutilation, and mental illness. It is exactly us that Cretella referred to in her undocumented tirade against a model of care that appears to rub against the grain of her and her cohort's conservative values. Yet, if we are to extract any positive message from Cretella's attack on the GAM, it is to remind ourselves that we have miles to go before we can demonstrate, in evidence-based terms, the actual psychological outcomes for all of the children who have received our services within a GAM and all that might follow in their footsteps in the future.

Some of that work has already been done, as when our colleagues in the Netherlands demonstrated that the TGE youth treated in their clinic with both psychological and medical interventions were on par with the general population in their age group in measures of psychological well-being (de Vries et al., 2014), and in Olson and associates' ongoing research at the University of Washington, which is consistently demonstrating that young transgender children who have been allowed to socially transition are also on a par with a matched group of cisgender peers in various measures of psychological functioning (Olson, Durwood, DeMeules, & McLaughlin, 2016; Olson, Key, & Eaton, 2015). Four major gender clinics in the United States—housed at University of California, San Francisco, Benioff Children's Hospital; Children's Hospital Los Angeles; Boston Children's Hospital; and Lurie Children's Hospital of

Chicago—are presently engaged in a National Institutes of Health longitudinal study to investigate the effects, both medical and psychological, of gender affirming medical interventions (puberty blockers, masculinizing and feminizing hormones) provided to eligible patients as part of their gender care. Our greatest hope is that more studies are proliferating as we write and that more federal and private funds will be invested in research endeavors to validate best practices for TGE children. As the results of these studies are consolidated and as more studies are initiated, we can expect to gain a better understanding of which components of the GAM work and which aspects need to be either improved or discarded as either ineffective or potentially harmful to children's growth and development.

Generating Our Own Research/Evaluation Questions

To say that we finish this volume with no unanswered questions would be to turn our backs on the beauty and significance of never-ending evaluative endeavors. So, what are our questions for the future, questions that anyone having read this volume might want to take up under their own banner of investigation?

To begin with, it is time to convert the controversial question "Can a young child know their gender?" into the more meaningful question "Why do some children follow a pathway that aligns their assigned sex with their true gender while others carve a path that overrides assigned sex at birth with an authentic gender defined by other factors?" Within the GAM, we could even imagine putting forth the investigative query "If gender lies between our ears rather than between our legs, would it not be better to assume no gender at all until a child lets us know what theirs is?" In this endeavor we could seek out the families, although small in number, who have consciously chosen to wait until their child lets them know and compare their children's gender development with that of children who have been told from birth on, "You are a boy" or "You are girl." How do the children not given that message consolidate a true gender self? If they were to prove to have better mental health outcomes than children who have lived with an expected gender since birth, might that push the GAM to invite parents to desist with such expectations and follow in the footprints of the families who took the radical step of dispensing with gender assignations until they come from the child?

Swinging to the other side of the equation, whether young children should be allowed or encouraged to socially transition from one gender to another remains controversial. Those who operate within the "watchful waiting" model have expressed the reservation that such early intervention is premature and potentially inhibiting—cognitively locking the child into a permanent sense of a gendered self when they were still in the throes of exploration and discovery. Would such cognitive inhibition prevent the child from being gender expansive in the sense of evolutionary unfolding of the gender self over the course of childhood? We have presented evidence in this volume of the ex post facto test of social transitions—when transition is an appropriate move in a child's life, that child blossoms in mental health and sheds emotional stress and psychological dysfunction. However, we have yet to measure that observation systematically across aggregate groups and now is the time to do so, before too many more years of facilitating social transitions go by only to discover that the cautionary tales were well founded.

Many parents have come to us with deep reservations regarding anticipated medical interventions in their child's future as their child moves toward puberty and beyond—GnRH agonists to stanch an unwanted puberty, hormones to facilitate a wanted puberty. Parents worry about the yet-unknown physical side effects or the permanency of the interventions, and they wonder about the social constructs of gender and why their children could not just be happy with the bodies they have, rather than the gender tropes of male/female physical presentation orchestrated by the culture. As more children and youth challenge the social constructs of gender and push the boundaries to "all and any" to replace "either/or," perhaps the parents have a point. Maybe our GAM, endorsing stages over ages in proffering interventions for gender consolidation, needs to pause and ask, "Why does a child have to change their name to authenticate their gender; why can't Susie just be a person's name rather than a girl's name, and why does someone have to grow breasts to claim their female self?" If we channel these questions into a research modality, the present GAM will be put to the test as we compare the mental health outcomes of the children who have broken out of the gender binary completely with the children who abide by the boxes but request social and later medical interventions to be able to do a switch to the other box. Are we comparing apples and oranges here, or are we seeing historical shifts in the meaning of gender in which the GAM would do well to take heed and continue to ask itself the questions "What is gender, anyway? Who says so? What responsibility do we have for shaping that conversation and challenging our own protocols that may inadvertently endorse outmoded binary modes of experiencing and living in one's true gender?"

A Gender Affirmative Specialist's Work Is Never Done

As the free flow of questions generated above shows, we should never take for granted the goodness of the model from which we work—in this case, the GAM. As the late President John F. Kennedy asked us not what our country could do for us but what we could do for our country, so too must we now ask what we can do for the GAM, and more important, for the children who receive services within this model. We hope we have provided sufficient evidence that in this moment of history it is a best practice model for ensuring the gender health of TGE children and youth. But just as each child's gender is an interweaving of nature, nurture, and culture, over time, these factors also influence the evolution of our models of care—as culture changes, as science uncovers more of nature's contribution to gender development, and as we are differently nurtured over time in our own gendered selves, we must leave room for alterations in the GAM. Let us ensure that the work is never done.

References

Cretella, M. (2017, July 3). "I'm a pediatrician. How transgender ideology has infiltrated my field and produced large-scale child abuse [Blog post]." *Daily Signal.* Retrieved from https://www.dailysignal.com/2017/07/03/im-pediatrician-transgender-ideology-infiltrated-field-produced-large-scale-child-abuse/

de Vries, A. L. C., McGuire, J. K., Steensma, T. D., Wagenaar, E. C., Doreleijers, T. A. H., & Cohen-Kettenis, P. T. (2014). Young adult psychological outcome after puberty suppression and gender reassignment. *Pediatrics, 134,* 696–704. http://dx.doi.org/10.1542/peds.2013-2958

Olson, K. R., Durwood, L., DeMeules, M., & McLaughlin, K. A. (2016). Mental health of transgender children who are supported in their identities. *Pediatrics, 137,* 277–282. http://dx.doi.org/10.1542/peds.2015-3223

Olson, K. R., Key, A. C., & Eaton, N. R. (2015). Gender cognition in transgender children. *Psychological Science, 26,* 467–474. http://dx.doi.org/10.1177/0956797614568156

Index

About the Editors

Colt Keo-Meier, PhD, is a clinical psychologist whose expertise is in clinical work, research, and training in the health of transgender people of all ages. He is an assistant professor in the Menninger Department of Psychiatry and Behavioral Sciences of Baylor College of Medicine, lecturer and researcher in the Psychology Department at the University of Houston, and is completing his MD at the University of Texas Medical Branch, where he is a student scholar in the John P. McGovern Academy of Oslerian Medicine. He maintains a small part-time private practice in the Houston/Galveston area of Texas. Dr. Keo-Meier is a cofounder and board member of Gender Infinity, an organization dedicated to promoting justice, hope, and equity through the advancement of relationships, knowledge, and resources that empower transgender and gender expansive individuals. He helped develop the National Association for School Psychologists' (NASP) and the American Psychological Association's (APA) joint *Resolution on Gender and Sexual Orientation Diversity in Children and Adolescents in Schools*, the NASP Position Statement on *Safe Schools for Transgender and Gender Diverse Students*, and the APA and the Substance Abuse and Mental Health Services Administration's report on *Ending Conversion Therapy: Supporting and Affirming LGBTQ Youth*. He is a chapter work group member for the hormone therapy chapter for adolescents and adults of the World Professional Association for Transgender Health Standards of Care Version 8. His research has focused on understanding the mental health effects of hormone therapy and the experiences of parents of young transgender people. Dr. Keo-Meier is a transgenderqueer White man who has thrived because of his experience of acceptance and unconditional love from his parents, Cambodian American genderqueer spouse, and long-time family and friends.

Diane Ehrensaft, PhD, is a developmental and clinical psychologist, associate professor of pediatrics at the University of California San Francisco (UCSF), and director of mental health of the Child and Adolescent Gender Center, UCSF Benioff Children's Hospital. She specializes in research, clinical work, training, and consultation related to gender expansive children, and she publishes and lectures nationally and internationally on this topic, as well as making media appearances. Dr. Ehrensaft is presently coinvestigator in a four-site National Institutes of Health grant studying the effects of puberty blockers and masculinizing and feminizing hormones in gender expansive and transgender youth. In addition to being the coeditor of this volume, she is the author of *The Gender Creative Child*; *Gender Born, Gender Made*; *Mommies, Daddies, Donors, Surrogates*; *Building a Home Within* (coedited with Toni Heineman); *Spoiling Childhood*; and *Parenting Together*. She is a chapter work group member for the World Professional Association for Transgender Health Standards of Care Version 8 and also is on the Board of Directors of Gender Spectrum, an organization providing education, advocacy, and support to families, schools, and community to build gender inclusivity. Dr. Ehrensaft is a founding member, board member, and senior clinician of A Home Within, a national organization that offers pro bono psychotherapy and serves the emotional needs of children and youth in foster care.